JUST FOR
ONE DAY

For Mum and Dad.
You were right, I should have got a proper job.

JUST FOR ONE DAY

ADVENTURES IN BRITPOP

LOUISE WENER

EBURY
PRESS

5 7 9 10 8 6

This edition published 2011
First published in 2010 by Ebury Press, an imprint of Ebury Publishing
A Random House Group company
Originally published by Ebury Press in 2010 as *Different for Girls*

The Random House Group Limited Reg. No. 954009

Addresses for companies within the Random House Group can be found at
www.randomhouse.co.uk

A CIP catalogue record for this book is available from the British Library

Designed and set by seagulls.net

ISBN 9780091936525

To buy books by your favourite authors and register for offers visit
www.randomhouse.co.uk

The Random House Group Limited supports The Forest Stewardship
Council® (FSC®), the leading international forest-certification organisation.
Our books carrying the FSC label are printed on FSC®-certified paper.
FSC is the only forest-certification scheme supported by the leading
environmental organisations, including Greenpeace. Our
paper procurement policy can be found at
www.randomhouse.co.uk/environment

MIX
Paper from
responsible sources
FSC® C016897

Printed and bound in Great Britain by Clays Ltd, St Ives plc

CONTENTS

PART I

PART I

HOME TAPING IS
KILLING MUSIC

It's a typical Sunday teatime in the spring of '79 and I am twelve. My parents are enjoying a packet of fondant fancies in front of the *Holiday* programme while I scurry around the house making last-minute preparations for the top 40 singles broadcast on Radio 1. You might imagine listening to the radio is a largely passive activity, requiring little or no advance planning, but in this case you'd be entirely wrong. If you were serious about such things, and I was, you'd know the task at hand wasn't simply to *listen* to the top 40 countdown, but to capture its edited highlights on a hand-held tape cassette recorder. The resulting compilation could then be played repeatedly – my mother might say incessantly – over the coming week, until a new set of movers and shakers had climbed the chart, and it was time to begin the entire process all over again.

With half an hour to kick-off, I run through my checklist of very important jobs.

Job one: Locate tape recorder. Last seen in hands of older brother. Most likely use, the covert playback of *Derek and Clive* tapes in his bedroom with the door shut. I can't be certain – the sound is muffled, even with my ear pressed tight to the lock – but these contraband recordings seem largely to consist of two men swearing and giggling, and some jokes about lobsters and cancer. My brother thinks this stuff is very funny. He is clearly quite odd.

Job two: Locate suitable WHSmith C90 cassette tape. Again, more difficult than it sounds. I only have a dozen or so of these treasured oblong boxes and some are so worn from repeated tapings of the top 40 countdown, I've had to reinforce perished sections with Sellotape. These mended sections are inherently problematic. Not only do they cause ruinous blank spots – in the middle of 'Ladies Night' by Kool & The Gang, for instance – they are also liable to snag in the machinery at any moment, resulting in hours of patient salvaging, untangling and re-spooling.

Job three: Re-acquaint self with auto-reverse function of tape recorder. As hard as I try, I will never get the hang of this. At least once each Sunday I lose focus for a moment and find myself recording on the wrong side of the tape with potentially devastating consequences. I once went over a cherished *Top of the Pops* recording of Boney M.'s 'Brown Girl In The Ring' with Barbara Dickson singing 'I Know Him So Well'. It still upsets me to think about it.

Job four: Practise hitting pause button with thumb until reflexes are lightning fast. We don't want a repeat of last week's debacle in which I somehow managed to lop off the front and back ends of 'Heart Of Glass' whilst capturing 'Bright Eyes' – a song about a dead rabbit – in its entirety.

Job five: After due consideration and much soul-searching, I've decided not to record over 'Bright Eyes' just yet. For now it keeps a treasured spot on my least worn C90 cassette tape. Don't get too comfortable, Art Garfunkel. We'll review things again in another week.

With minutes to spare and all the necessary recording equipment in place, there's just time to run through my inter-pretive dance routine to 'Wuthering Heights'. I've been perfecting it for weeks and I almost have it down. It begins with a flurry of high karate kicks, segues into some manic twirling and the occasional head-over-heels, and ends in a series of star jumps accompanied by a lengthy series of winks and some protracted batting of the eyelashes. The eyelash segment is fundamental to the routine's success. In the most recent issue of *Jackie* magazine, Kate Bush says – she is quite emphatic – that the secret to a great performance is talking to the audience with your eyes. My older brother says – he is quite emphatic – that the secret of Kate's performance is wear-ing a skimpy leotard without a bra on underneath.

In case this isn't obvious from the outset, I wasn't the coolest of twelve-year-olds. If I had been, I wouldn't have grown up to be a pop star. It's a little-known equation that ambition flourishes in direct proportion to the level of embarrassment you experience as a child. To put it another way, if you grow up with parents so disinterested in your social wellbeing they let your half-blind grandmother choose your glasses for you when you're six and make you wear the same style – National Health, pink plastic – until you are fourteen, they've only themselves to blame when you turn up on their doorstep, decades later, bran-dishing a platinum album saying I told you so.

There are other impediments to my coolness. I have chronic asthma. I've already sprouted my first spots. I live in a dull Essex suburb and have parents who are at least a decade older than those of all my friends. As my big sister – who is twelve years older than me – never tires of saying, Mum had me late and by mistake. I was a cap baby. I made it through the twin obstacles of latex and spermicide just in time to greet a pair of forceps, in the middle of a notable football match, on 30 July 1966. If nothing else, I like to think this demonstrates a certain level of pluck and ambition. If nothing else, my mum would like you to know that if you ever have to be on the wrong end of a pair of forceps, it's advisable to avoid them being operated by a doctor who is missing seeing England win the World Cup.

From the ages of ten to twelve – as disco fades and punk combusts, and the New Romantics ride into town with their blouses flapping – I'm rarely to be seen without my Panasonic cassette recorder. It's a cherished Christmas gift from my Auntie Dolly, my dad's eldest sister, and a particularly generous one at that, given cassette players are relatively expensive and my Auntie Dolly – being from the Jewish side of the family – doesn't believe in Christmas.

I love the Panasonic immediately. It's pleasingly heavy, with chunky white buttons and an extra important red one that emits a satisfying clunk when you depress it, along with the play button, to record. I begin by taping music from the telly. In a scene that's played out in a million households across the land, I spend Thursday evenings crouched in prayer beside the television set, Panasonic held aloft, capturing such seminal performances as David Soul (Hutch from *Starsky and Hutch*!) singing 'Silver Lady'. I'm big on the soundtrack to *Evita* around this time, and even bigger on the soundtrack to *Grease*; especially 'Summer Nights' with John Travolta and Olivia Newton-John, whose transformation from geek to goddess never fails to delight me. Mum worries that Olivia

Newton-John's shiny black trousers are too tight. And rightly so. Apparently they had to sew her into them.

Recording these songs is almost a performance in itself. The important thing is to get the levels just right to minimise hissing and – cross fingers, hope to heaven, pray to the spirit of The Fonz – make it through the song from start to finish without my father leaning forward from his corner armchair – everyone in our family has a strictly ascribed viewing position – and shouting, 'When can we turn this rubbish over?' I develop a sixth sense about when he's going to do this. Less likely during The Three Degrees and Peaches & Herb, more likely during Sex Pistols and Lene Lovich. Almost instantaneous during Village People.

The world changes at the end of the seventies. Sid Vicious dies and a female prime minister is elected, but I'm less interested in the death of punk and the rise of Mrs T than I am with events much closer to home. While Sid is mourning Nancy, Dad pops off to the high road and returns with a brand new Amstrad music centre. The Amstrad is a thing of beauty. It has a smoked glass door, wide silver dials and a raft of flashing lights that pulsate like the control deck of a spaceship when you listen to 'Xanadu' in the dark. Most ingenious of all, it has a built-in cassette deck which means you can record albums directly onto tape, with the simple depression of a single button. As labour-saving devices go, this is as revolutionary to me as the purchase of a washing machine, at around the same time, is to my mother.

The year 1979 is when I switch from hovering in front of the radio speakers with my Panasonic and start making cassette copies of my big brother's albums. Suddenly, out of nowhere, it's feasible to have a music collection of sorts without saving up for weeks on end to buy each and every record that you love. As is the way with the advent of the new, some small thing is often lost in the process. I don't yearn to listen to the tape cassettes of my brother's Barclay James Harvest albums now, but I'd give anything to have one of those *Top of the Pops* recordings with their clumsy clicks and bonkers compilations. The Boomtown Rats fading into Showaddywaddy, Gloria Gaynor segueing into 'Up The Junction' by Squeeze. The Skids next to Chic, The Jam and Ian Dury next to Dollar. There was no thought to form or consistency in the tracks that I taped, no self-consciousness about what was credible or cool. They were simply tunes that I liked, all of them pop songs whose pedigree was indistinguishable from the other.

Most of all, I'd like that tape of 'Brown Girl In The Ring' that I lost. What a recording that was. I'm fairly sure it was punctuated by my dad leaning forward from his corner armchair and demanding to know when we could turn this rubbish over.

WHO ARE YOUR INFLUENCES?

There's music playing at home as I'm growing up, but none of my family are musical. Mum sings around the house but never pop songs, only religious music and hymns. Quite often she'll do the washing up humming the best bits of Handel's *Messiah*, or hang out the washing, merrily crooning her way through 'Wings Of A Dove'. Mum likes no contemporary music at all, unless you count Perry Como, and this is because she wasn't allowed to listen to music as a child.

Mum had a very strict upbringing. Her father was a formidable man: a veteran of the First World War trenches who was brought up in a Methodist children's home. He believed young people should be seen and not heard, and thought music, make-up, cigarettes and alcohol were sinful. When she was a girl, Mum was taken to regular Bible meetings by her father. She'd watch him slip into a trance and speak in tongues, while disabled people were dragged to standing from their wheelchairs so God could heal them. Members of the congregation would wail and faint around her, and my mother would clamp her eyes shut, petrified, and try to think of nice things, like Perry Como.

Dad likes music a lot. He loves jazz and blues and on Sunday afternoons the house is filled with the sounds of

Sinatra, Gershwin and Ella Fitzgerald and the tunes of big-band supremo Duke Ellington. Dad's music is wartime music. He taps along to all his favourites – Cab Calloway, Louis Armstrong and Nina Simone – and the cupboards are stuffed with mint-condition vinyl 78s, some of which he's owned since his war years in the forces. Mostly he listens to records on his own but sometimes I sit and listen with him. He wants me to like this stuff, to appreciate its quality. And I do. Just not as much as I appreciate Captain & Tennille and Sheena Easton.

Sheena Easton is the luckiest girl in the world. She has become an overnight pop success on account of Esther Rantzen plucking her from obscurity and featuring her in a TV show called *The Big Time*. One minute Sheena's studying to be a singing teacher, the next she's got two singles in the top ten. Amazing! Perhaps I should write to Esther Rantzen. On second thoughts, that's pointless. I wrote to Jimmy Savile loads of times in the seventies asking if he'd fix it for me to be on *Top of the Pops*. Or meet a Dalek. Or be in a film like Tatum O'Neal in *Paper Moon*. He never wrote back to me once.

It was the same with *Opportunity Knocks*. When me and my best friend Bernice Cohen applied to be on Britain's favourite talent show, aged seven, we didn't hear a peep out of Hughie Green. It's Hughie's loss. You should have heard our rendition of 'Hard Day's Night'. You should have seen our accompanying interpretive dance moves. There was a hand-jive interlude and handstand section that was prize winning all by itself. On second thoughts, I'm not sure we ever sent off for the application form. I've half an idea we spent the postage on a strawberry cone and a bag of sherbet pips.

This is the thing with being famous. As Roy Castle was forever reminding us at the start of *Record Breakers*, it takes hard work and 'dedication' to be successful. You have to want it a lot. You can't afford to be distracted by the lure of ice creams and sweets. It also helps if you can find something that you want to be famous for. This part is easy. I may have a way to go on the dedication front but from a very early age, I've always suspected the thing I might like to be famous for is music. I play tapes and records every spare minute. I spend hours in my bedroom scribbling words and making up tunes. I'm away from school for days on end when my asthma gets bad, and singing along to my favourite records makes my lungs feel a little less wheezy.

Best of all, music is transporting: a way for a shy, dreamy kid to be something more substantial, more glamorous. A way for me to be somewhere else. Not stuck at home watching the trade test transmission while Mum trundles back and forth to the launderette. Not sat in the bathroom with a towel on my head, face held over a sink full of eucalyptus-scented steam. Music is like food. It's like presents. If simply *listening* to it is this good, imagine how it must feel to play and perform it, and get to live in a mansion, and own a hot tub and hang out with Tony Hadley to boot!

Wearing out my turntable this weekend are 'So Lonely' by The Police and 'My Perfect Cousin' by The Undertones. Next week it's 'Enola Gay' by OMD and 'Different For Girls' from my big brother's new Joe Jackson album. These are some of the songs that welcome us into the eighties and you can only feel optimistic about a decade that begins with a number-one hit ('Coward Of The County') for Kenny Rogers! OK, so maybe Kenny Rogers isn't the most auspicious start, but by

February it's 'Atomic' by Blondie, swiftly followed by 'Working My Way Back To You' by The Detroit Spinners. Listen to that one now. See if it doesn't make you feel good. Music has an endless capacity to do this. I can still remember the exact time a record first made me feel content and immensely much better about the world.

I have just wet myself in fear and surprise. I am six. I am standing in the middle of the school sports hall and the headmaster, an old-fashioned and slightly sadistic sort, is bellowing at me. Everyone is staring. I have done something wrong. I have bought four toys at the lunchtime jumble sale, even though it was made absolutely clear that each of us was *only* allowed to buy three. I couldn't stop myself. The one-eared donkey in the knitted green hat with unspecified brown stains on its fur was calling my name. It was only a penny. Where was the harm? Who else would be fool enough to buy themselves a stained one-eared donkey?

All my purchases are confiscated. I walk back to the classroom with sodden pants. My teacher wonders why I didn't buy anything and I lie and say there wasn't anything I liked. I spend the day in wee trousers. I am gutted about the donkey. And the doll. And the two chipped elasticated bracelets. I don't tell my mum what happened when she comes to pick me up. Mum's pragmatic in such circumstances and would doubtless say it served me right for being greedy. In any case, I know something else that will help. It could have been 'Can The Can' by Suzi Quatro. It could have been 'Paper Roses' by Marie Osmond. But when the chips are down and the trousers are damp, what you really need are the curative powers of Elton John.

It's entirely Elton John's fault. I could have done something sensible like grow up to be an accountant but I'm going
to have to do something daft like try and become a songwriter
now, all because of 'Goodbye Yellow Brick Road'. I have no
idea what the song is about, but its sweeping, soaring chorus
is happiness and melancholy and escapism distilled into a
sound. As the record spins, the day is forgotten. Sitting there
on the shag-pile rug in our dining room in 1973, the plot of
my future is all mapped out. A new and lasting disdain for
rules and authority figures. A conversion to the transforming
powers of pop. A sudden determination to make more than
my fair share of purchases from life's lunchtime jumble sale.

EMMANUELLE

Today I am going on a date. Sort of. At least I think I am, except I'm not really sure.

What it amounts to is this. A boy in the year above me called Robert Frankel has asked if I want to come to his house to watch a video on Saturday afternoon. I don't think I fancy Robert Frankel. I am thirteen years old and my heart belongs to Hawkeye from *M*A*S*H*. And a little bit to Sting from The Police. Even so, I say yes. I've just come out of a home economics class in which I earned a lowly mark of two out of ten for pineapple upside-down cake, after Bradley Bird turned my oven up to full when I wasn't looking and practically set the thing alight. Robert catches me at a moment of weakness and it's only after I've committed to the video visit that he tells me both his parents will be out.

That Saturday morning, my stomach is knotted with apprehension and I almost don't go over to Robert Frankel's house in case it turns out he wants to get off with me. Everyone I know is getting off with someone, but I'm not clear on the details of what this means. I assume it involves French kissing, which I currently have no desire to do – and most especially not with Robert Frankel – yet a part of me just wants to get it over and done with so I can forget all about worrying about French kissing and get on with my life.

It becomes clear soon after I knock on Robert's door — and I don't know why I've not realised this before — that the reason I don't fancy him is because he's a bit odd. His way of getting me to like him — if indeed that's what he's aiming for — is by offering me a Diet Pepsi and regaling me about the time he and his older brother once gave someone they didn't like a shit sandwich to eat.

'It was brilliant. Steven pulled his pants down and crapped onto a copy of *Look-in*.'

'I see.'

'Then we spread a dollop of it between two slices of Sunblest.'

'I see.'

'Then, right, and this is the *best* bit. We used a whole jar of fish paste to disguise the smell, so he didn't even know it was *there*!'

'That's… um… disgusting.'

'I know!'

Building on this winning opening gambit, Robert says it's time to watch the video. If I'd had any sense I would have turned round and left there and then but, fool that I am, I decide to give Robert another chance. The reason I give him another chance is that I'm dead impressed his family have a VCR. I'm desperate to get one but they cost a small fortune and there is no chance on earth that my dad will buy one. Dad's not in the least bit interested in taping episodes of *Dallas* and hunting out pirate copies of *Private Benjamin* and *The Blue Lagoon*. Dad can see no benefit whatsoever in an evening spent quaking behind your fingers, watching *Driller Killer* and *I Spit On Your Grave*. Actually, Dad has a point. I've heard what goes on in some of these films — the hacked-off limbs, the exploding heads – and the idea of them scares me to death. I'm keen to examine Robert's new video machine at close quarters but I'm really hoping he doesn't want us to watch *Cannibal Apocalypse*.

Horror is not, and has never been, my cup of tea, but by the middle of 1980 all anyone wants to watch are video nasties. The boys are swapping them at school: psyching each other out with their appetite for gore and competing over their heroic lack of squeamishness. The ones who have a video player tucked under their TV sets are held in highest regard by those who don't. These are the kids in the know. They have access to the films and illicit secrets we've been wondering and whispering about in the playground for years. Some of them know what a Deep Throat is. Some of them have seen *Confessions of a Window Cleaner*! I've always wondered what that window cleaner needed to confess. Perhaps I'm about to find out.

'You're going to love this,' Robert says, pulling an unlabelled video from its brown paper wrapper. 'Just wait until she pukes and her head spins round.'

'Is this the one… you know… about sex with the window cleaner?'

'No. No way. It's *The Exorcist*!'

It turns out Robert is a video nasty fan. He has no idea that I'm an uninitiated horror virgin and, immune to my unease, he pulls the curtains, dims the lights and sits down beside me on the sofa. He smells of Paco Rabanne aftershave – probably his brother's – and he's wearing white towelling socks with his penny loafers. He rests a clammy hand on my shoulder and winks. This is awful. I don't want to watch this scary film. I am worried that I'll show myself up and faint at the gory bits. I don't want this boy to kiss me, either. I am worried that I won't know what to do. What do I do with my tongue? Swirl it round and round, or keep it still?

The film is worse than I imagined. *The Exorcist* scares me so much I can't breathe. I don't want to turn away or look like it's bothering me all that much, but my face has turned pale and my body is set so rigid it might snap. The instant Linda Blair stops vomiting bile and twizzling her head, I leap to my feet, grab my parka and bolt for the door. As I tug my coat over my arms it finally dawns on Robert that his tactics aren't working and, in a last valiant attempt to make me stay, he repeats a popular playground rumour about the *Blue Peter* presenter Valerie Singleton and the pop star Joan Armatrading, and asks me if I know what a lesbian is. I'm fairly sure I do, but the *Blue Peter* element has thrown me ever so slightly and I find myself unclear on the finer details.

'Well, thanks all the same,' I say, and scoot off home, thankful that I got off pretty lightly. Without having to eat a shit sandwich or be French kissed.

At home, I ring the doorbell with some relief. I'm later than I expected but it's odd that no one seems to be in. I ring again. Still nothing. I open the door with the spare key under the bin, convinced there's been some sort of emergency and that one of my parents has spontaneously combusted or been carted off to hospital. Inside, there's a note on the kitchen table. It reads: 'At cinema. Dinner in fridge.'

I am shocked. My parents never go out. By that I don't mean my parents go out occasionally, or once or twice a year on birthdays and anniversaries, I mean my parents *never* go out. I am thirteen years old and my mum and dad have never left the house past the 6pm early-evening news curfew, unless it's to go to a wedding or some other family function. My parents are spectacularly anti-social.

I watch TV while I wait for them. I turn all the lights on to calm my *Exorcist* fears and though I'm desperate for a wee, I don't venture upstairs for terrifying certainty that if I do I'll instantly be possessed by the devil. At nine o'clock I hear my dad's car pull up and the two of them breeze in as if nothing is out of step, as if it's entirely usual for me to see my parents come home this late in the evening after an impromptu trip to the local cinema. For want of anything better to say, I ask them what they went out to see. My mother looks pained. My dad looks shifty. There is an uncomfortable pause.

'*Emmanuelle in Soho*,' my mother says, finally. 'But we saw it by mistake. We bought tickets to see *The China Syndrome*.'

I almost fall over. This is too, *too* strange. Not only have my parents been out together at night for the first time in thirteen years, they've been to see a soft-core porn film. This is the kind of film that gets traded at school. Robert Frankel probably has a copy in his house! As if that wasn't enough, my mother now wants me to believe they wandered into the wrong screen of the Odeon cinema and sat through 90 minutes of French people humping one another before they realised one of them *wasn't* Jack Lemmon.

I don't know how to take this. I swallow my parents' *China Syndrome* line because the truth is a little too much to bear. My mother is the kind of person who turns the light out when she goes to the toilet at night in case someone can see her silhouette through the inch-thick frosted window in the bathroom. This is not common discussion material between the two of us and it's only thanks to my older sister's copies of *Cosmopolitan* and an illuminating conversation in my best friend's storm porch that I know anything whatsoever about the facts of life.

I'm so thrown by this turn of events and so distracted by the threat of impending demonic possession that I make a final error of judgment. Right there, out of the blue, I hear myself asking my mother if she's heard the rumour about Valerie Singleton from *Blue Peter*. I don't know why I do this. Perhaps I feel we're entering a new phase in our relationship; perhaps I think that after an hour and a half sitting through *Emmanuelle* by mistake she'll be able to enlighten me about the finer points of lesbianism.

This is the final straw for my mother and after what's clearly been a stressful evening, she packs me straight off to bed an hour early. Given the kind of day I've had, this feels like cruel and unusual punishment. Thankfully, there's a brand new issue of *Jackie* magazine with Debbie Harry on the front that I've hardly scanned to restore good order to the world. I am entering my teens, it's the dawn of a brand new decade and everything feels awkward and strange. I take comfort in the fact that it couldn't have been like this for the pop stars in *Jackie* magazine. I bet Sting never got sent to his boxroom. I bet Kate Bush knows what a lesbian is.

BATTLESHIPS

I'm trying very hard to like Adam And The Ants today. I'm trying not to sing 'Super Trouper' under my breath or hum 'Bette Davis Eyes' by Kim Carnes. I'm trying especially hard not to wonder aloud about the lyrics to 'Vienna' by Ultravox. What is Midge Ure on about? I have no idea. I'm sure it's something deep and profound because the video is black and white and extra moody. But I really need to concentrate on 'Stand And Deliver'. *Kings of the Wild Frontier* is where it's at.

The reason I'm trying to like Adam And The Ants is all down to my crush on Richard Grant. After the Robert Frankel debacle, I have set my sights higher up the boy chain. Richard Grant is gorgeous. Everyone fancies him. He has dark curly hair and wears Kickers to school, and has a tattoo of his name on his forearm that he made with the point of a compass needle and a bottle of Quink. Last week Richard brought his ghetto blaster to school, cleared away the desks and chairs in our classroom and got everyone dancing to 'Ant Rap' in the lunch break. After 'Ant Rap' it was 'Stand And Deliver', then a change of pace to 'Baggy Trousers' by Madness, at which point the dancing fell apart, collapsing into a legendary class-room 'bundle'.

A bundle can happen at any time of the school day, so it pays to be on your guard. When you least expect it one of the boys will yell '*Bundle!*' and all of them will spontaneously leap on top of one another, scrapping and punching, and crushing whoever happens to be on the bottom. If you get in the way you're fair game, but girls aren't generally expected to join in with the bundling. We're much too sophisticated for that. We prefer to spend our break times sending each other to Coventry for hours on end, orchestrating elaborate séances with makeshift ouija boards and working out new ways to make each other faint.

The latest craze at break time is to stand behind our 'friends', furiously pumping their arms up and down, then squeezing and compressing their stomachs, trying to get them to pass out cold. One girl cracked her head on a radiator as she fell and had to go to hospital last week. The teachers have banned us from doing it any more so we've moved on to hypnosis instead. Vivienne, the class bully, tried to hypnotise Sponge, the girl with the curly hair, into putting her hand into a lit Bunsen burner. I fear it's only a matter of time before someone tries to hypnotise me into doing something perilous on account of my National Health spectacles.

I don't know what I'm thinking, imagining I can find an *in* with Richard Grant. It's pure fantasy, of course, but imagine how it would feel, having the most popular boy in the class fancy you? I'm not sure that anyone will fancy me, ever again. I'm sure word has got around that I don't know how to kiss or watch a horror film. I'm sure boys would rather play a game of battleships with me than clash teeth and swap saliva. To prove the point, my friend Susan has just told me that I'm not invited to a get-together she's having at her house this weekend because everyone is going to be getting off with each other. Susan is going to pull people's names from a hat and pair them up. She thinks there might even be an orgy. She doesn't think there's any point in me coming and pairing off, because I'm nerdy and won't know how to do it.

I'm gutted not to be invited. It's also a bit of a relief. Half of me wants to go to Susan's house but half of me misses the days when you could punch a boy on the shoulder to show you liked him and not have to worry if your bra strap was showing or how to do orgies. I'm desperate for someone else to fancy me, especially Richard Grant, but I'm at that crossroads where sexually motivated activities still seem embarrassing and silly. Even so, I think the two of us would get on really well because both of us are crazy about music. I recently heard him saying that he likes Adam Ant's old punk stuff the best. What old punk stuff? I need to find out. This might be a job for my big brother.

'You think your friend sniffs glue?'

'That's what Susan says.'

'And he has a tattoo?'

'Made with Quink. Mum says it will give him blood poisoning if he's not careful.'

'He likes Adam And The Ants?'

'Yep.'

'And you want to know about the punk years.'

'Yes. I do.'

Geoff is eight years older than I am. He's already at university and seems immensely confident and cool: grown up in a way I will never be. He can do no wrong in my eyes and I look up to him in all things, despite the fact he's recently permed his hair and spends a good deal of his time jabbing at his curls with a wooden afro comb. The two of us have always been the best of friends. He taught me how to climb a tree and play cricket and did brilliant card tricks for my friends. Because he quite likes to experiment on his kid sister, he showed me how to do quadratic equations when I was eight and read the whole of *Animal Farm* to me when I was ten, while I was trying to watch *Scooby-Doo*. I didn't have helicopter parents but I occasionally had a helicopter sibling.

I've been missing him a lot since he's been away. I liked hanging out with my brother and his friends. No one seemed to mind me being there, stealing biscuits and listening in to their conversations, watching them playing football at the park. I liked how they were with one another. Easy and honest, playing card games and Subbuteo and larking about, and there never seemed to be any of that confusing, bitchy exclusion that there is with groups of girls. This stuff is coming into its own now, becoming increasingly more difficult to read. Last term I sat next to Susan in double French, this term she wants to sit next to Paula. Last week Paula said she wanted to sit next to me instead, but Susan said something to her and now she doesn't. It flips around like this from day to day. You walk into school on a Monday morning never knowing if you're going to be in or out.

It would be nice to have my sister to ask about these things but she left home when I was six. She moved to Nottingham then on to Leeds when she got married, and now Geoff's gone too I'm starting to feel like an only child. The house is quiet with just the three of us – me, Mum and Dad – but when Geoff's home during the holidays, the whole place seems to spring back to life. He's full of exotic stories about getting stoned and going to concerts and hanging out with his new college friends. It all sounds amazing to me – the demos, the lectures, the parties – and I've just seen and smelt a square block of something called hash that he's pulled from his jeans pocket. If I promise not to tell Mum and Dad what he's doing, Geoff's promised to let me watch him smoke it in Dad's car.

As well as educating me to the effects of marijuana, Geoff sees it as his role to toss stink bombs at my relentlessly technicolour pop palette. It's because of him that I was watching the *Today Show* the evening the Sex Pistols swore at Bill Grundy. When John Lennon was shot I was glad, all of a sudden, that my brother had made me listen to Lennon's strange (to me at least) solo album, *Shaved Fish,* when it first came out. 'Imagine' and 'Give Peace A Chance', everybody knew. But none of my nine-year-old friends were singing along to 'Cold Turkey' or 'Woman Is The Nigger Of The World'.

Without digging around or asking any embarrassing questions about why I need to know, Geoff steers me through a potted history of Adam Ant: the wild punk years and the Malcolm McLaren period. Later he digs out a cassette recording of the Ants' first album, the oddly named *Dirk Wears White Sox*. It's boring and weird and I hate it.

'That's because it's a bit more underground.'

'What does that mean?'

'More experimental. Less of a commercial imperative.'

'I see. Geoff?'

'Yes.'

'Are you a communist now you're at university?'

He thinks for a moment. Takes out his afro comb and has a quick jab at his perm in the rear-view mirror.

'No,' he says. 'Why do you ask?'

'Grandpop thinks you are because of your long curly hair.'

'Really?'

'Yeah. He said to Mum that if you like hippies and pinkos so much, you ought to go and live in Russia. Can I try some of your joint now?'

'No you can't.'

Armed with my new Ants information, I wait for my moment with Richard Grant. It takes days – possibly weeks – but one afternoon I spot him, alone in an empty classroom, in a low-risk-for-bundle situation. He's cramming pencils into his Gola bag and I sort of go over and shuffle about for a bit and then I say, 'Hngh, have you ever heard *Dirk Wears White Sox*?' Richard looks startled. 'Bit different then, wasn't he? More... uh, underground.' He's visibly confused, wondering how someone like me could possibly know something like that. He rubs his chin, which is code for not believing what you're hearing. We rub our chins a lot in class 2b.

Richard Grant will nod at me on occasion after that but won't actually speak to me until the day I ditch my glasses and grow into my oversized blazer: Mum thinks it's a good idea to buy school uniform that's at least four sizes too big, to maximise length of wear. It's a long way from an orgy or a game of battleships but even so, it's a minor triumph in my 2b world. It's also an important lesson when it comes to men and music. Know your subject if you want to impress a boy.

MOON BOOTS

My top two ambitions for 1981 are:

a) Owning a copy of *Dare* by The Human League.
b) Owning a pair of burgundy-coloured moon boots.

Moon boots are fantastic and surprising. They look like the kind of footwear Neil Armstrong would pack into his overnight bag before climbing aboard his rocket but are, in fact, designed to be worn in inclement weather: snow blizzards, for instance.

To the casual observer, like my mother, it might appear that the thick rubber soles, sturdy laces, Day-Glo colours and heavily insulated padding would be best suited to a person living in Canada, say, or Alaska. They'd certainly come in useful if you were called upon to drive a team of huskies across the Antarctic but, as my mother cunningly points out, there are no huskies in Gants Hill – only Dobermanns – and, in the unlikely event there were to be a blizzard, I could keep my feet warm with one of the two pairs of black and yellow striped toe socks she bought me for Christmas.

As enjoyable as it is to have a knitted acrylic pocket for each of your toes – and legs that look like giant bumble bees – the goal here is not to keep my feet warm. I'm not desperate for moon boots out of a misplaced fear of frostbite, but because they are supremely cool. More importantly, if I get a pair now I'll be in at the very start; I'll be an early adopter of the fashion. It'll make up for being the last one in my class to read Judy Blume, get bellbottom jeans, and have one of those pens that you wore round your neck as a pendant.

The problem with getting moon boots is this: I only have £5 of Christmas money left and if I buy them I won't be able to afford *Dare* by The Human League. I love The Human League. They are my new favourite band, a million times better than Adam And The Ants.

The three main reasons I love The Human League are:

1) 'Don't You Want Me' is a superbly catchy meditation on fame and unrequited love that made me want to work out a brand new interpretive dance routine the moment I heard it.
2) Phil Oakey has brilliant hair – jet black and asymmetric – as do the two girl singers: Joanne Catherall (the brunette one) and Susan Ann Sulley (the blonde one).
3) Amazing but true – the two girl singers were discovered by chance at a disco (probably doing an interpretive dance routine of their own) aged sixteen and seventeen. One day they were ordinary schoolgirls worrying about how best to bunk off double hockey, the next they were worldwide international pop stars. Just like that. No preamble. No previous pop star experience necessary.

This free-for-all attitude to band membership is exactly what is great about The Human League. Above and beyond their insanely hooky synth-pop they have proved, by the very nature of their inception, that instant pop mega-stardom is a real possibility. On the right night, at the right disco, displaying the right heavy fringe and sulky dance moves, Phil Oakey might pluck you from suburban obscurity, buy you a Malibu and Coke and catapult you to the top of the charts. If it can happen to Joanne Catherall and Susan Ann Sulley, there's a chance it could happen to me. Especially if my spots clear up. And I'm wearing my brand new moon boots.

On Saturday morning, like most Saturday mornings, I go shopping with my best friend Bernice Cohen. She lives at the end of my road and we've been best friends since the age of four. We've spent our childhood summers playing outside on the streets until dusk, and in the winters we have lived in and out of each other's houses as if they were our own. In some ways we're a slightly odd pairing. Her family are gregarious and open whereas mine are reserved and bookish. Her mum hugs you like a bear when you go round to tea, tells wonderful rude gossip about the next-door neighbours – there's a persistent rumour that the Mednicks are wife-swapping with the Davids – and makes the best chips I have ever tasted in my life. Her dad is a taxi driver who reads Harold Robbins whereas my dad is a civil servant who consults medical encyclopedias on account of his hypochondria and his stomach ulcers.

At Bernice's house, which is fanatically tidy and clean, we eat the good chips and seek out the dirty bits in Harold Robbins. At my house, which is mismatched and messy, we look at pictures of people with smallpox and take each other's blood pressure with my dad's stethoscope and his sphygmo-manometer. I have spent long periods of my childhood worrying about getting hypertension or ending up in an iron lung. I'm beginning to realise this might be slightly peculiar.

Now we're fourteen, we discuss our future plans for our lives. Pop dreams aside, I already know I want to go to university, like my brother and sister, but Bernice thinks she'll leave school in a couple more years. I will never get married, because marriage is pointless, and I'll never have children, because my sister has two of them already and it seems like *unbelievably* hard work. Bernice is undecided. She isn't ruling out either option. The two of us are cast from different moulds but our conflicting aspirations matter not a jot at this stage. I am Penfold to her Danger Mouse. We are two thirds of our own Charlie's Angels. She's one of those generous kids who is almost always sunny and kind, and I think the two of us will be best friends forever.

There are no record shops or moon-boot shops in Gants Hill – the Essex suburb where we live – so the two of us will have to take the bus into Ilford. Unlike Gants Hill, whose main attraction is its Wimpy Bar, Ilford is very cosmopolitan indeed. Fascinatingly, it has the highest density of shoe shops of any high street in the country (two Freeman Hardy Willis, a Saxone, a Curtess, two Dolcis, a Trueform, a Clarks, and a Lilley and Skinner) which, along with it being the birthplace of Noel Edmonds of *Multi-Coloured Swap Shop* fame, is something to be immensely proud of.

On the fifteen-minute bus ride into Ilford I outline my predicament to Bernice. She instinctively understands the complexities of the situation and while she's unable to provide a definitive answer one way or the other, she kindly offers to let me tape the twelve-inch of 'Under Pressure' by

Queen and David Bowie that she's planning to buy today. Of course, this ought to be the perfect solution. Wait until someone else I know buys *Dare* by The Human League then tape it from them. But it's not the same. I want the cover and the vinyl and most of all I want the lyric book so I can sing along to every track, including the lesser-known ones like 'Darkness' and 'Seconds', without getting any of the words wrong.

Our bus comes to a stop outside Bodgers department store, an old-fashioned emporium that stocks everything from girdles to goldfish and is our first port of call every Saturday. It's not so long ago that we were shopping in here with our mums. Scuffing our lace-up shoes in the park the next morning, embarrassed about the brown jumpers they'd bought us. But now we're off the leash, thrillingly free to dip our fingers into pots of cherry lip gloss and sparkly Biba eye-shadow; free to drench ourselves in clouds of Opium perfume and save up for matching hacking jackets and drainpipe jeans.

'I shaved my legs for the first time last week.'

'*Wow*. Did you?'

Bernice shows me her handiwork in the changing room.

'You've got cuts all over your ankles.'

'I know. And my legs look like a plucked chicken.'

'You going to do it again?'

'I think so.'

'Do you think we should pluck our continuous eyebrows?'

'Good idea. Let's go to the cafe for Coke and crisps next. And afterwards we can go and buy tweezers.'

We're both aware of trying to look more grown up and attractive these days but neither of us is the type of kid who would ever consider going on a diet. After a visit to the

swimming baths last week we rewarded ourselves for navigat-
ing the twin water-borne perils of verrucas and sticking plasters
by eating: toast and Cup-a-Soup from the pool canteen, a stick
of candyfloss, a cola float ice-cream sundae, a shared bag of
pick 'n' mix from Woolworths and, to gird ourselves up for
the mile-long walk home and lay a decent base for dinner, a
bag of chips each and a fat pickled cucumber. Despite this level
of gluttony being a regular occurrence, the pair of us were
distinctly average sized. Which just goes to show, it's not bad
diet that's making the nation's youth obese, it's the fact
they're downloading all their music instead of trudging up and
down the high street for hours on end each Saturday, crushed
with calorie-burning anxiety vis-à-vis moon boots and The
Human League.

Conveniently enough, Our Price record shop is located directly
next door to Curtess Shoes, my favoured moon-boot outlet and
the place I will get my first Saturday job. The exact pair of moon
boots I want are in the window. As I stare at them through the
plate glass I am overwhelmed by their plastic burgundy
gorgeousness. There's not a shred of doubt in my mind. I am
definitely going to buy them and it's only out of a sense of fairness that I accompany my best friend into Our Price, while she
makes her planned purchase of 'Under Pressure'.

I spot *Dare* the moment we walk in. The luminous white
cover with its close-up of Phil Oakey's heavily made-up face is
staring straight at me from the album racks and all but ordering me to buy it. Before I know what I'm doing, the record
sleeve is in my arms and I'm racing to the back of the
shop and thrusting the last of my Christmas money
over the counter. My mother was right: what use is padded

footwear in the temperate climes of suburban Essex? So long, boots. The new year belongs to The Human League.

What happens next is that it snows. It snows all week and the week after that. Gants Hill is coated in a deep icy drift that sticks around for the whole of February and on into March. On the walk to school each morning *everyone* is wearing moon boots. Bernice has a pair and, gallingly, in an act of decidedly un-best-girlfriend-like behaviour, they are burgundy. No matter. I console myself with the fact I know all the words to the lesser-known *Dare* tracks, 'Darkness' and 'Seconds', and hum them defiantly under my breath as I trudge through the slush in my plimsolls and bumble-bee toe socks.

It doesn't help. 'Darkness' and 'Seconds' were a bit of a let-down if I'm honest, with little obvious contribution from Joanne Catherall and Susan Ann Sulley. As the cold water seeps into the knitted acrylic pockets that are my toes' final barrier against frostbite, it strikes me that I'd rather have moon boots and toasty feet than be able to sing along to a morose electro-pop song about the assassination of John F. Kennedy.

Things come to a head some months later when I attempt to revive my passion for The Human League with a trip to Uppercuts, Gants Hill's premier hair salon. I ask the barber, Brian, to cut my hair like one of the girls from The Human League. Unfortunately for me, Brian thinks Phil Oakey *is* one of the girls from The Human League and instead of giving me the cute crop and blunt heavy fringe that would mark me out as a future pop star at any self-respecting Sheffield disco, I end up with a lopsided mishap that makes me look like Deputy Dawg with one of his ears missing.

At home, as I rummage through my drawers for a suitable bobble hat in which to see out the remainder of 1981, I wonder what my mum will make of the way I spent the hair-cut money she gave me. I dig out my cassette copy of 'Under Pressure', by Queen and David Bowie, and listen to it from an entirely new perspective.

HINDLEAP WARREN

There are two types of people in this world: sporty and not. I'm not. I can handle an innings or two of back garden cricket but anything involving nets and pucks or navy-blue gym knickers results in a complete collapse of hand-eye-body coordination akin to physical dyslexia. Even now, as an adult, I get a brief rush of panic if somebody takes out a Frisbee at a picnic.

'Who fancies a chuck about?'

'Great. Be right with you. Just going to polish off this second tub of spicy hummus. Shame to waste it.'

My athletic prowess is such that in my first term of secondary school I collapsed with an asthma attack during the 1500 metres and my mum had to come to the nurse's office and collect me. After that I was made to use an inhaler in the changing rooms, minutes before every games lesson. It was a clunky old-fashioned prototype – not the discreet pressurised kind you see these days – and made an incessant high-pitched *weeeeee* sound when you sucked it.

Having the inhaler is a curse. From the moment I first use it, I know beyond doubt I'll always be the second to last kid picked for school sports teams – second only to fat, smelly Stacey – and that I'll never, not *ever*, be asked to wear a shiny black netball sash that bears the immortal words: *goal attack*. Those black sashes were as covetable as Simon

Le Bon's home phone number. They might just as well have read 'Miss World'.

The goal-attack squad are beautiful and popular: Sharron Davies blondes with long legs and rosy complexions. All the boys want to go out with them and all the girls want to be their best friend. The reigning queen bee is Hailey Collier, who has frosted hair and looks a bit like Thereza Bazar from Dollar. Her second-in-command is called Samantha. Samantha has chunky thighs from all the trampolining she does, but no one dares point this out, on account of her being first lieutenant to Hailey Collier.

Every Tuesday after netball practice, the goal-attack girls dive head-first into the communal showers with their bottles of Flex, as if they haven't a care in the world. This is because they *haven't* a care in the world. They don't have AA-sized boobs, they have proper C cups. They don't have spots or glasses, or wavy hair that dries funny in the wind and is a curious shade of orange after an ill-advised experiment with a carton of market-stall henna. They have long swishy tresses that they tie into perfect ponytails, and thick plaits that reach down their backs. They have more than three friends. They think Ryvita tastes nice. They are an alien life form. I hate them.

Me and fat Stacey hop from foot to foot in the showers and wave our toes under the dribbling water jets. We wrap ourselves in towels and splash water onto our shoulders to make the sports mistress think we've been in properly when we haven't. Me and fat Stacey have had our periods for six weeks in a row now but Miss Watkins has finally twigged what we're up to and forced us to take a shower after games. I don't need a shower. I've done no running about whatsoever. I've loitered at the back – in wing defence – examining the quicks of my nails and scowling at Samantha and Hailey in case they throw the ball in my direction by mistake. Fat Stacey could do with a shower, though, if I'm honest.

Given my longstanding aversion to team games and sports, it's something of a puzzle that in the summer of 1981 – with my lopsided Oakey haircut still growing out – I find myself on a weekend outward bound course in the Chilterns with Bernice Cohen. The likeliest explanation is that I've mistaken an outward bound course for being a bit like boarding school in the manner of Enid Blyton's *Malory Towers*. Either that or my parents forged my signature on the application form so they could get me out of the house and go to see *Emmanuelle* by mistake again.

'So,' Bernice says, as we unwrap our egg sandwiches on the coach, 'what do you think it's going to be like?'

'Non-stop midnight feasts and a bit of lacrosse, probably.'

'What's lacrosse?'

'It's something that posh girls do at boarding school.'

'It's not a sport?'

'I don't think so.'

We nod our heads. We tuck into our egg.

'Did you remember to pack your waterproofs and torch?'

'What are we going to need *those* for?'

'It said in the info pack, bring torches. Knee pads and helmets are supplied.'

I have made a gargantuan error. This is nothing at all like *Malory Towers*. There are no midnight feasts. No lacrosse. The entire weekend will be filled with one nightmarish activity after another: assault courses, rock climbing, tree-top rope-walking, cross-country running and death slides. Unless I can find a way to sign up for the pottery tent ten times in a row, there's a distinct possibility I won't make it out of here alive. I can feel all eyes upon me as we unpack our cases: wondering how soon I will crack. The only tool in my armoury – thanks to my brother – is an uncanny ability with an overarm spin ball. There is, unfortunately, no possible use for spin bowling that I can see in the entire Hindleap Warren itinerary.

It feels like a never-ending school day. Hell without the blessed release of the school bell. Flat on my belly in the mud, trying to wipe the grit from my glasses, while Collier and her sidekicks streak past me. Gritting my teeth on the high tree-top ropes, doughty and determined, while the boys yell at me to hurry up, or express their mass desire to see me fall. There's a quiet moment as I queue up for the death slide, only punctuated by my inhaler going *weeeeee*.

Afterwards, in the dormitory, Hailey and Samantha parade around in their bras and knickers, saturating their bodies in Impulse deodorant. They are brazenly flouting teenage convention. Don't they know you're meant to get changed in public by employing a Houdini-like contortion behind your towel? There is no way on earth I am going to do this. I'm sticking to what I know. Wriggling and bending and dislocating my shoulders to get out of my towel and into my top. My body is less than perfect. I have two strawberry birthmarks on my right arm, and a huge irregular one – the size of a palm print – in the middle of my chest, exactly where my cleavage ought to start. I go to enormous lengths to hide it. I can change in and out of a PE kit in ten seconds flat without ever appearing naked below the chin. Every day I pin my school blouse shut, to stop its lapels from flapping open and revealing the dark, scarlet stain. I don't own a single low-cut item of clothing. The most revealing top I have is a round-necked T-shirt.

This summer I went to a London hospital to learn how to disguise my birthmark with camouflage make-up. I sat there with the nurse as she brought out her pots of NHS powder and grease and taught me how to trowel it onto my skin. I was excited to go – I imagined some blemish-dissolving alchemy, akin to invisible ink – but the stuff is so thick and badly coloured it makes the damn thing look even worse. I hate it so much I've thought about covering it in bleach to see if it will fade. I have fantasised about taking a knife to it, and cutting it out of my body.

My mum insisting it's a nice shade of red and my dad saying it's shaped like a map of Africa and pointing out the exact location of Sierra Leone – top left-hand corner – only really helped when I was a kid. It doesn't help now. Not in the dormitories. I'm embarrassed enough about my emergent breasts as it is, without having a map of Africa stencilled in between them. The perfect girls will stare. Or something worse. I haven't forgotten being chased home from junior school by a group of kids with sticks for having the mark of the devil on me. I know. It's ridiculous. If I'd had any sense I would have stayed at home with the curtains shut until I was at least eighteen.

The only bright spot in the whole weekend is that it has to end soon. The downside of it ending is that our instructors have saved the worst activity until last. The finale to the most torturous 48 hours of my life so far is a night hike through the woods.

What this foolhardy activity amounts to is a cross-country run by two dozen children in the dark. The three-mile round trip is steep and slippery and takes in various challenging obstacles, the most notorious of which is 'the pipe'. The pipe is a narrow tunnel that's been dug through the side of a grassy hillock and, despite repeated assertions to the contrary, looks like it might collapse at any moment. It's just wide enough for a fourteen-year-old (not fat Stacey, though, not a chance) to crawl through whilst lying flat on their belly. There's rain water at the bottom and it's intensely claustrophobic; especially when your torch gets wet and the light goes out, and you can't see where the end is because it's pitch dark outside, and all you can hear is the person up ahead of you yelling 'Rats!'

I get ten yards through the pipe before my Private Benjamin moment strikes. I am reversing. The instructor sees my feet emerging from the tunnel and all but shoves me straight back inside again. I refuse to crack under the weight of his ridicule. I ride out damning accusations that I have let everyone down and failed to get into the spirit of outward bound. The goal-attack girls crawled through without a whimper, he tells me. Some of them liked it so much they asked if they could go round again.

I will not be deterred. After 48 hours of bad food, barracks life and the agonising embarrassment of communal showers, I decide I can't take any more. It's time to make a stand and, contrary to all expectations, this might be my moment in the sun. I appear to have incited a rebellion. The last few behind me are also refusing to go into the tunnel: one girl is sobbing and threatening to sue for child cruelty. The instructor is beaten. He grudgingly waves us round the final obstacle to the rewards of a lukewarm mug of cocoa, one last dreaded shower and an early night.

It's not a great night in the dormitories. Several of the kids have caught stomach bugs. Everyone is blaming the food but it seems more likely they've ingested stagnant water in the pipe because it's only the kids who went through the tunnel who spend the night pooing and throwing up. This makes me very happy indeed. I'm just drifting into a contented sleep – imagining a subtle correction of the universe against the supremacy of goal-attack girls – when I find myself dreaming that it's raining. It's raining in my bunk. Warm rain. A slow and intermittent drip. There's a stain on the cover of my sleeping bag that definitely wasn't there when I went to bed.

If there's one piece of advice I will pass on to my children it's this: never sleep in the bottom bunkbed on an outward bound course. You are gambling with your life. There will always be a bed-wetter hiding somewhere in the vicinity and the last place you want a bed-wetter is fast asleep, directly above your head, with only a paper-thin mattress between you and them. I head to the bathrooms for a second time that night, the only consolation being that I get to use my shower gel on my own.

When we return from Hindleap Warren, Bernice's mother – who punctuates every third sentence with a spritz of Mr Sheen – is so appalled by the tales of poo and sick that she marches Bernice straight upstairs and gives her a bath with a mug of Dettol mixed into the water. My mum does the next best thing. She cooks roast lamb for tea with mint sauce on the side and, as a special treat, she lets me eat it in front of *All Creatures Great and Small*. As I watch James Herriot thrust his hands up the umpteenth cow's bottom I am forced to reassess my recently expanded career ambitions. I'm quite keen on animals at this stage and I've toyed with the idea of becoming a vet. It suddenly becomes clear I will never make it as a vet, since it might require me to be outdoors covered in wee a good deal of the time. Veterinary science is discounted once and for all from my list of prospective careers. That only leaves actress and pop star.

THE KIDS FROM FAME

Bernice's cousin Dilly is a mixture of actress and pop star. She goes to stage school, has a small part in *Annie*, the West End musical, and is officially the first true extrovert I have ever met. There are no extroverts in the Wener family, unless you count my Auntie Hylda who likes to get up and sing at family weddings. At the merest provocation, after one too many Snowballs, she'll hitch up her skirt and belt out a version of 'It's Not Unusual' that would put Tom Jones to shame. She makes my mum giggle and has a sense of humour that can best be described as fruity. Everybody loves her to bits.

Auntie Hylda aside, we are not known as a family that likes to break into spontaneous song without good reason. My dad will do a spot of Sinatra after a couple of gins, my mum might sing you the books of the Bible (all 66 in order, from start to finish) if you ask her nicely, but the chances of one of us standing outside C&A on Ilford High Road belting out the score to *Jesus Christ Superstar* on a Saturday afternoon is less than nil. Dilly is doing just that. She's halfway through 'I Don't Know How To Love Him' and she's attracting a bit of a crowd. Her voice is knockout. Loud and powerful with what seems to me to be an unfeasible range. She starts off low then swoops up to the high bits without losing any of her strength. After assorted songs from *Superstar,* Dilly performs a choreographed version of 'Hot Lunch' from *Fame*. People are clapping. It's amazing. This must be what it's like to go shopping with Irene Cara!

Bernice and I love *Fame* so much, we have recently travelled to Roman Road market and invested in matching all-in-one leotards, the kind with built-in leggings that reach to the ankles. Mine is purple and Bernice's is electric blue. We spent ages choosing them, squeezing our bodies into the shiny nylon sausage skins behind a makeshift curtain, bending our bodies double to check the size of our bums in the small chipped mirror. On the tube journey home, we clasped our precious packages to our laps – matching legwarmers and headbands included – and dreamed of imminent stardom. Our plan was to save up our pocket money and take modern-dance classes after school. Before you knew it we'd be performing mid-air star jumps on the way to double maths and pirouetting on the canteen tables during our lunch hour. It could only be a matter of months before our talent was discovered and we were transferred to the New York High School of Performing Arts on a full-time scholarship.

We only ever went to one class. It turns out that dancing is very difficult indeed and not unrelated to sport. While everyone else was wrapping their legs around their ears and falling to the floor to do the splits, Bernice and I were creaking around the room, as lithe and limber as a couple of arthritic pensioners. It was a sobering lesson. For months I'd fantasised that my inner kid from fame was Coco Hernandez, only to discover it was Doris Schwartz.

Bernice's cousin Dilly is exactly like Coco Hernandez. She's a little older than us; she can sing, dance and act, and she's recorded an actual pop song in a studio. She has long curly hair, dyed a startling shade of burgundy, wears legwarmers with a short grey ra-ra skirt, and a sweatshirt cut open at the neck, so it hangs off one shoulder. She's very good-looking, but in a young Barbra Streisand way more than a goal-attack way, so I can't even dislike her for that.

Dilly is only visiting for the week but already she's making her mark. First she has half of Ilford High Road eating out of her hand, now she's come over to my house and charmed the pants off my dad. She does this by kissing him on both cheeks and telling him he's the spitting image of the film star Walter Matthau, who just happens to be my dad's third favourite person in the universe after Duke Ellington and Groucho Marx. I distinctly remember Dilly getting first pick of the fondant fancies that afternoon and me beginning to like her slightly less.

After tea and Mr Kiplings we crank up the Amstrad music centre and Dilly plays us her newly recorded song. She thinks it sounds like Toyah Willcox and it sort of does, but without the annoying lisp, or a tune you could hum along to without listening to it at least 50 times. Even so, Dilly's cassette tape is remarkable. There are real instruments playing, with drums and guitars and synthesisers and everything, and Bernice and I are massively impressed. Dilly tells us the track has been mixed by a producer and we both say, 'Wow, amazing', even though neither of us has the foggiest idea what this might mean.

When Dilly packs her tape away I experience a deep and lasting attack of envy: a palpable sense of unfairness. Based on no good evidence whatsoever, I have the overwhelming feeling I could do much better. She might have a producer and a big stage-school voice, but music is my thing. It belongs to me. I am rubbish at everything else. I might do OK at schoolwork but what's the point of that when your siblings – who both got into grammar school – have done much better than you already. I need to have something of my own. This girl is stepping on my toes. She can't just wander in with her burgundy hair and her off-the-shoulder sweatshirt, wow the whole of Ilford, and march all over my pop dream. I am suddenly overcome with competitiveness. I think this might call for some drastic action.

I am fifteen years old around the time of Dilly's stay and just about to join a local youth club. On the evening of my inaugural visit, with a renewed sense of purpose, I make the life-altering decision to embrace blurred vision and ditch my hideous glasses. I shut them in their case with their stupid yellow cleaning cloth and make a vow not to open it ever again. No more steamed-up lenses. No more cunning and original quips, like, 'Fuck off four eyes'. The effects are almost instantaneous. The social order is not yet established at youth club and stripped of the jam-jar spectacles, I can feel my self-consciousness slipping. I'm the new girl in the room, welcomed in on a level pegging. It's not quite worthy of Madonna – and it will be a good while yet before the image change resonates back at school – but for me this is the beginnings of a reinvention.

More miraculous still, someone has finally fancied me and asked me out. It can't have come a moment too soon. When the proposition comes I'm mere hours away from getting off with crater-faced Jonathan. Crater-faced Jonathan wanders the youth club at closing time, offering cubic zirconia stud earrings from a paper bag to any girl willing to kiss him. You have to admire Jonathan's ingenuity. His father is a jeweller.

I was desperate to break my duck. In some ways it seemed like a fair trade.

The boy who saves me from imitation diamond jewellery is called Scott. His favourite record is 'We Will Rock You' by Queen. He backs up his romantic advances by offering me not one, but *two*, packets of Matchmakers: mint and orange. If you're as short-sighted as I am now – in an alleyway, in a very bad light – he bears a passing resemblance to Nik Kershaw. He makes my stomach queasy. I have kissed him with tongues. It wasn't entirely without incident – there was a bit of tooth collision, some chipped enamel – but I can finally throw away my game of battleships.

The evening before Dilly goes home she lends us her can of pink, glittery hairspray. The three of us paint neon skunk stripes in our hair – just like Toyah – and spend a couple of hours backcombing our fringes and rehearsing 'It's A Mystery' and 'Go Wild In The Country' by Bow Wow Wow. A week or so later, Bernice and I are at the Odeon to see *Raiders of the Lost Ark* when there's a bit of a hiccup with the film. The Odeon is a grand old building, the nicest thing about Gants Hill. It has steep, tiered balconies and a single giant screen, and there's a working cinema organ at the front of the stalls, left over from the fifties from when it used to be called the Savoy. Every so often someone still plays that rickety organ, grinding out old music-hall numbers between the trailers and the main event. Today, while the problem with the film projector is getting fixed, the organist steps up to fill in.

After ten minutes of plinky-plonky music hall, I have a strange thought and it's this: if Dilly were with us now, what would she do?

'No way.'

'I'll buy the Butterkist.'

'No chance.'

'I'll get the hot dogs.'

'I'm not going to do it.'

'Fair enough. But what if I told you there was a really easy way to get free cubic zirconia earrings?'

Before you know it I've convinced Bernice to come up to the front with me and we're having a quiet word with the organist to see if she knows the chords to any Bow Wow Wow songs. Together we mug our way through a few choruses of 'Go Wild In The Country' while the organist gamely improvises behind us. In the end, when we finish – by collapsing and running out of words rather than through any real intent – half the Odeon cinema whistles and claps. It feels strange. It feels wonderful. I would never have done this in my glasses. I might not be Coco Hernandez, but deep down in the genes, I always suspected there was a touch of my Auntie Hylda.

SO GOOD I
BOUGHT IT TWICE

My brand new copy of 'Eye Of The Tiger' by Survivor, the theme tune to *Rocky III*, is warped. Warping is a common hazard with vinyl. Only last weekend my brother came home from university to discover his *Best of The Stranglers* was past its best. We had a heated discussion about my promising to keep his albums in their sleeves and out of direct sunlight in future and an illuminating conversation in which I learned the lyrics to 'Golden Brown' were about heroin, and the lyrics to 'Peaches' were about bottoms.

I'm particularly annoyed about the warping of 'Eye Of The Tiger' because I haven't had the chance to play it yet. I pulled it fresh from its cover just this afternoon and watched in horror as it wobbled on the turntable, its wild undulations sending the stylus skidding back and forth across the vinyl. It's a blow. I was very much looking forward to miming along to the spectacular high notes in the chorus whilst pretending to be heavyweight boxing champion of the world.

Survivor's uplifting single is number one in the charts and I'm buying it as a prelude to a planned outing to see *Rocky III*. I am a big fan of the *Rocky* films. I had a poster of Sylvester Stallone on my wall when I was nine, next to David Soul and Orinoco Womble. I grew out of my Soul and Womble phases but have retained a residual loyalty to Rocky Balboa. This is because *Rocky I* is a work of genius.

There are people who will try to tell you that Martin Scorsese's *Raging Bull* is the best boxing film ever made, possibly the best film of the eighties. They are wrong. OK, so Robert De Niro put on a bit of weight to play the role of Jake La Motta. Big deal, he ate a few cakes. Sylvester Stallone wrote his own script!

Rocky did the iconic punching the wall scene long before Jake; Balboa did steady-cam before *Raging Bull*. LaMotta is a self-pitying wife-beater with whom we feel no sympathy or engagement. Rocky is a dumb but noble hero, fighting for the one chance he's ever had in the whole of his miserable life, and the future of his timid, specky girlfriend, '*Adrian!*' Worst of all, *Raging Bull* has a crappy ending. With no explanation of why or how, the thuggish Mafia stooge LaMotta suddenly morphs into an affable, Lenny Bruce-style club comedian. It's deeply anti-climactic. The damn thing's not even in colour!

Compare this to the ending of *Rocky*. It's the fourteenth round. Rocky goes down. Adrian is standing at the back crying. Mickey, his trainer, pleads for him to stay down and take the count. The music builds. Rocky gets to his feet, bloodied and barely able to see. He tells the ref he's OK, dredges up his last shred of strength and smashes into the champ's damaged ribs. Rocky survives the round. And the next. Against all odds the underdog goes the distance, which is all he ever dreamed he could do. Adrian runs to him. She embraces his beaten body. Whole cinema stands up and cheers!

Rocky versus *Raging Bull*. Round one knockout.

*

I bought my warped copy of 'Eye Of The Tiger' at HMV in London's Oxford Street. There's no local HMV, so I'm not going to be able to exchange it before I see the film. For the only time in my life, I'll have to buy a single for a second time.

I ask for 'Eye Of The Tiger' at the counter of my local branch of Our Price. The boy behind the till is wearing a Stiff Little Fingers T-shirt and I can't work out why he's giving me that funny look. He goes to get my record but I can tell he doesn't really want to touch it.

'Don't you like this single?'

'Fnah,' he says.

'Have you heard it?'

'Yeah, I've heard it. It's shit.'

'Oh. What do you like then?'

He points to his T-shirt.

I have never heard Stiff Little Fingers. They may very well be completely brilliant. I am open to his musical tastes. I think he should be open to mine.

'You know what else is good?' I say, casually.

'What?' he says, putting my record in a bag like it's a radioactive isotope.

'That song by Bill Conti. "Gonna Fly Now". They play it when Rocky's running up all those steps outside the Philadelphia Museum.'

He shakes his head in disgust.

'Fuck's sake,' he says. 'Do you like *any* kind of music that's not been in the *Rocky* soundtrack?'

Of course I do. I was thinking about asking him for a copy of 'The Look of Love' by ABC, but I'm not going to bother now.

At home I hold my breath to see if my replacement slip of vinyl is warped. It isn't. I put it on the stereo and play it six times in a row. The high notes are a triumph. It was worth buying twice. Listening to 'Eye Of The Tiger' makes me feel like a heavyweight champion: at the very least a heavyweight champion's girlfriend.

The following week I go to see *Rocky III*. It's not as good as some of the others in the series and I'm prepared to admit that the *Rocky* sequels are a mixed bag, quality-control-wise. But you've got to feel sorry for Stiff Little Fingers. I know why he was looking at me funny now. I bet he was a Jake La Motta fan.

58 SO GOOD I BOUGHT IT TWICE

DEAD CAT

It's one thing massacring a Bow Wow Wow song in front of a hundred teenagers high on Kia-Ora, it's quite another doing a gig in front of 12,000 people at Wembley Arena. Even so, having been there, having *seen* it, this is the thing I most want to do in the universe.

I'm at my first ever concert. We don't call them gigs yet, at least I don't and my brother doesn't and it's him and his girl-friend who are taking me to see the last ever London performance by The Jam. I'm not going because I particularly like The Jam – though I will after tonight, which is a bit of a shame since they are two dates away from splitting up – I'm going because my cat has just died and my brother has wangled me an extra ticket because he thinks it will cheer me up.

To be honest, I'm not too bothered about the concert. I'm in mourning. I've had Stanley, the cat, for five years and we've seen each other through some pretty rough times. Fleas and worms: him not me. Big school, teenage angst, the Phil Oakey haircut: me not him. Home life has grown increasingly difficult in the years since my brother left home. My parents' marriage is strained. My relationship with my father is at a low. I rattle around the house with my head down, avoiding my parents' eyes, caught in the middle of their arguments. Theirs is an odd married madness, a years-old being togetherness that I can't yet make good sense of or understand.

Lately there's been more war than peace in our house and on fraught Friday nights and silent Sundays, I escape for hours on end with a pair of headphones plugged into a socket. It's almost good enough, but the thing that makes it work is Stanley fast asleep on my lap, kneading claw marks into my favourite album cover. He was black and white. He was really cool.

'He's dead then?'

'Yup.'

'What of?'

'Vet said cat-flu or something. Because we never gave him any vaccinations. We should probably have taken him in earlier. You know, when he started losing all that weight.'

'What did Dad say?'

'Nothing. He hated the cat. He says we can move into a flat now, because we don't need the garden any more.'

My brother's girlfriend offers a thin smile. Unsure at her boyfriend's family's ways.

'Well, never mind. Here's your ticket. It's The Jam. The farewell tour. This is going to be bloody great.'

I put my hands in my pockets. I shrug. Really, how good can it be?

The Jam concert is a little piece of magic. I am overawed by the size of the place. We take our seats, high up in the auditorium, and gaze down at the stage, sparsely decorated with unfamiliar equipment. I have never been in a room with so many people and the sight of thousands of music fans crammed into their seats, with hundreds more crushed tight against the stage, is exhilarating in itself. They are giving off steam, an evaporation of neat sweat and tension, and a cloud of excitement sits heavy in the air, waiting to burst with its rain.

As the lights dim the crowd rise to their feet. They let forth a roar that feels like a punch: it is Cup Final day and the first goal has just hit the net. The band take their places and they seem so small, so slight, I worry that they won't be able to hold us, that they haven't the goods. And then the music starts. It's provocatively loud, filling the space around us with muscle and melody and grit. I am lost for the hours that they play, so transformed by seeing 'A Town Called Malice' – the one Jam song I love – take shape in the flesh, with all its fire and spit, that it leaves an indelible mark.

The first thing I do when I get home is tape every one of my brother's Jam albums. I label the cassettes as neatly as I can, track listings included, and spend some quality time studying the lyric books before I have to give the original copies back. Once I'm done with memorising the words to 'Going Underground' and 'Beat Surrender', the album I fall in love with is *Setting Sons*. It's less Vespa and parka than *All Mod Cons*, more crafted, satirical and Kinks-ish. It's crammed full of stark English narratives about wasted lives and class rivalries that seem to chime with my teenage self, as if I've discovered a secret.

The band sing about beating 'the system', about council houses, rusting bicycles and holy Coca-Cola tins. It's a decaying inner-city landscape, not my Sunday car-washing suburban one, but its bitter-sweetness resonates nevertheless. And then I find the track 'Smithers-Jones'. I don't think I've ever heard a pop song with lyrics about a ground-down, pinstripe-suit-wearing middle-aged man before and I have the feeling The

Jam have been spying on my family because it could almost have been written about my dad.

I decide Smithers-Jones is a civil servant, just like Dad. He's clearly posher and likely much richer, because his name is double-barrelled, but essentially they seem cast from the same mould. He's a commuter from the suburbs, he's done everything right, but he's blithely underrated by his bosses. Smithers loses his coveted promotion on the whim of his superiors, Dad lost out on his because his socialist convictions meant he once had the temerity to go on strike. Even so, Dad and Smithers both make the best of it. They take the same tube journey to work each morning, at 8am sharp, carry a briefcase and umbrella under their arms and eat the same sandwich for lunch every day: in Dad's case it was always cheese and Marmite.

Much of my father's generation worked like this. They left school with the qualifications their class afforded them, took a job for life, something dependable, and supported a wife, home and family until the gold-plated watch on retirement. Dad ended up in a job he didn't like all that much, that left him frustrated and unfulfilled. Against the dictates of a bullying father, he'd nurtured a dream of going to university to study law but the Second World War got in the way and before he knew it, he was demobbed and married and mortgaged and that's how it happens; plans are put aside and you end up with no room to manoeuvre.

It was a similar story for Mum. She had always wanted to be a nurse but settled for being a housewife. She started her nursing training in her teens but never completed it, and was always filled with regret. Mum says she gave up nursing to get married but I think the thing that swung it was the surgeon who once threw an amputated leg at her during an operation, to make sure she was paying attention. The Health Service was different in those days. My parents' discarded ambitions are the ghosts in our house as I'm growing up, the presence that soaks up all the light. Their lives seem claustrophobic to me, put away, boarded up, but their days haven't always been this plain. Dad's had his fair share of adventures. In 1940 he joined the RAF, aged eighteen, and fought through the Second World War. He was stationed in West Africa and when I was a child he'd make up stories about crocodiles that he'd seen and show me black and white pictures of mud huts and jungles and lions. He travelled the oceans on troop carriers, always sleeping on the deck to stand a better chance if they were hit by torpedoes. He was an engineer. He flew bombers. He lost great friends and family in devastating ways and fought off malaria four times.

We grew up with Dad's stories about Nazis and crocodiles and post-war austerity and listened just as eagerly to my mother's domestic counterpoint: her younger sister Freda scrabbling around to find her knickers when the air-raid sirens sounded in the middle of the night; my nana rushing her family to the garden bomb shelter accompanied by the eerie buzz sound of the doodlebug bombs as they flew overhead. After the buzz came the ghostly silence which meant they were about to explode and a slice of shrapnel the size of a plate once missed Mum by inches, lodging itself in her garden gate. In 1940, while Dad was joining up, Mum was being evacuated from the East End Blitz to the quiet of the Yorkshire country-side. Finding she didn't care for it all that much, she promptly ran away to find her mother.

In 1945, quite by chance, Dad won a lottery that saw him stationed in Paris in the days directly after liberation. He told us dreadful stories of female collaborators being dragged through the streets with their heads shaved, and wonderful ones about drinking champagne at the Moulin Rouge. There were beautiful women everywhere, jazz clubs and alcohol and abandon and for a 23-year-old man it must have been the most extraordinary party ever, in all the world.

Growing up with older parents meant I heard a different set of back stories to most of my friends. I was conscious, early on, that a world existed somewhere that was graphically opposite to mine. When Dad listened to Duke Ellington and Ella Fitzgerald on Sunday afternoons, he was back in the narrow streets of Pigalle and Montmartre, drinking and living and dancing. Music was instant pleasure and relaxation for him, a direct route to some previously experienced otherness that was almost unimaginable to me. Music was his route of escape. Records have begun to feel like the means to mine.

I'm approaching a musical crossroads. I'm eating up The Jam and The Smiths and now there's Dexy's Midnight Runners and David Bowie and I seriously can't *believe* there is something out there as good as David Bowie. Most of my classmates are into Shakatak and Imagination – soul-pop is big in this part of Essex – and while I'm a long way from ditching Doris Schwartz completely, I'm sensing 'Hungry Like The Wolf' has less relevance to my life than I might previously have imagined.

In essence, the Jam concert has confused me. All of a sudden, I suspect there might be some subtle difference between being in a rock band and being a pop star but I'm damned if I know what it is. I've never met anyone who's been in a band. I wonder how you go about joining: how you find one, how you begin. Perhaps the process is simpler than I think. For all I know Paul Weller might have started out just like Bernice's cousin Dilly, singing excerpts from *Jesus Christ Superstar* on Woking High Road.

WHEREVER I LAY MY HAT

After years living away up north, my sister has moved back to Essex. Her children are four and two and because she's only a few miles up the road now, I have taken on the job of some-time babysitter. This is easy enough. Eat biscuits. Watch TV. Scan through my sister's well-thumbed copy of *The Joy of Sex* and point out the weirdest bits to Bernice Cohen. We've done starters and main course. Now we're trapped in the sauces and the pickles.

'Why would you want someone to tie you up and tickle you with a feather?'

'God knows.'

'I am *never* doing sixty-nine.'

'No. Me neither.'

'Or the bum sex.'

'No way!'

'Would you ever do it with a man who had a beard?'

'*Never*. Beards are disgusting.'

'Quick, let's put the book away before your sister gets home. I don't want her asking us if we've started masturbating again.'

This is the kind of thing my sister does now I'm sixteen. She comes home from a night out, waits until her husband has left the room, claps her hands together and says, 'So, girls... are both of you still virgins?' Not content with our mumbling replies and reddened faces, she presses on with a knowing smirk and demands to know if we've started masturbating yet. It's excruciating. She doesn't even whisper it. She thinks she's Claire Rayner or something.

I should have known this kind of thing was going to happen when my sister came back. She has always been loud and uninhibited. When she was still living at home she used to change the lyrics to The Monkees' song 'Daydream Believer' from 'Cheer up Sleepy Jean' to 'Cheer up have a wank', and sing it at full volume in the bath. Even at the age of six I suspected this was inappropriate lyrical material for Davy Jones.

When she had her second child my sister videotaped the birth in all its close-up, life-affirming glory and offered to show it to every friend, neighbour or relative who came to visit. There are a couple of our more traditional cousins who still haven't got over the shock. I'm guessing they didn't fully appreciate its life-affirming glory. For my part, the hours of torturous screaming and bloody close-ups only served to reinforce the confounding, nightmarish, idiotic folly that is trying to force something the size of a baby through your front bottom. I will not be doing this any time soon. There is no way I'm getting pregnant at the age of 22, putting on a smock dress and filling my bookshelves with Dr Spock and Sheila Kitzinger and recipes for 101 ways with mince.

My sister's bookshelves have a lot of Germaine Greer on them as well. And something by Erica Jong which purports to be about the fear of flying but is really about something called zipless fucking. She may be a stay-at-home mother for the moment, but my sister has new ambitions to be a radio journalist. I suspect she might even be a feminist. I think I might like to become one too.

I remember the time I first started thinking seriously about feminism. I was lying on my bed at my most mopey, listening to Yazoo, with a hot-water bottle on my stomach and a packet of Feminax open beside me on the dressing table. As I stared at my poster of Edvard Munch's 'The Scream' and wondered at the pointlessness of my own existence, my mum peeped round the door with a Caramel Wafer and a steaming hot cup of sugary tea. What I should have said is, 'How thoughtful, thanks very much.' What I said instead – in a sneery teenage voice – is, 'How come Dad never makes the tea?'

My dad doesn't cook. He doesn't clean. He and his brother grew up with three big sisters and a mother who did everything for them. To the best of my knowledge he has never washed up a dirty cup or simmered so much as a boiled egg. Family legend has it that when my mum came down with the Hong Kong flu in 1968 and was forced to her bed (Mum will only abandon her post at the coal seam of housework if she's delirious or has accidentally amputated a digit with a blunted breadknife), my dad fed the entire family on jars of my baby food for days. Mum thinks this is funny. What's wrong with her? She should be *furious* about it. Dad ought to know how to operate the cooker and make boil-in-the-bag fish, at the *very* least. The fact that he doesn't is fantastically old-fashioned and sexist!

'How come Dad never does the Hoovering?'

'Your dad works very hard at his job.'

'How come Dad never cooks?'

'He doesn't know how.'

'Well, I'm never getting married, but if I do, I'm going to be the one who goes to work and the man can stay at home and do all the Hoovering.'

'I see.'

'And change all the nappies.'

'I thought you said you didn't want children.'

A vision of my sister and some stirrups.

'You're right. Oh my *God*. I forgot for a second. No, I don't.'

It turns out that sexism is not only confined to the home. The more you look into it, the more you discover it's a revolutionary and all-encompassing concept. The legacy of our suffragette sisters was brought home to me just last week when a careers advisor came to visit our school. I filled in one of his stupid forms along the lines of: Do you want to spend the rest of your life a) changing nappies b) typing c) on your boss's knee taking dictation, and my answers all pointed to a future career as an air hostess. This is so sexist! What about doctor, or engineer or astronaut? I'm pretty good at sciences, as a matter of fact. I'm up with Ohm's Law. I'm down with Pythagoras. If only I'd correctly remembered that speed equals distance over time when I sat my physics O Level, I could probably have grown up to be Marie Curie.

It turns out that everything can be sexist: careers advisors, *his*tory, make-up, dieting, advertising, wages, my brother's poster of the tennis girl with her bum hanging out, even pop music. A prime example is Paul Young, who I've recently written off as a sexist pig on account of the lyrics to 'Wherever I Lay My Hat (That's My Home)'. Paul is the kind of guy who loves them and leaves them, breaks their hearts and deceives them, but if he tries to lay his hat in Gants Hill he'll be for it, I can tell you!

Paul Young is destined for my musical bargain bin – along with the J. Geils Band and their *very* sexist song 'Centerfold' – and will shortly be joined by Robert Palmer on the release of 'Addicted To Love'. By this time I'll be deep into my right-on, old-school feminist phase and the site of four robotic, lip-glossed sex-pots cavorting behind Robert Palmer, pretending to play their instruments while their boobs jiggle up and down, will send me into an apoplectic rage. In revenge, after I've finished shouting abuse at the TV set, I'll have a super unflattering butch haircut that makes me cry, and makes my boyfriend ask me when I decided to become a lesbian. That will teach them.

Bernice Cohen isn't that interested in borrowing my new copy of *The Women's Room*. She most definitely doesn't want us to build a bonfire in the back garden and set fire to all of our bras. I think she might be right about continuing with the leg shaving but I've decided to experiment with my armpits. I'm less interested than I was in spending our Saturdays at Roman Road market these days, trawling the stalls for bargain handbags. Handbags are probably sexist, and besides, I want us to go to Camden Town instead. Bernice wants to know why I was in a mood when we went to McDonald's for lunch the other day. I don't *know* why. I just was. We're off with each other lately. Something is picking at the seams of our friendship, and I'm not sure exactly what it is. It might be that she's decided to give up her A Levels and leave school at the end of this term. It might just be that Bernice likes The Commodores.

'Come on, admit it. "Three Times A Lady" is the best.'

'It isn't. It's rank.'

'But *you* like Toto.'

'No I don't.'

'And Bonnie Tyler.'

'That's different!'

'No it's not.'

Our musical tastes have recently begun to diverge, along with our opinions on burning bras. Top of my wish list of concert tickets this year are Dexy's Midnight Runners, The Police and Heaven 17. Top of Bernice's list are Lionel Richie and Kool & The Gang. But it's not time to worry yet. The two of us still have masses in common. When it comes to the utter fabulousness that is David Bowie, both of us are in agreement and rock solid.

HELLO MILTON KEYNES: PART ONE

I can remember being in the bathroom. Sunday night is bath night and I've just been reluctantly stripped of my clothes and set about with a hot, soapy flannel. Later, as I'm admiring my wrinkly fingers and keenly hoping the rest of my body will follow suit if I stay in the water long enough, the sounds of 'Space Oddity' drift up from the record player downstairs. I am four or five. I love this song. It's as familiar to me as a nursery rhyme, except this one is about spaceships and rockets and I'm immensely more worried about Major Tom than I will ever be about the fate of Humpty Dumpty. How will he get down? Is he still floating about up there now? That bit where he asks you to tell his wife he loves her. It's sad. What if my family die in a spaceship? What if I do? It's almost as worrying as that other song I know called 'Chirpy Chirpy Cheep Cheep'. Sample lyric: 'Where's your mamma gone? Where's your mamma gone? Far *far* away.'

It feels like David Bowie has always been there, like The Beatles and the Rolling Stones and all my father's old Fats Waller records. I can't remember a time when I didn't know the words to songs like 'Love Me Do' or 'Life On Mars' or 'Ain't Misbehavin''. There's always been an image of Bowie somewhere in the house: looking like a fairytale prince on the cover of *Hunky Dory*; made up like a beautiful, kooky girl on the cover of *Aladdin Sane*. He's different again as Ziggy Stardust and I think I'm quite old, ten or eleven, before I realise these faces are all the same person. Bowie was always intriguing to me, even as a very small child. I felt I knew what The Beatles and all the others were about, but with Bowie I was never quite sure. He makes no concessions, offers no explanation; he explicitly insists that you come to him.

Take 'Ashes To Ashes'. I'm sitting in front of the telly with my mum and dad, who are eagerly waiting for *Rising Damp* to come on, and here's this ghostly clown drifting in and out of shot, darkly singing about astronauts and junkies. He's here in my living room and yet he's not here, since he seems to bear no real relation to anything in it. The song feels coded, indecipherable, but it takes me on a journey somewhere. I don't know exactly where it is that Bowie is taking me, I only know I want to keep on going back.

Now I'm older I want to turn Ziggy Stardust up to full volume and roar along to the bit where he sings 'Five years, my brain hurts a lot; five years, that's all we've got', even though I'm just sixteen and hopefully I've got lots and lots of years. I want to be overtaken by the gorgeousness of 'Starman'. I want to work out if I understand 'Low' or not. And the melodies are so unusual and the instrumentation seems so euphoric and plaintive and odd, and we haven't even touched on how he looks. The eyes. Those eyes. His funny teeth. He's not like you and me, is he? He's different. An outsider. And so it must be OK to be an outsider after all, because look at him, he's a star and he's a rock god. A wonky, imperfect, luminous, alien hero who thinks that we can all be heroes too. And you know when you hear that song, when you sing that song, that we absolutely can be.

Most kids in my class don't seem to get Bowie at all, but me and my best friend know much better. This summer he is touring and playing at Milton Keynes Bowl. The concert is pivotal. Non-negotiable. We can take or leave our planned outings to The Police or Lionel Richie, but must score tickets to David Bowie or die. When they come in the post, we pin them next to our Bowie posters and count down the weeks until we see him, comparing the intensity of our crushes on our idol and wearing out our copies of *Changes Two*.

The wait is finally over. It's a hot, simmering day in late July. Bernice and I have driven to Milton Keynes with two boys we've befriended at youth club on the sole basis that one has a car and the other knows the way to the M1. I don't remember their names but I remember I wore two badges on my T-shirt that day: one depicting Bowie in his cocaine Ziggy heyday, one showing him as the character Jack Celliers in the film *Merry Christmas Mr. Lawrence*. I saw that film three times. I cried when they buried him up to his neck in sand.

The stadium is vast and the four of us have set up camp near the lip of the bowl, miles from the stage, but with space to spread out and sunbathe and ensure we look our best for the start of the concert. Bernice and I have come prepared. First up we change into bikini tops and shorts and coat ourselves in Ambre Solaire tanning oil. It offers no protection whatsoever from the sun but smells so sophisticated and exotic we apply it almost like perfume. I still search it out at the chemist shop, twisting off the cap and secretly inhaling its amber sweetness. It smells of back-garden cricket matches with kitchen stools used as stumps, and camping holidays in the rain when you applied it in the morning, just in case. It's a heady mix of sunburn and scorched suburban lawn, with a top note of Jerry Hall and the south of France.

Still shiny with oil, we go to work on the lemons we've brought, slicing two in half and squeezing the sticky juice onto our hair. By the time Bowie comes on we'll be brown as nuts and have blonde highlights in our crimped mousy tresses, as cool and pale as Debbie Harry's. Once we've changed into our ra-ra skirts and white Essex heels, we'll doubtless look so fantastic that David Bowie will pull us from the crowd and invite us to sing the chorus to 'Heroes' with him. In addition he will quite likely kiss us. And marry us.

The pair of us idle away the rest of the afternoon fantasising about what we'll wear to our pop-star wedding, and tucking into the bag of corned-beef sandwiches my mum has insisted we bring to keep us going while we wait for the Thin White Duke to come on. I should stress here that my mum doesn't actually call Bowie the Thin White Duke. She calls him that funny boy whose silly records you're always wasting your money on, who could do with a corned-beef sandwich or two himself.

Our valiant attempts to create an outdoor beauty salon aren't altogether successful. By show-time our hair is still irrefutably mousy – but irresistible to wasps – and our skin is baked red and beginning to blister. Undeterred, we set out to claim prime position: tottering forward in our spiky heels, snaking our way from the periphery to the centre, where the crowd is at its thickest, tight and condensed like a knot. From here we inch forward, row by row, body by body, drawn by the music, compelled to get closer to its source. By the time Bowie pounds into 'Heroes' we are yards from the front and the whole crowd, its giant mass, is moving. I can't see, can barely move, and I catch Bernice's eye and we fleetingly acknowledge the crushing certainty that neither one of us is a) likely to get on stage and sing the chorus to 'Heroes' or b) end up married to David Bowie. I lose sight of her after that, the bodies suck her forward and push me back, and I'm on the point of turning round when I'm scooped onto someone's shoulders, suddenly held aloft like a child.

Once in the air, I can't tear my eyes away from Bowie. He wears a peach-coloured suit and his hair is coiffed curly and blond. He seems at once a mirage and something quite ordinary, since here is proof that he's a human being and not an alien. There is something shocking in the realisation that your idols exist in the flesh and something disquieting in knowing so many people share your crush. He is singing my favourite song in the universe, a song whose ownership I take, in part, for granted. How can it possibly be that so many thousands of other people know the words and like it just as much as, if not even more than, I do? Do they like 'Modern Love' too? And *Hunky Dory*? When they listen to 'Changes' do they think Bowie is calling their name in the hushed drop-down section before the chorus?

I want to close my eyes and go home. I want to take this music away with me, so I can own it again. The Thin White Duke isn't simply an object of my lust and adoration, he is far more important than that. Bowie is the sticking plaster I apply to my teenage awkwardness, and there is only so much of him to go round. This music, up close, it seems astonishing. I'm just not sure I'm ready to share it.

As the song fades out and the crowd erupts, I turn my head for a moment and look back towards the bank, to see how far we have come. The bodies stretch forever, faceless and elated; a dark sea of joy, peppered with camera flashes and lighter flames. I suddenly get it, let go of the panic and the claustrophobia and surrender to the shared experience. It's a gorgeous sight. It must look unimaginable from the stage. One day. Maybe. Many years from now. I will stand on this stage and find out.

FLASHDANCE

Long before Bowie there was Springsteen. I have loved Bruce since the summer of '81 when I was fourteen, and first stumbled across my big brother's copy of *Born to Run*. The Boss wore a black leather jacket on the album's cover and held a battered guitar, strung seductively low across his hips. He smiled wryly, in profile; cheeks rough with stubble, brown eyes softly crinkled at the edges. He looked impossibly handsome and poetic.

Bruce, I now realise, was then, and has remained, the enduring template for my ideal man: dark, swarthy, rough around the edges, rock star. You may jest about beefcake muscles and shortness of stature but how could you fail to be attracted to a man who can keep a straight face while imploring you to climb aboard his Harley-Davidson and 'strap your hands across his engines'. Springsteen is the ultimate mix of sensitivity, intellect and machismo, not to mention the fact he could quite likely build you an American-style front porch from a pile of timber and a packet of nails in under an hour, wearing only a pair of Levis and a sweat-soaked vest. I am imagining Bruce Springsteen making me a porch right now. I am liking it. It's going well. There is room for a barbecue set and everything.

At the age of fourteen, I doubt I cared much about Springsteen's carpentry skills but I did care, to the point of obsession, about the album *Born to Run* and in particular its opening track, 'Thunder Road'. 'Thunder Road' might just be the most romantic song ever written. Its vision is exhilarating and jaded in equal measure, and its narrative is positively cinematic. This is *Romeo and Juliet*, *Rebel Without a Cause*, *Pretty Woman* and *West Side Story* all distilled into one 4min 49sec epic.

The imagery is quintessentially fifties American but when I listen to 'Thunder Road' I'm forever cruising the mean streets of Ilford in the late summer evenings of the early eighties. My brother is just home from college and we're marking his return by borrowing my dad's car without his permission. While Bruce sings from the cassette player about stagnating small towns, burnt-out Chevrolets and the grandeur of the open highway, we pootle past the Odeon cinema, take a left at the Beefeater restaurant – the poshest eatery in town that will one day grow up to be a Harvester – and take a turn onto the A406 which leads directly to Southend and the Essex seaside. We know each word by heart and sing along at the top of our voices, reserving extra emphasis for the song's crescendo where its heroes strike out to 'case the promised land', speeding towards adulthood and freedom.

Over the years, at moments of both sadness and celebration, my brother and I have recreated this scene in a variety of different ways: drunk, sober, often with friends, always faithful. I firmly believe that in the event we were ever to fall out with one another and stop speaking for a period of years, the resolution would come in the shape of *Born to Run*. One of us would turn up at the other's place with a copy of the album tucked under their arm and even before the slow-burn piano and harmonica intro to 'Thunder Road' had faded out, all would be good with the world again. Bruce's music has the power to do this. He charts every scar, every canker of the bruised and battered American Dream but he never abandons all hope for it. At the heart of a Springsteen tune, there remains the lasting chance of redemption.

There is, however – and I hate to say it – one niggling problem with Bruce Springsteen. In general he chooses winningly apposite names for the heroines of his songs – Rosalita, Kitty, Mary – but in 'Born to Run' the woman he invites to strap her hands across his engines is called Wendy. *Wendy*. Now, I obviously mean no offence to anyone called Wendy, but Wendy's the kind of name that makes you think of flame-grilled burgers, or the cute kid in Peter Pan, not a biker-chick temptress who's just about to climb aboard Bruce's 'suicide machine' and teach him the meaning of true love. He might as well have chosen Janet, or Doris, or Pauline, or Louise, for that matter.

My issue with Springsteen's Wendy builds slowly over the months and reaches its peak in the weeks just after my seventeenth birthday. Through most of the last few years, I have kept my Springsteen fetish to myself. I know of no other teenager in my social circle that likes his music and so listening to his albums is something I do alone in secret; in much the same way as I like to mime along to Joe Dolce's 'Shaddap You Face' while bleaching my moustache with Jolen in front of the bathroom mirror.

Everything changes when a new boy called Simon comes onto the scene. He's an imposter at our Gants Hill youth club, shipped in by mistake from the rather more upmarket environs of Gidea Park, a couple of miles to the north, with its driveways and mock-Grecian columns. What he's doing slumming it here is anybody's guess but he quickly infiltrates our tight-knit group and becomes its resident alpha male. He is skinny and tall, with vivid blue eyes and tight curly hair that looks like it's a perm but isn't. You wouldn't say he was great-looking exactly, but he's definitely something out of the ordinary. He has a place at university. He drives his own car. He has a ravishingly attractive younger sister who he cunningly persuades to accompany him at every opportunity, which ensures the boys appreciate him nearly as much as the girls do. Simon, it must be said, is almost certainly not a virgin.

Of course, all this pales into insignificance when it emerges that Simon's favourite rock star of all time is Bruce Springsteen. Not only does he like Bruce Springsteen, he has been to see him play live. Several times. He has even seen him play a gig in America! It's fair to say I am besotted by this interloper and without warning, the period before Tuesday night youth club morphs from being a relaxing hour spent eating Wagon Wheels in front of *Grange Hill* to an elaborate ritual of leg shaving, hair scrunching and spot camouflaging, topped off by the careful application of Barry M Dazzle Dust eye-shadow. It should be noted that the use of Dazzle Dust eye-shadow is a precise and perilous procedure. Too little and you miss out on the hi-watt neon glittery effect, too much and the loose particles migrate directly to your eyeballs, coating them in a dusty slurry and ensuring a nasty case of conjunctivitis.

For the moment, at least, I have decided not to burn all, or any, of my bras. Thanks to Madonna I am coming to realise that it's entirely acceptable to fight for equal pay and still embrace under-wire and Dazzle Dust. Girls can do anything they like. Any day now I will ask a boy I fancy out myself, instead of waiting around for him to ask me. Actually this is highly unlikely. I'm still too awkward and gauche and unsteady, but I'm developing better tactics to hide it. It helps that I look better than I used to. I have stopped going to Uppercuts. I am laying off the market-stall henna. The asthma that my doctor thought would fade in my teens really has. I'm beginning to feel less vulnerable and geeky. I am ready for a boyfriend. A proper one.

Happily I'm a dab hand with the Dazzle Dust and sooner or later the inevitable happens: I end up getting off with Simon. It's a coup. I am smitten. He is all I can talk about to anyone and there is barely room in my head for thoughts of anything else. A single sighting can keep me going for an entire week at least, and in between times I get my fix playing records that both of us like. Things appear to be going fine – in that on-again off-again, unspecified teenage way – until it becomes apparent that snogging on the back seat of his car while listening to cassette tapes of *The River* is not going to cut it forever.

'So, then?'

'So.'

'You like me?'

'Uh… yes.'

'I really like you.'

'Well, that's good then.'

'Your parents are away this weekend, aren't they?'

'No. I don't think so. Is that *both* your hands up my skirt?'

'Relax a bit. You don't want me to think you're a prick tease. Do you?'

Shit. What should I do? Thanks a bunch, Madonna. I knew I should have grown my leg hair and burned my bra.

What follows is straight from the agony pages of *My Guy* magazine. Simon might quite like to sleep with me but I'm not sure I want to sleep with him back. I'm intimidated by his experience and my lack of, and when I summon the nerve to tell him this, he assures me he doesn't mind and is happy to wait. Clearly his idea of waiting and mine are somewhat divergent because two hours later he chucks me. In fact, he does far worse than that. The very next day he gets off with my second-to-best girlfriend. Her name – what else could it be? – is Wendy.

I am inconsolable. Not only have I lost the first great crush of my teenage life, and the camaraderie of my second-to-best girlfriend, I am now unable to listen to one of my favourite albums of all time without editing out its title track. Springsteen's ode to Wendy is no longer a lyrical blip, it is a personal betrayal to me. I am broken. I haven't even got the appetite to finish the bowl of coffee-flavoured Angel Delight my mother has rustled up in the kitchen in a last valiant attempt to cheer me up.

Days after Simon gets off with Wendy they go out on their first official date. Word filters down that Wendy has been out shopping and bought a brand new tiered gypsy skirt for the occasion. And some fringed pixie boots. And a set of hair combs festooned with beads and ribbons and various dangly bits which she hopes will make her look sexy and Madonna-ish and I hope will make her look like the bass player in Kajagoogoo. I fear the hair combs won't last the evening. They're coming off. Along with the new skirt and the pixie boots. It's only a suspicion, but I have the feeling Wendy is putting out. I wonder if she's been to Marie Stopes.

So that I don't spend date night weeping alone in despair, my best friend Bernice Cohen persuades me to come to the cinema with her. I tell her it won't do any good, that it's point-less, that a sweaty hot dog and a bag of popcorn are paltry salve to a wound as deep as this, but Bernice is insistent. We sit together in the dark. We share the popcorn. I'm more miserable than I've been in my life. And then the film starts.

High up on the screen a girl is dancing. She wears a black leotard and legwarmers and appears to be auditioning for something. She's awkward at first: she stumbles and trips, then picks herself up and carries on. She looks stronger now, more confident. The soundtrack soars and before you know it, this girl is turning cartwheels and practically flying. My spirits are lifting. As hard as I try, I can't stop smiling. The girl in the leotard is Jennifer Beals and precisely six seconds after I first lay eyes on her she has replaced Irene Cara as the girl I most want to be in the world. Five minutes in and I'm wondering where I put my leotard; another ten and I'm vowing to give dance classes another try. Half an hour later I am seriously thinking it might be a good idea if I took up welding. Who needs Simon and Springsteen? What kind of a name is Wendy, anyway? The important thing to remember is this: in the midst of personal tragedy, there is always *Flashdance*.

OTHER PEOPLE'S MUMS

We have a lot to worry about in our teenage years: seal culling, Musical Youth, global cooling, how to work the layered look, what love has to do with it, how to meet Nik Kershaw, how Prince can be so short and yet so sexy, how to survive an impending nuclear war.

I'm quite worried about nuclear annihilation in the eighties and spend a good portion of school lunch breaks discussing what to do when the three-minute warning comes. Or is it four minutes? Either way there's not much you can do in 240 seconds – we all said we'd have sex or boil an egg – and there would barely be time to paint yourself white and duck and cover before you and your entire family, and everyone you knew in the world, were irradiated and burnt to a crisp. It wasn't a comforting prospect. I think this might have been the reason my friends had a habit of wearing badges made out of shrunken crisp packets around this time. We'd take an empty bag of Golden Wonder, place it on a layer of foil under a hot grill, and the heat would make the plastic shrivel, to the point where you could attach a safety pin to the shrunken packet and wear it on your lapel. Our parents thought this was ridiculous but they failed to understand that these charred, shrunken packets weren't simply a fad, they were direct visual representation of our teenage fear of dying in a nuclear holocaust. Those weren't Quaver packets on our school blazers, they were victims of an H-bomb blast.

In 1983 I went on a CND march with my mum. In truth, I hadn't realised Mum had any strong feelings about nuclear disarmament one way or the other. Obviously she couldn't be in favour of nuclear bombs, per se – what with the radiation, mutilation and death and everything – but the way she sometimes sniffed disapprovingly whenever the Greenham Common women came on the news meant I hadn't exactly pegged her for an anti-war crusader.

There was a lot of political discussion going on in our house, but hardly any from Mum. My dad and my siblings (both politics students) were always at it around the dinner table, railing about the miners' strike and that bloody awful woman, Margaret Thatcher. In the seventies I remember the National Front marching through Ilford (there was a time when it seemed like it was every other weekend) and my dad and my brother going out to protest against them. Dad could remember the Blackshirts marching through the East End streets where he grew up and, hearing him talk about it when I was little, I grasped my first shaky understanding of prejudice and anti-Semitism. It took a while to understand the wider ramifications. We were a nation raised on *Love Thy Neighbour*. I remember my brother explaining to me – around the same time he took the stabilisers off my bike – why it wasn't OK to call the Pakistani boy on our street Chocolate Drop, like everybody else did.

I have always wanted to listen in and absorb these conversations, even more so now I'm beginning to work out how I view the world myself. As far as I can ascertain, it's all pretty simple and depressing. *Everything* is *really* bad. And *unfair*. Why isn't anybody doing anything about it? I will do something about it. I have recently written a poem about Flight 007, the Korean airplane that was blown up by the Russians. It is truly terrible. The Russians are terrible. Do you know people get shot just trying to climb over the Berlin Wall? I may write a poem about it. Or one about what a lunatic Ronald Reagan is. Can you believe it is *his* hand on the button? Thatcher was re-elected this year. I wrote in my diary: Heaven help us. The Tories are *awful* but everyone loves them round here. Where's the world heading? Why can't we all just get along? I will read *1984* next year. I think it would be good to read it, you know, *in* 1984.

Last night, over dinner, Dad went off on one of his tangents. He outlined his vision of a futuristic socialist utopia in which all heavy industry was hidden underground and driven by giant computers that can wirelessly communicate with each other across the globe! He may be pinstripe and Marmite sandwiches on the surface, but I'm beginning to realise that Dad's a bit radical, or maybe just plain nuts, for where we live. And anyway none of it really matters, because we're all going to be annihilated by the bomb. Maybe I should ask my brother if he'll let me listen to his copy of 'Blowing In The Wind' again. I might like it better this time.

Astonishingly enough, Mum wasn't all that interested in reading my Ronald Reagan poetry. She rarely joined in with these conversations. She'd ferry back and forth with the teacups and the cakes, and busy herself at the sink, raising her eyebrows at the folly of all this nonsense. But today it's her that wants us to go. Without warning, on the day of the CND march, she puts on her best blouse, calls me down from my bedroom and tells me we're going to the tube station. Her decision is so uncharacteristically spontaneous she hasn't even had time to make Dad his lunch or fix us a picnic of corned-beef sandwiches. There are 300,000 protesters in London that day, three million marching across Europe. The streets are filled with banners and peace signs; music is playing, people are singing. It's optimistic, peaceful and sunny.

Jon Stewart, Sleeper's guitarist, has come down from Sheffield that day too, and he's in the march somewhere with his own mum. When I go to school on Monday I find this pattern repeated with lots of my classmates. Kids with ordinary net-curtain-washing housewife mothers find themselves unexpectedly yanked away from their stereos and dragged up to London to join the march. It's not what I would have expected. These are friends whose mothers are hooked on Valium 'for their nerves'. Mums that have never had a job, driven a car or had any money they can call their own. There is one mum I've never seen without a pile of ironing under her arm in all the seven years I've been going round to their house. The ironing board is always up in that kitchen. The house is immaculate, neat and shiny, like a pin.

I like the idea that these quiet women were filling out the crowd that Saturday, leaving their husbands on the sofa, travelling on tube trains, coaches and buses with their teenage children, to add their voices to the protest. I was proud to be walking with my mum. We'd never done a thing like that together, never had anything approaching a political debate. But Mum had been there before, seen real bombs and the effects of a war on people's lives and I could see that it meant something for her to be there. It made me think that maybe Mum had more to say than she let on. Perhaps she just doesn't like arguments. Perhaps she'd rather keep the peace. Perhaps it's just that the rest of the family are so opinionated, she could never find a space for her voice.

Jon took the coach back to Sheffield after the march. A few months later a television company came looking for extras to be in an anti-war film called *Threads*. Jon and his mother were recruited and lay on the streets of Sheffield playing corpses, while vegetable soup was ladled over their bodies to represent them vomiting from radiation sickness. Jon met a girl that he fell in love with. She had prosthetic burns all over her arms. He had fake blood pouring out from one eardrum. He can't be certain, but he has a feeling his bloody ear and her burnt arm are just visible on screen.

JUST THE JOB

Jobs I would quite like to have this week:

a) Tossing gladioli at Morrissey on *Top of the Pops*.
b) Being uptown girl to Billy Joel's downtown man.

In truth, I have the feeling neither job would pay particularly well, given that crowds are perfectly happy to toss gladioli at Morrissey for free and 'uptown girl' is just another way of saying girlfriend, which isn't strictly a job.

I have recently purchased *Hatful of Hollow* by The Smiths. Bernice has recently purchased *Innocent Man* by Billy Joel. This could be taken as further evidence of our increasing divergence in musical tastes if it wasn't for the fact that I secretly like *Innocent Man* as much as, if not a bit better than, *Hatful of Hollow*. This is exactly like the time Bernice bought *Guilty* by Barbra Streisand and I bought *Peter Gabriel* by Peter Gabriel. 'Games Without Frontiers' and 'Biko' were all well and good, if a bit depressing, but no match for the power-ballad magnificence that is 'Woman In Love'. I only meant to borrow it to tape it. I ended up keeping it for a month. I nearly gave myself a hernia trying to reach those high notes.

My closet weakness for Billy Joel is causing me some unlikely teenage angst. What next? Barry Manilow? Cliff

Richard? ZZ Top? Are all attempts to shrug off my suburban mores sheer pointless, optimistic folly? Does an appreciation for *Innocent Man* mean I've become a provincial Essex housewife by proxy? Am I destined to shop at Bodgers all my life? Is liking this stuff in my genes? Perhaps U2's 'Pride' cancels out Joel's 'Uptown Girl'. Perhaps I'm immune from liking Barry Manilow by virtue of liking The Psychedelic Furs. Actually, you know what? It's been ages since I've listened to *Guilty*. I think a quick belt through a couple of Barbra Streisand songs might be just the thing while I work out how to get a new Saturday job.

I haven't done particularly well with jobs so far. I've already been sacked from three. From Curtess Shoes, for holding my nose when encountering cheesy feet and sending someone home with a pair of boots in two different sizes. From a spell as an Avon lady for using up all the make-up samples myself. From a high-street cafe for taking extended loo breaks when I got bored and coming across a bit stroppy when one or two of the customers failed to leave even a tiny tip. I need to knuckle down. I need to expand my horizons. Find a Saturday job away from the pallid confines of Ilford High Road.

I think what I'm hoping for is this. Evidence of a wider world outside. Proof that suburbia is not my heartland: a sign I can fit in somewhere grander and more exotic. I want a job in the West End of London. I want to stroll along Argyll Street with a sense of purpose, nodding at girls with one-day tube passes in their pocket and a spare fiver to spend at the salad bar in Garfunkel's. I might walk to Trafalgar Square in my lunch hour. I could visit an art gallery, something I've never done before. I could soak up the twinkly Christmas atmosphere in Regent Street and tut at the out-of-towners who don't know which way to go on the escalators.

I'm bound to earn more than I did as an Avon lady so I won't have to scrounge off my mum. I can save up for that fantastic yellow dress, the one I have a hundred-watt crush on and will *literally* change my life forever if I buy it. In the evening I will travel back on the tube with all the other Saturday girls and moan about how hard it is being on my feet all day. It's ridiculous that this is something I should want to experience, but I do.

I feel romantically drawn to the world of work lately, and all the independence it represents. Some of my friends have full-time jobs now. Some of them even seem to like them. They are taking driving lessons and moaning about National Insurance and replacing their ancient Pierrot bedspreads with cool stripy ones that they've bought themselves from Habitat. They pay their parents rent and contribute to the weekly shop and they talk – in slightly superior tones – about supporting themselves. If I get into college this autumn, it will be years yet before I can say the same.

The job I find is at Mothercare in London's Marble Arch. After a few strolls down Argyll Street and some salad lunches at Garfunkel's, it soon becomes clear that the job is not particularly horizon-expanding or exciting. A Saturday job is just a Saturday job, wherever it is, and the fact that this one is at the opposite end of the Central Line instead of a bus ride away means the day seems to last twice as long. My principle tasks involve arranging packs of nappies, re-pricing maternity bras and getting bossed about by a pack of self-important supervisors who prowl the shop floor in matching brown nylon tabards. They seem like normal people, but they're not. They take their role very seriously.

After one particularly stimulating morning – mopping up kiddy wee in the toy department – I head to the staffroom for something to eat. I'm expecting the usual scene: girls in brown uniforms eating sandwiches on plastic chairs while Gary Davies blares at full volume from the radio. Today the atmosphere is a little different.

At the centre of the room, on the low banquette that runs across one wall, a petite, skinny woman in a leopard-print, pill-box hat, wearing a black skirt and batwing jacket, is sprawled out in what can only be described as a compromising position. The woman is Paula Yates. I've been so caught up with kiddy wee I've forgotten a film crew are coming to the shop to film a segment for a baby show on Channel 4, and that Yates is its presenter.

Paula is lying on her back, legs akimbo, ankles wrapped around her friend Jools Holland's neck. She's laughing, a cool lusty giggle, and flirting outrageously with the dark-haired pianist from Squeeze, who looks exceedingly dapper in his silk navy suit. As she reclines on his lap, spiky hair bleached and ruffled, cracking quick, easy jokes, the staff nibble quietly at their Nimble and pretend she isn't really there.

I imagine that I'm rather less subtle. That I stare at her open-mouthed over my cheese roll and my can of Um Bongo. This is the woman from *The Tube*. She's *met* Debbie Harry, danced with Cyndi Lauper and quite likely sniffed Nik Kershaw's hair. Now here she is, right in front of me. A beacon of free will and rebellion in the land of the brown nylon tabard.

She seems to me then, on TV and spied briefly in the flesh, a cross between a rock star and a fifties starlet: confident, vivacious and unashamedly vulgar, practically an entirely new species of womankind. I can't quite summon up the nerve to talk to her, but when she leaves to finish filming I dash down to the storeroom she's been using as a makeshift dressing room to have a quick nosy around.

The tiny space is dishevelled, littered with shoes, hat boxes, piles of expensive make-up and designer dresses, and taking pride of place on a clothes rail, a red military-style jacket decorated with brocade and golden buttons. Laid out over a coat hanger behind it are a dozen or more colourful leather belts. Faced with this bounty, I find I just can't help myself. I reach for a pink knotted number on the hanger, scrunch the soft leather into a ball and bundle it into my bag.

I knew getting a job in the West End was a good idea. I knew exciting things would happen the moment I ventured forth from Gants Hill roundabout. This might be the evidence I was looking for. There *is* a wider world out there and the fact I like *Innocent Man* doesn't mean I want in on it any less. Just as a precaution, I should probably go home and spend the rest of the weekend reassessing my take on *Hatful of Hollow*.

I wear that stolen belt every weekend for the rest of the year. It makes me feel special: it's a talisman, a slice of unfettered blonde ambition that might just as well have belonged to Madonna. Hidden beneath its buckle is a vision of womanhood completely at odds with the suburban housewifery I've grown up with. I covet a piece of its otherness. I take a piece of its punk rockery, wrap it up and store it in my pocket.

THE METHOD

Look at them now, the goal-attack girls, crowded round the radio in the sixth-form common room; listening to 'Our Tune', oohing and ahhing, humming along to Matt Bianco. They've all been elected prefects this term, and wear stripes on their blazers to prove it. They hand out detentions to the first years, like dolly mixtures, and swoon each time they hear 'Hello' by Lionel Richie. They think I'm weird because I fancy David Bowie (*yeuch*, he doesn't even have the same colour eyes!) but I've recently discovered weirdness confers its own status; that a bit of difference gives you an edge. The trick is not to push it too far. You don't want to end up completely ostracised like Samantha Benson who likes Siouxsie Sioux and paints her lips black, and wears lace gloves and leggings under her uniform.

I've worked hard on this small advantage over the summer. I have shortened my school skirt, bought a pair of yellow slouchy boots, and vowed to wear my blazer sleeves rolled up at all times. A good portion of each day is spent pulling up my slouchy boots, tugging my skirt down, and pushing my sleeves back past my elbows. I am a cross between Sheena Easton and Crockett and Tubbs.

This is going to kill them, though. This will flip their world upside-down. Underneath my arm is the latest copy of

Jackie magazine and I am in it. These girls might be prefects – confident, clear-skinned team captains – but *I* am in a *Jackie* photo story!

I've joined a local drama club. Ten kids, church hall, Monday evenings, improvising teenage arguments, earnestly rehearsing plays like *The Crucible* and *Educating Rita*. The teacher's name is Ronnie and I like her a lot. She's fat and loud, direct to the point of rudeness, and the first person I've ever met that eats lentils for pleasure. She sits there with her script and a Tupperware tub, scooping lentils into her mouth, barking out director's instructions. We spend entire lessons pretending to be animals. Others pretending to be trees. Quite how she thinks she's going to translate her vision of the Stanislavski method to a dozen sulky, New Romantic Essex kids is uncertain, but she's damned if she's not going to try.

Ronnie's Monday night drama club is loosely aligned to a stage school in London. This means nothing at all to us until the day she walks in and says they need a girl to be in a *Jackie* photo story. Someone has dropped out. Would I like to fill in? I want to kiss her.

In fairness, I'm out of my *Jackie* phase by now – I read about clitoral orgasms and sexual intercourse in *Cosmopolitan* instead – but *Jackie* is seminal, its beams of insight stored in my brain for posterity. I have performance tips from Kate Bush and Debbie Harry. I have relationship advice from Cathy and Claire. I've learned that Farrah Fawcett-Majors' favourite colour is yellow and that Woody from Bay City Rollers is 'shy actually', and afraid of ghosts. I know how to put a dab of lip gloss in the centre of my bottom lip to make it look fuller, and how to apply highlighter to my brow and shader to my cheeks, to make my eyes look bigger and my face look thinner. I have washed my hair in beer and vinegar (not at the same time) and I've studied the lines at the side of my palm to see how many children I will have. I have taken a thousand personality quizzes with questions like 'Do you fancy the idea of yourself in a matching lavender nightie and negligee?' to discover that I am: personality B), mostly moody.

Jackie has cult status in our school. Being in it will elevate me from back-bench no-mark to queen of the sixth form in the blink of an eye. The photo shoot is tomorrow. I will take the day off. This will be amazing. The most glamorous day of my entire life.

The photo call is at an address in Harlesden: fourteen stops along the Central Line, thirteen more along the Bakerloo. I'm meant to be there by nine so I get up at six, shave my legs, paint my nails, scour my cheeks with Apricot Scrub, and take a stuffed smoky tube train at 7.30. Standing for 27 stops in the rush hour is not especially amazing or glamorous and I'm beginning to realise how Dad and Smithers-Jones feel now. No matter. Best concentrate on stopping my hair from going frizzy in the heat and humidity by patting it repeatedly and adding dollops of wet-look gel straight from the tub. Luckily, I've had it cut recently. A layered, flicky triumph that's short at the sides and long at the back and only looks like a mullet in retrospect.

I check my bag every couple of stops, to make sure I have all component parts of the two outfit changes I was asked to bring. Outfit one is a pair of drainpipe jeans, with zips at the ankle – the ones where I have to lie down and hold my breath to do them up – matched with my favourite purple sweatshirt and tennis shoes. Outfit two is a flared floral mini-skirt that cost £15 from Topshop and is the most expensive thing I have ever owned, matched with thick belt, cap-sleeved T-shirt, and three-inch-high white stiletto heels.

I wonder if there will be someone there to do our make-up. I've brought everything I own just in case: eye-shadows in shades that range from cerise to navy, pan sticks and tinted Clearasil, and two roll-on lip glosses in flavours of Mighty Mint and Very Cherry. I'm already wearing two layers of my favourite lipstick in the must-have shade from Miss Selfridge, a pale metallic violet, called Iron Lady. I ummed and ahhed for a long time about the ethics of making this purchase since it was clearly named for our lady prime minister. And then I thought, to hell with it. What's more important, empty protest, or having purple lips?

This part of Harlesden isn't all that nice, if I'm honest. I wonder if I have the right address. A small terraced house on a scruffy street, with the bin kicked over outside it. There are four bored kids mooching around inside – my photo-story comrades – and a harassed-looking photographer who is middle-aged and wear-ing a dirty tank-top. I change in the bathroom and reapply a layer of Iron Lady, then the photographer tells me what I'm meant to be doing. I'm going to play the nagging girlfriend. My boyfriend is sick of me trying to change his looks and his clothes. I will chuck him then run into him at a party. He is going out with a beautiful girl who has made him look cool just by being nice to him! He looks handsome and trendy. I am gutted when I realise what I'm missing.

This is easy. I can nail this character. I draw on everything Ronnie has ever taught me and throw myself into the role with conviction and gusto. The photographer says I'm over-doing it a bit and can I just, you know, pretend to look naggy, then sulky.

It takes a long time. There's lots of waiting around. They reward us with tea and Bourbon biscuits at the end of the day and then I get on the tube and go home. When the magazine comes out Dad thinks it's 'bloody silly' and Mum thinks they missed my good side, but the goal-attack girls are wildly impressed. Seconds later, they are cross. And confused. How come they aren't the ones in *Jackie*? How come the swotty quiet one with the slouchy boots got to be in a photo story? What's going on? Has the whole world gone completely mad? Is 'The Power Of Love' by Frankie Goes To Hollywood the best song ever written, or *isn't* it? Suddenly they are questioning everything they have previously held dear; doubting their own magnificence for the very first time in their lives. Victory! One nil to me.

I'm on some kind of list after the *Jackie* adventure, and get sent to a few proper auditions. One is for an Opal Fruits advert. The waiting room is full of angelic-looking teens accompanied by their brash, pushy mothers. When my time comes in front of the camera, a lady with giant shoulder-pads asks me to eat a green Opal Fruit and look zingy. I say that will be hard because I don't really like the green ones, but Shoulder-pads doesn't have a sense of humour. She ushers me out before I get the chance to look zingy. The next is for a Timotei advert but my mullet lets me down and the last is for the lead in a feature film directed by David Puttnam, the man who made *Bugsy Malone*. I'm excited by this one and start rehearsing my Oscar speech as soon as I get the call.

At the audition, twenty girls who look a bit like me line up in David Puttnam's office. The producer walks up and down between us, picks out five he likes the look of and sends the rest of us away. That's that then, I'm not going to grow up to be Jodie Foster after all. I cheer myself up on the tube journey home by eating a packet of onion ring crisps and humming the theme tune to *Chariots of Fire*.

I carry on with Monday night drama club but decide this acting lark is not nearly as glamorous or interesting as it's cracked up to be. I cross actress off my list of careers. Vet is long gone. That just leaves pop star.

WEST END GIRLS

I am on-again off-again friends with a girl at school called Nicole who will one day grow up to work in fashion. She's starting a foundation degree in art at the end of this year and she may, or may not, be thinking about becoming a lesbian. She has recently shaved off the hair on one side of her head and taken to wearing androgynous clothes. The things we have in common are a shared loathing of the goal attacks, and a mutual love of Prince and The Revolution.

Nicole thinks she's cooler than me – crazy fool – and the reason she thinks this is because she hangs out at legendary eighties nightclub the Wag. When I say hangs out, I mean she's been there once and got in, which is no easy feat because the door policy is notoriously tough. Sade and Boy George go to the Wag Club, as do the girls from Bananarama. It's stuffed full of models and scenesters and, most important to Nicole, designers like Jean Paul Gaultier and John Galliano. If Madonna were in town, this is where she would strap on her crucifix and conical bra and shake her booty.

Nicole and I are in the middle of a lengthy discussion about the video to 'When Doves Cry' – she thinks it's good, I think it's creepy and worry that Prince must have ended the day covered in dove poo – when Nicole announces she's going to the Wag Club on Saturday night, and asks if I want to come along. Of course I do! I might get to meet Bananarama. They'll most likely be on a wild night out with Fun Boy Three. One of Bananarama might fall over and break her leg on the dance floor while we're there, and the other two Bananas will be left shorthanded. In the midst of their confusion, one of them will be bound to notice my scruffy mullet hairdo and artfully layered nightclubbing outfit, and ask me to take her place and save the day.

I'm getting ahead of myself. First we have to get past the Wag Club bouncers.

It's 1984 when I start going to West End nightclubs. It's a big step up. Previous to this, Saturday night outings have consisted of a visit to Pizza Hut, a video session at Bernice's house and a rare night out at a pub or the bar of the Essex County Country Club. The Essex Country Club is frequented by Tottenham Hotspur footballers, but I've never met any when I've been there. Only white-sock-wearing wide boys called Dave, who work as estate agents and drive Ford Capris.

The nightclubs my friends and I have broken our teeth on are nothing at all like the Wag. They are all based in and around Leicester Square and are tourist-trap havens, the kind that have ladies' nights and let all the girls in free. They have names like Xenon and Peaches and Busby's and are decorated in an S&M confection of black leather, rubber and shiny chrome. The most famous of our nightclub stops is the Hippodrome, which takes up an entire corner of Leicester Square. On the hour, every hour, the Hippodrome's famous lighting rig gets lowered from the ceiling where it flashes and revolves in time to the theme tune from *Star Wars*.

We travel 'up west' by car once a month – a couple of the boys in our group learning to drive has hugely expanded our domain – and travel back not long after midnight. We have a brilliant time. We dance to 'Sign Of The Times' by The Belle Stars and 'Automatic' by The Pointer Sisters, and slow dance with boys we've just met to 'Last Christmas' and 'Your Love Is King'. We make dates with Italian men and northern lads in pressed white shirts, that we have no intention of keeping. The point is to get fancied by at least one boy before home time and spend the rest of the evening dancing round our bags to 'Girls Just Want To Have Fun'. We have the odd rum and Coke, or a spritzer, but none of us really drinks. Or does sex. Almost all of us are virgins. Our year at school was known as the virgin sixth.

All that wandering around trying to get fancied – rushing to find your friend to tell her you've been fancied, rushing back to the boy to see if he still fancies you, hiding with your friend in the loos when you've decided you don't fancy him after all – is hungry work and it's traditional in our little gang, because we're so rock 'n' roll, to take a fuel stop on the drive home to Gants Hill. In the very early hours we detour to an all-night bakery in Brick Lane to stock up on much-needed carbohydrates. We buy a still-warm bagel each (Bernice always buys a dozen to take home to her mum), and a cup of tea and a doughnut for good measure.

The bagel bakery is an institution, a little dab of New York in London's grubby East End, brightly strip-lit and filled with atmosphere and chatter. It's full of other junior clubbers, just like us. Canary-yellow eye-shadow, electric-blue eyeliner, moussed hair, scrunchies and mules. The only downside of the bagel bakery is the mirrors that run the length of one wall.

Lines of girls troop past them, lipstick kissed off, spots shining without powder, Dazzle Dust collected in mucky gloops at the corners of their eyes. We call them the mirrors of truth.

I wonder if Nicole will want to stop off for bagels after our trip to the Wag Club tonight? I wonder if she'll approve of my Wag night outfit? I'm at an age when I desperately want to look sophisticated and savvy and my hope is that I can hot-tail it up to London to the coolest club in the world and look so bored and impassive and effortlessly trendy that people will think I go there all the time.

'What are you *wearing*?'

'Don't you like it?'

'Isn't that jacket... a bit big for you?'

For our trip up to London's kinky Soho I've taken a leaf out of my new friend's book. I have ditched my usual staple of T-shirt dress, thick gold belt and high-heeled mules and gone for something, well, a bit more dykey. I have borrowed an old suit jacket from my dad and teamed it with dungarees and a bright orange off-the-shoulder top. I have invested in some shoes that aren't mules. They are patent lace-ups and they are flat, and I don't really like them.

Essentially I am wearing the exact same outfit as Nicole but hers manages to look edgy and cool and Bananarama-ish, whereas mine just looks like I'm wearing dungarees with one of my dad's suit jackets. The jacket is hanging off me, my dungaree bottoms are rolled too high, and I've neglected to add a colourful Swatch watch or a whimsical bandanna into the mix, to bring the whole outfit together. Nicole lends me one of hers. She has two. One on her arm; one tied in a knot like a washer woman, around her head.

We travel up by tube, high on excitement about what we might find, and take our place in the queue in Wardour Street. Every so often some funky-looking clubber saunters up to the front and is ushered through the velvet rope without waiting. My stomach gives a little fizz of excitement each time it happens because one of them is *bound* to be Bananarama. I wish the queue would go down faster. I want to get inside and besides, Nicole and I are running out of things to say to each other. It turns out there is limited currency to be had in Prince and the problematic dove poo.

Almost an hour later, we make it to the thick velvet rope. A bouncer looks us over and I can feel his eyes running over my clothes. I have prepared a lengthy speech, something about us needing to get inside because Nicole is designing Wham!'s outfits for their next appearance on *Top of the Pops*, but we don't need it. My dungarees pass muster and he waves us straight in. I can't believe it's so easy. It's a bit of a disappointment, if I'm honest.

The club is up a flight of narrow stairs. It's dark inside and the walls are dirty and there's no leather or rubber or chrome, or lights that revolve to the theme tune from *Star Wars*. It feels a little seedy and the atmosphere is subdued, like a house party that hasn't got going yet.

'It's great in here, isn't it?'

I'm not sure it's really all that great. We wander round for hours in the gloom. We buy ourselves some very expensive drinks. We chat to a couple of men in make-up who look a bit like Steve Strange from Visage. There's not much dancing going on. People cling to the walls, looking serious. Nicole wants us to cling to the walls looking serious too. We nod in time to the music. We don't say much.

I know the Hippodrome is unspeakably naff but I'm not sure this place is much better. I thought Nicole was really onto something: with her shaved head and her shiny patent loafers and her ability to draw fantastic likenesses of the Thompson Twins in the back of her scrapbook, but it's full of sullen posers in here. My dad's suit jacket is making me hot. Everyone is acting like there's something important and alternative going on, but there's not. No Sade, no Boy George. No Bananas.

The Wag was a scene of great debauchery in the eighties but there wasn't a sniff of it that Saturday. No people snorting coke off dwarves' heads, no couples having sex on the dance floor. No couples having sex anywhere that we could see. Who were those exotic people who went to the front of the queue? Where were they hiding? What were they doing? Perhaps they were nobodies after all.

Nicole and I left just before midnight, to catch the last tube train back to Essex. We didn't stop anywhere for bagels. Nicole raved about what a good night we'd both had and said we ought to do it every week. I've been thinking about elevating Nicole to joint-best-friend status lately, but after tonight, I'm not so sure. Maybe she thinks I don't get it. This new clique that she wants us to be part of. She might be right. Or it might be that Nicole's just no fun to go out clubbing with.

I fall asleep at one in the morning, cosy beneath my continental quilt, and dream about going to a nightclub that's really cool and filled with pop stars instead of bored androgynous people, shuffling around in suit jackets, wearing matching bandannas on their arms. It was a nice dream. I imagine life at the Wag Club was just getting started.

TWO TRIBES

Someone has just flushed my school bag down the toilet. What is it with toilets and school bags? There's always one stuffed down the pan, suffocating beneath a pile of sodden bog roll. Every week there's another mopey girl carrying a sopping satchel from class to class: wringing out the pages of her history homework, trying to work out if her Kit-Kat is worth saving, given that the layer of foil is still largely intact and the milk chocolate is only slightly damp inside.

I decide to give up on the Kit-Kat. *The History of the Corn Laws* has probably had it. The liquid foundation, the one I wear over my lips to make them look extra pale and matt, will have to go in the bin. My mini Denman hairbrush is full of wet, gunky tissue and the batteries in my pocket radio are leaking a substance like liquid rust. The one bright spot is that my homework on *Vanity Fair*, a book I haven't read, an essay I've plagiarised almost entirely from *Coles Notes*, is completely ruined. This might be a blessing in disguise. It means I won't ever have to give it in. Term is almost over. The year is almost through. Revision. Exams. Then leave school forever! Job done!

The school bag down the loo gag has tailed off since we started in sixth form. It used to happen once or twice a week. But everyone's matured now. We've settled down. The worst offender, a Rothmans-sucking, thin-lipped shrew called Vivien, has gone to work at Boots, and lunch boxes everywhere have breathed a heavy sigh of relief. It's months since anyone stole Susan Solomon's duffel bag, drove it to the dual carriageway and tossed it from a speeding car window where it languished on the central reservation all summer long. I've half an idea that if I went back to Gants Hill now, I'd still see it sitting there, pages of her O Level project on oxbow lakes mournfully flapping in the breeze.

The school bag thing is getting off lightly, to be honest. It's almost an initiation: it means you're on the radar, in the club. The real bullying is saved up for the special cases. The girl with the stutter who was cut to the quick with vicious jibes after her mother died, and went home crying every single day. The girl who was really smart, best in her class, who was systematically picked apart for being clever. Her mistake was having very big boobs. You weren't allowed be a swot with big boobs. Little by little they ground away at her until she gave up her college ambitions and settled for a couple of low-grade O Levels and a line of boys queuing up to finger her behind the science block.

Still, at least she wasn't suffering from a chronic bowel disorder that left her painfully thin. At least she didn't have a lazy eye and ginger eyelashes. The boys are at it too, crushing the life out of the weaker ones. The thin boy and the ginger boy. Their lives were miserable. I wouldn't have swapped places with them for anything.

I'm grateful to have missed out on the worst of all this – nobody's put my head down the toilet, nobody's punched me in the stomach – but it hasn't always been an easy ride. I've been sent to Coventry for weeks on end by girls I thought were my friends. I've had people write on the blackboard that

I'm ugly. I've had girls stop talking when I walk into a room, then pass secret notes about me behind my back. I've gone home at lunchtime rather than sit in a dinner hall with no one to talk to. It wears you down, the exclusion. It's shaming. You think you must be an awful person.

Bullying is endemic in this school, but things have been bearable for a couple of reasons: a small but tight knot of friends, and a tactic that mostly involves getting on with things and keeping my head down. I'm an expert at this. I can drift in and out of a room like a ghost. The goal attacks are largely benign these days, anyway. The Haileys and the Samanthas are happy to rub along, glad to be queen bees, civil and self-obsessed, so long as you don't get in their way. This was my big mistake. This was the move that cost me my Kit-Kat and did for my Philips pocket radio. I decided to stop keeping my head down.

When I was at my most introverted and miserable my mum used to tell me not to be so hard on myself. There is no way to express how much I resented her saying this. What does she know? Mum is almost a hundred. Her response to any upset is to pick yourself up, brush yourself down and get on with it. She has it all wrong. I wasn't being hard on me. *Other* people were being hard on me. Somewhere in the last few months, I have grudgingly had to accept she has a point. This is all smoke and mirrors, this stuff. I've spent years worrying about how people see me. The seemingly intractable task of your late teens and early twenties is making fresh sense of how you see yourself.

Last Saturday night I went to a party and wore my over-sized *Frankie Says Relax* T-shirt as a dress. It made a great dress, once I'd hitched it up with a belt and knotted it at the hip, and it may or may not have been the case that I felt a bit like Madonna once I'd had a couple of cider and blacks and danced about to 'Holiday' three or four times. I had rainbow-coloured make-up on my eyes. I wore footless tights and frosted lipstick and I'd tried really hard to look good. I didn't look like me. Not the me that people knew at school.

One girl, let's call her Donna, was shooting me dirty looks from the start. Donna and I go back a long way. Years ago, when we were kids, she used to get the others to call me 'it'. As in, look at it. Look what it's doing. No, don't let it join in with us. Tonight she glares at me from the corner, behind the safety of her drink, surrounded by her gold-hoop-earring friends. Things get increasingly frosty. A bump on the stairs on the way to the loos. Chief of the gold hoops telling me she's seen me with a boy that Donna fancies and ordering me to back off.

'Or what?' I say.

'Or there'll be trouble.'

We are almost eighteen now. We leave school in a few weeks. But we stand there with our arms folded, psyching each other out, both knowing this is sort of ridiculous.

Even so, the Donnas follow through. What it amounts to is this. I have stepped out of line. Aimed too high. Made a show of myself with my dancing and my *Desperately Seeking Susan* outfit, and snogged someone out of my league at the end of the evening. First *Jackie* magazine. Then the big part in the school play. Now this. Come Monday morning the bag down the toilet routine is reinstated to teach me a lesson. A shot across the bows. Watch out, swotty pants. Get back in your baggy blazer. Know your place. But I don't have a place any more. This is all about them. It is nothing at all to do with me. I'm pissed off about losing the radio but I don't give much thought to the rest of it. The Donnas are idiots. Mum was right. I've been much too hard on myself.

School days are the best days of your life. I couldn't wait to be shot of them. I counted down the months, like a giant advent calendar. You know that bit in *Poltergeist* where they keep urging the girl to go towards the light? That's what the end of school felt like when it came, like I'd stepped out into a bright, shiny sunbeam. Relax. Exhale. Relief. No more pretending to be stupid. No more sick feeling in the pit of your stomach on a Sunday night. No more pretending that you don't have plans.

Weeks pass. Exams come and go. Afterwards, when it's all done and dusted, there's another sixth-form party. We sit in someone's living room drinking beer and celebrating the end of term: the end of school. We listen to 'Two Tribes' with our teachers. We're out of uniform. They are out of their suits. We feel incredibly sophisticated and mature, hanging out like this with the head of history, the head of English, the head of French. But the gloss on our teachers is already fading, even from the cool ones; even from the one with the pierced ear and the bright red socks. Next term we'll be long gone, off to new horizons. Next term they'll be back in the classroom telling the same weary jokes about the War of Jenkins' Ear that I used to think were funny but on reflection already seem lame.

Someone puts on 'Perfect Skin' by Lloyd Cole and The Commotions, and the perfect-skin girls, with cheekbones like geometry, get up to dance. But their sheen is fading too. When the summer's over the Donnas and the Haileys are off to work behind the counter in Gants Hill supermarkets. Or local hairdressing salons. Or forget to take their pill and get pregnant. There are four of us going to university from this sixth form. Despite spending half my time drafting and re-drafting revision timetables with a multitude of pens and coloured pencils, my results will all come good. And I'll be one of them.

FISH FROM MARILLION

I am so glad to be free of school and so reluctant to commit to three more years of education, my big plan is to defer my place at college and take a gap year. The gap year is a marvellous invention. It offers untold freedom and limitless possibility for personal growth. I could volunteer to lay water pipes in Sub-Saharan Africa, tour Southeast Asia on a dollar a day, learn French or Taiwanese or how to hang-glide, or, *or* I could hang about in Gants Hill looking for a part-time job in a clothes shop, whilst getting fat on McDonald's with my friends.

Through a mixture of chronic indecision, blind panic and prevarication, I have singularly failed to come up with anything interesting or life-enhancing to do in my gap year. I have negotiated a twelve-month sabbatical from life's weary treadmill – much needed after the exhausting teen years of getting up at midday, learning how to crimp my hair without scorching it, and repeating rumours about Marc Almond having his stomach pumped of a gallon of spunk – and what do I plan to do with it? Spend it dossing about on the sofa and signing on at the DHSS.

My parents are not unduly worried. In part this is because I'm the last of three children and they've used up all their energy worrying about the first two, and partly because we're simply not a go-getting, up-and-at-'em, travel-the-world-in-a-camper-van type of family. The Weners don't have adventures – unless you count the foolhardy moment my mum once swapped Heinz beans for Crosse & Blackwell – and we are, by and large, an indolent bunch. In fact, so laissez-faire is my parents' attitude now they've hit late middle age, I'm fairly sure I could sit here for any number of gap years, let's say six, before they'd finally get around to asking me what I plan to do with the rest of my life, and if I fancy egg or just peas with my chips for dinner.

After six months of doing next to nothing, save from cursing myself for not making the great escape to college the instant it became humanly possible, I come up with a semblance of a plan. I'll get a job in a shop, save up some money and run off to spend a few months as a volunteer on a kibbutz in Israel. Kibbutz is practically a rite of passage for a Jewish girl growing up in Gants Hill. My sister went when she was my age and when I ask her about it now, she makes it sound like one long bohemian, hippy holiday. In my head it's endless hot days skinny-dipping in a pool, while intense boys and cool girls strum Bob Dylan songs on acoustic guitars, debating Arab–Israeli politics and smoking marijuana. I've not done any of these things. I suddenly find I'm unduly keen to do all of them.

It's only after I've saved up £200, signed up for the trip and sorted out a rucksack that I remember you have to work hard on a kibbutz – get up at four o'clock in the morning to beat the heat of the day, spend eight hours mucking out chicken sheds or picking cotton – and that my sister couldn't hack it and left after less than two weeks.

No matter. I'm hardier than she is and I'm packing for all eventualities. My washbag is crammed with home comforts designed to stave off any material hardship: Sage & Comfrey spot cream from The Body Shop, a talc and soap set, also from The Body Shop, and I have just enough money left over to buy an atomiser of Anais Anais perfume in duty free. I also have a Walkman and a dozen or so cassette tapes that will see me through any tough times, the most important of which are *Let's Dance* by David Bowie, *Setting Sons* by The Jam, *Life's a Riot With Spy Vs Spy* by Billy Bragg and assorted tracks by The Style Council.

It's a cold morning, overcast and foggy, and hardly past dawn when the time comes to set off for Gatwick. This is it! I'm leaving home. A world of adventure is waiting and it begins the moment I step foot outside the storm porch. I pick up my rucksack but it's so unwieldy I can barely balance it on my shoulders. This is partly due to the sheer weight of Body Shop products I've shoved into its many side pockets and partly because the damn thing is ancient. It's made of heavy orange canvas, has a rigid metal frame that's bigger than I am and hasn't seen the light of day since my sister first took it on kibbutz some twelve years earlier.

Mum holds the door open as I struggle with my luggage, and I suddenly notice that she's crying. I get the feeling this is not entirely down to her distress at watching my knees buckle beneath the weight of the demon rucksack, and has more to do with me being the last of her children to fly the nest. Even so, her reaction throws me for a loop and I almost don't make it through the door. Mum's fantastically stoic – all post-war rationing and the Blitz and stiff English upper lip –

and I'm not used to seeing her being so openly emotional. How will Mum cope without me? How will I cope without Mum? What if kibbutz is Hindleap Warren all over again?

'Off you go,' Mum says, tightening her emotional corset at the sight of mine cracking. 'Keep in touch, love. Have a wonderful time.'

I hug her very tightly and promise to phone the moment I get there and every week after that on the days when I'm not writing letters.

I hardly pick the phone up the entire time I'm there.

Day One

Flight was amazing. We had red wine in little bottles with our lunch. I have the WORST rucksack out of everyone. Embarrassing. There were soldiers at the airport carrying machine guns. Some of them were women!

Day Two

I'm sharing a room with two girls. They are both really friendly. I have made friends with a cool American girl called Janice. She comes from Milwaukee, has a tattoo of barbed wire on her ankle, and has slept with most of the good-looking boys on the kibbutz. She once had sex with a boy in the toilets, even though she still had her tampon in!

Day Three

Have skinny-dipped!!

Day Four

Am in love with an Israeli film director. He doesn't direct many films because he lives on a kibbutz, but he does write fantastic poetry about being depressed. Example: *I am so heavy I need a crane to lift me from myself*. Amazing. I will definitely lose my virginity any day now.

Week Two

Have skinny-dipped again! Have smoked marijuana. Couldn't stop eating prawn cocktail flavour crisps dipped in peanut butter. Have not learned to play acoustic guitar yet, or discussed the finer points of Arab–Israeli politics.

Week Three

Israeli film director is in love with someone else! Devastated!! Very short Texan is in love with me. He's into some weird mystical stuff called Kabbalah. He says he's seen things I can only imagine! He smokes a lot of marijuana. And listens to Jefferson Starship.

Week Four

Have lost my virginity!!!!!!
To a Jewish sex therapist called Alvin!!!!!!!!!!
He is ten years older than I am. He has a *beard*! Wait 'til I tell Bernice Cohen!

It was good. It was OK. It was sort of, I don't know, a bit gynaecological. I hope it gets better than this. What if it doesn't? He's a sex therapist, for God's sake. He should be completely brilliant at sex. Maybe it was *me* that was rubbish. I don't think so, though. It turns out there's not very much to it. You just sort of have to lie there and shuffle about a bit. I wonder why I didn't have an orgasm. Is there something extra you're supposed to do? Should it have lasted longer or shorter than fifteen minutes? Do I feel any different? Yes I do! Relieved mostly. That it's over with. I don't know why I was making such a big deal out of it. I wonder if people can tell? Just by looking at me, I mean.

Janice thinks I look different. Less eager. But she thinks the sex therapy angle is just a line. She thinks he uses it to get virgins into bed with him.

'Janice?'

'Yes.'

'Have you… in fact, slept with him?'

'Of course!'

To the best of her knowledge Al has slept with three other virgins here already. Perhaps the four of us should get together and compare notes. He probably used the same tactics on all of us. A trip out to the monastery for wine, some sweet-talking New-York-style therapy speak then bam, before you know it, it's 'let's take the bus down to the beach'.

I realise this doesn't sound good. It makes him sound like a bit of a git. On top of it all I might have given you the impression that he looks a bit nerdish, when he's actually OK-looking. Less Woody Allen with facial hair, more Al Pacino in *Serpico*. Scruffy. Hippyish. Handsome. I'm as certain as I can be that I'm just another notch in his insatiable quest to bang teenage English virgins, but even so, all things considered, I think it could have gone a lot worse.

I want to have sex lots more times before Al leaves in a couple of weeks. Janice says you have to do it at least ten times before it gets any good. I must try *very* hard not to fall in love with him.

Week Five

Up at 4am again today. Went to canteen for breakfast. Ate bread and tomatoes and strange green jam. Rode tractor over the fields just as the sun was coming up. Listened to 'Walls Come Tumbling Down' by The Style Council on my Walkman. Romantic.

Week Six

I love being outdoors all day. My favourite job is pruning the avocado trees. Today we stopped for lunch in the shade and ate watermelon and delicious cheese.

Week Seven

There is a lot of wife-swapping going on here.

Week Eight

Have fallen hopelessly in love with sex therapist. Today he flew home to New York. Devastated! Am taking up smoking. Went with him to the airport to say goodbye. Told him that I loved him even though I had promised myself I wouldn't. He gave me his necklace to remember him by. There was no talk of seeing each other again – we both have to be realistic – but he had some parting words of advice. He says whatever I do I'm not to sleep with weird short Texan who's into Kabbalah because – in his professional opinion as a psychoanalyst – he's a bit fucked up. I told him that I absolutely won't.

Week Nine

Have slept with weird short Texan. Oh well!

Week Ten

Jerusalem is beautiful. Got lost in the Arab quarter. Drank mint tea.

Week Eleven

Watched Live Aid!! Amazing. Half the kibbutz crammed round a portable TV set in the canteen. Queen and David Bowie were brilliant but Bono was SO cheesy. Dancing with that girl in the audience. Yeuch. This will probably be the end of U2.

Week Twelve

Bernice Cohen in Israel for a holiday! Went to visit her in Tel Aviv. Stayed overnight in her room at the Hilton. Bumped into Fish from Marillion!

It's all going dizzyingly fast. I am ticking off life experiences faster than I can say Yasser Arafat. I am living alone for the first time. Making my own decisions and, miraculously, it's going OK. I love the camaraderie of this place: the work, the sharing, the sense of belonging, the fact that people have come here from as far away as China and Argentina and that everyone has a story to tell. It's not a religious kibbutz: it's tiny and liberal, 100 people at most. Everyone looks out for one another, like some extended dysfunctional family. There are no children here, or any people over the age of 40. There are parties on the beach, nights spent camping in the desert, boyfriends and cigarettes and sex. Not to mention bumping into the man who wrote Kayleigh in the lobby of an international hotel.

I leave for home on the last possible day before term starts. My spots have healed in the sun, I have lost my virginity, I have put on a stone in weight because of all the crisps and peanut butter, but you can't really tell because I'm tanned the colour of a conker. I have a bottle of duty-free Kahlua in my rucksack and Fish from Marillion's autograph in my pocket. There is no way university is going to top this.

ONCE IN A LIFETIME

Manchester is perpetually grey and damp. My tan peeled the moment we hit the M6 and, in a moment of madness, I appear to have signed up for an English degree whose first year is devoted to transcribing Anglo-Saxon texts from some ancient, indecipherable, runic alphabet. It's fair to say things aren't going well. I'm pining for the tractors and the sunshine. I am not getting on with the runic alphabet.

To top things off, I think the accommodation office must have made a mistake. I've been put into a flat with six textile technologists who've never met a Jewish person before and want to know if I do strange things on Friday nights. They're obsessed with calories and dieting and at least two of them are seriously anorexic.

If I'd come straight from Gants Hill to Manchester I'd probably have been ecstatic to spend my days studying ancient *Englisc* and my evenings working out the calorie content of chips with curry sauce, but so far university seems a lot like school without the added comforts of home. The joy of owning my own jar of powdered coffee is somewhat mitigated by the girl in the next-door study-bedroom playing 'Spirit In The Sky' by Doctor & The Medics 1600 times a day. I suddenly feel homesick and lonely and just want to leave and go back to the kibbutz. Instead of this, I dive headlong into a long-distance relationship with the very short Texan which gets me into all kinds of trouble.

The key to maintaining a long-distance relationship is talking to one another as often as possible. Luckily, there's a payphone outside my student halls that accepts reverse charges calls. At a prearranged time, several evenings a week, the Texan calls from Israel and I say, 'Yes, operator, I accept the long-distance charges.' This is great. We can talk for hours! For free! I can't understand why *everyone* isn't doing this.

The university bursar comes to find me in term two. I've run up a bill of £300 on the payphone and my place at university is under review. I may or may not be expelled, depending on how soon I can pay the money back. This is bad. I have no idea how I'll get the cash. I could ask the Texan to contribute but we've just split up after I made an ill-advised visit back to Israel over the Christmas holidays that he paid for. We stayed in a youth hostel in Jerusalem. It was freezing cold and snowing and I chucked him on the second day when I realised Alvin the sex therapist had been right all along, and I'd been blinded to the Texan's weirdness by the weed and sunshine.

We sat out the rest of the week together. The Texan spent every day crying while I went to bed in all my clothes to keep warm and developed boils on both my cheeks from the filthy sheets. On Christmas Day I phoned home from a call box and pretended to be enjoying myself. I could hear everyone chatting and laughing and rustling crackers in the background. I could almost smell the turkey and the pudding and taste my mother's glass of Harvey's Bristol Cream. It sounded warm and happy. It was the worst Christmas Day of my life.

*

We come to an arrangement, the bursar and I. I agree to pay my debt by the end of the summer and he agrees not to have me thrown out of university. As a parting shot he asks me how I like my course and I lie and say I love it when in truth I'm failing at everything. I can't translate any of the ancient English and seriously doubt I'd want to read it even if I could. Dispiritingly, everyone else in my group has studied funky, dead languages before and already seem to be fluent in Latin and Norse. I have a lot of catching up to do. The only bit of Latin I know is *et cetera*.

'Well, good,' says the bursar. 'At least you're enjoying your studies.' And then he reaches into my waste-paper bin and stubs his cigarette out onto a Clearblue pregnancy-test box that's lurking at the bottom. He blushes and pretends not to notice. And I say, 'Really, it's fine. It was negative.'

Term three is a big improvement on terms one and two. I make great friends with one of the textile technologists, ditch the Old *Englisc* and switch to Combined Arts: a hotch-potch course where you can pick and choose from all the arts disciplines and spend afternoons discussing Vietnam and Virginia Woolf and watching old Alfred Hitchcock films. Better still, I'm just about to find a brand new boyfriend.

I recognise the boy standing behind me at the NatWest queue on Oxford Road. He's in my politics tutorial. He's from Sheffield and he's funny and smart, and he wears a long black trench coat that's two sizes too big for him. He offers to buy me coffee at the union cafe and lights my cigarette with a vintage Zippo, which I think is fantastically cool.

He invites me to a Pernod promotion at his hall bar that weekend and I'm just thinking I might rather like him when he delivers the killer of killer blows. We're talking about music that he likes and I like, and then he mentions he plays guitar and might be looking to start a band. I take a long drag on my Consulate. I stare deep into his eyes and say: *I have always wanted to be in a band.*

Jon Stewart has been in a band before. He has all the experience I will ever need. He has an amp and an electric guitar and he's written actual songs, and he's just invited me back to his halls to listen to his songs and check out his record collection. It doesn't start well. He likes Devo and Kraftwerk, which I think are beyond pointless, and he also likes The Cure but not the good songs like 'Boys Don't Cry'; he likes the bleak goth stuff like *Faith* and *Pornography*. He doesn't like Bowie or The Jam and I'm just thinking this might be a bit of a blind alley when he digs out something by Talking Heads, a band I've never listened to before. The song is 'Once In A Lifetime' and I love it so much I make him play it to me a dozen times in a row because I can't get enough of it and must fill myself up with it, in case I get run over on the way home and this is the last time I ever hear it.

' Once In A Lifetime' is colossal. It seems to sum up where I've come from and what I'm running from: it's even better than The Jam's 'Smithers-Jones'! If the boy in the long black coat likes this song, then there might be some chance for us after all. In truth it's a done deal by then.

I'll spend the summer working off my phone debt and backpacking round the Greek islands with the textile technologist. We'll dance to 'Inbetween Days' by The Cure a thousand times: blaring from every harbourside taverna and beachside disco that we visit, as if it's the only record owned in the whole of Greece. We'll sleep on the sand, fall in and out of love at least a dozen times a night, live on bread and peaches and ouzo and pretend we think retsina tastes nice. I'll still have that damn orange rucksack. When I come back next autumn I'll move into a shared house with Jon Stewart and form a band. Several bands. But for now we need to start at the beginning:

Me: How long will it take to learn guitar?

Jon: I can teach you three chords by tomorrow.

Fantastic answer!

Me : When I go into a guitar shop, how do I stop the men who work there from scoffing, redirecting me to Miss Self-ridge and fobbing me off with a pink plectrum?

Jon: Learn how to play the solo from 'Stairway To Heaven'. Ask for a jumbo can of Fast Fret. Spend some quality time discussing humbucker pickups.

Write all this down. Find out what it means later.

Me: What's a middle eight?

Jon: It's that 'meanwhile back at the ranch' part of a song. A break between the repetition of verse and chorus. The classic song structure is: intro, verse, chorus, verse, chorus, middle eight, choruses out.

I take note. I will hardly ever deviate from this form.

Me: There's one thing that's always confused me. Why do some guitars only have four strings?

Jon: Because... uh... that one would be a *bass.*

Me: I see. I see. And what would be the point of bass guitar, exactly?

Jon (realising the mountain he has to climb): You really don't know anything at all about being in a band, do you?

*

He was right. I knew absolutely nothing. But I still think I had a point about the bass guitar.

IRONING OUT
THE CREASES

The university band I formed with Jon Stewart never really took off. This is because a) it was a jazz band, b) it was rubbish and c) we were too busy attending to a wardrobe full of dope plants to fully master the subtleties of swing and syncopation. Growing marijuana requires careful attention – you have to ensure a stable temperature and fix up a complex lighting rig raised by a series of strings and pulleys – and there's only so much time for band rehearsals when you're busy exploiting the luxury of a grant-funded education by watching *Neighbours* twice a day and making a definitive list of top-ten foods to eat when you're stoned. Number-one answer: candyfloss.

I was hoping my first band would be a cross between The Jam and The Bangles but I'm not sure The Lime Street Blues Band fitted the bill. We played a curious mix of jazz and blues including assorted tracks by the 1930s' jazz quartet Hot Club de France, made famous by guitarist Django Reinhardt and the violinist Stéphane Grappelli. The disappointment of Hot Club de France, for me at least, was that all of its music was instrumental. With no vocals to speak of I was relegated to the Linda McCartney role, flapping around at the back with a cowbell and a tambourine. As a courtesy, to stop me complaining, I was allowed to step up to the mike every ten minutes or so and croon an old standard like 'Summertime' or 'Cry Me A River'. Every once in a while I'd turn my skills to the band's blues element – not the most obvious milieu for a slightly uptight white girl from Gants Hill – and knock out something about somebody's no-good baby leaving them. My outfit was a second-hand black dinner jacket and matching leggings. My tuning was occasionally a little off.

The reason we started a jazz band isn't clear, but probably had something to do with Jon knowing a student called Hannan who played the harmonica, and me knowing a student called Anthony who played the double bass. More importantly I knew a wine bar, The Larch, opposite my old student halls, that was offering money to bands who wanted to play at their acoustic jazz nights. It seemed like a good way to start. We earned £25 per week for those gigs, which would have come in useful, split four ways, if we hadn't decided to pool all our takings and save up to buy our own public address system – the means of amplification required by every live band – otherwise known as a PA.

There is something about being in a band that makes boys compelled to own their own PA system. I have never been able to work out why. Venues have PAs in them already – if they don't they're hardly worth playing – and there's only so many times you can lug your equipment up three flights of stairs, set up an impromptu gig in someone's bedroom and wait for a drunk fresher to pour a pint of beer down one of your speakers.

Even so, as soon as the idea was mooted, Jon, Hannan and Anthony were convinced saving up for our own PA was the way to go. They scoured the pages of *Exchange and Mart* and drove from Manchester to Rochdale to buy one. They returned, suffused with macho pride, like revolutionaries who'd taken control of the means of production. I think it made them feel a little less like wine-bar sell-outs and fractionally more like The Clash. For eighteen months our PA lived behind the sofa. It got taken to a couple of student parties and a blues festival in Salford. Someone poured beer into it. It broke.

I'm not sure playing Muddy Waters at The Larch got me any closer to playing Wembley like The Jam, but it wasn't a complete and utter loss. I learned how to count time so I knew when to come in at the beginning of a song – which had previously been a bit of a problem – and after one particularly off-key rendition of 'Cry Me A River' I decided to take singing lessons with a music teacher called Antonio in Manchester's Piccadilly Square. Antonio, a retired opera singer, taught me the difference between head voice and chest voice and packed me off to learn a different Italian sonata as homework every week. With all this blues and light opera knocking around, what I desperately needed was a bit of down and dirty rock 'n' roll to even up my musical education. Which must have been why Jon and I thought it would be a good idea to go to America on student work visas and spend three months working as singing waiters on a floating restaurant.

I have just sung the US navy song 'Anchors Aweigh' for the hundredth time. We sing it at midday, when the tourists board the boat for lunch, and again in the evening when the second wave of tourists board for dinner. I have 45 covers in my section. That's a lot of lobster bibs and jacket potatoes to hand out. That's a lot of lobster shell and half-chewed corn on the cobs to collect in my slop bucket when the customers have finished. I have just put squirty cream on someone's frozen margarita. They are not happy. Squirty cream is just for the daiquiris.

This is the tenth time tonight I've said, 'Hi, I'm Louise, I'll be your waiter for this evening. After dinner and a scenic tour of Boston harbour I'll be performing "I Wanna Dance With Somebody" by Whitney Houston with the *Spirit of Boston*'s house band. If you have any special requests, be sure to ask the captain, who will try his hardest to accommodate you.'

Here's a secret. The moustachioed man in the white cap and epaulets wasn't really a captain. He was the alcoholic with chronic halitosis who prepped the vegetables in the boiling hot galley in the bowels of the boat. The only reason they let him up on deck at show time was because he fitted the captain's brocade jacket. The main way he liked to accommodate people was by creeping up behind the waitresses and whispering that he'd like to lick their asses while they were busy with their cartons of squirty cream.

This might have been the worst summer job I'd ever had if it wasn't for the fact that Bostonians of pensionable age, in their white shorts and baseball caps, are fantastically generous tippers, especially if their waiter is English. Two or three times each day, once we'd established that I wasn't Australian, I'd be asked what it was like to come from a place (London) that was foggy all the time, and if I knew the queen. Cordial answers such as 'A bit chilly actually' and 'Yes I do and she's very nice' would elicit tips of up to $50 a night. This was a lot of money in 1988, especially since Jon and I were living in a shared clapboard house on the outskirts of Boston and paying no rent at all since we'd cunningly agreed to sleep outside on a pair of mattresses, perched on a tiny wooden balcony.

Two months of Whitney, lobster bibs and 'Anchors Aweigh' earned us enough money to take a Greyhound bus down to Florida, fly to Jamaica and spend a month living in a shack next to a reggae studio on the kind of powder-white beach I thought only existed with Judith Chalmers sitting on it. All in all, it was the perfect post-university holiday, only slightly marred by someone – I'm fairly sure it was the sex-obsessed vegetable cutter – stealing all the cassette tapes from my luggage on my last night as a singing waitress. As an act of kindness – or malice, depending on your perspective – he left me with a lone Psychedelic Furs compilation. On the two-day, 1500-mile bus trip from Boston to Miami – a perfect initiation into the discomforts of touring, as it turned out – I listened to 'Pretty In Pink' so many times I'd drift into an achy sleep in my seat after my fifth packet of Twinkies and come round convinced I was Molly Ringwald. Perhaps it was a sign. Perhaps becoming a redhead was the way forward. I could dye my hair ginger and go back to wearing spectacles, just like the girl out of Fairground Attraction.

By the time Jon and I returned to England that autumn, a new kind of female singer was taking a grip on the British charts: Eddi Reader, Tracy Chapman, Tracey Thorn, and some teenage girl with a man's voice, from Basingstoke, who couldn't keep her eyes open when she sang, called Tanita Tikaram. They all played acoustic guitar and, as far as I could determine from my limited grasp of musicology, had a dominant note of folk and jazz in their songs.

It was time for The Lime Street Blues Band to prove its usefulness. College was over. We were moving to London and this time I was determined to do the music thing properly. I wasn't just fantasising about being in *The Breakfast Club* on that Greyhound bus journey to Miami: I was coming up with a bona fide plan.

SADE

It turns out our plan has a few holes in it. It goes something like this: *come to London, find a room in a shared house, sign on, write some chart toppers, get a huge record deal, sign off, move to Hawaii.* The shared house and DHSS parts are easy – we are old hands at that – but the chart toppers are proving elusive I've finally mastered the three chords that should have taken me a day to learn, but every time I manage to scrape a tune together, it sounds disturbingly like a Latvian entry in the Eurovision Song Contest. Obviously there is work to be done.

While we set about finessing the finer points of chart topping, Jon and I duly sign on and take part-time jobs when funds get so depleted we can't afford to buy guitar strings or Pot Noodles. In the summer of '89 I'm waitressing at London's Tower Hotel, and Jon's working at a homeless shelter in Islington. I'm listening to Lisa Stansfield on a loop as I serve deep-fried Camembert to city boys, and Jon is listening to John Peel on the radio as he navigates the nightly uproar of fist-fights and overdoses.

By the end of the year we've officially had our first break. I've mastered a minor chord, we have a set of seven songs and we've formed a new band called Strange Fruit, after a Billie Holiday song. Strange Fruit is me, Jon and Anthony, our old double-bass player, and I like to think the vibe is very 10,000 Maniacs. But without a drummer. Or any amps. There's a touch of 'Crash' by The Primitives, a dab of Transvison Vamp, and it might just be the case that I've listened to 'Manchild' by Neneh Cherry once too often, because our style is difficult to pinpoint. Strange Fruit defy genre specification. But not in a good way.

Undeterred, we rehearse for several hours each day because we have a very important gig coming up. In two weeks' time we play the Mean Fiddler in Harlesden – upstairs at its acoustic room – in front of a genuine record company executive: the fabulously named Lincoln Elias.

The way we meet Lincoln Elias, who is just about to sign Jamiroquai, is this: one day my brother, who's driving a mini-cab for the summer to fund his PhD, gives a ride to a dapper-looking fellow called Russell. It turns out Russell is connected. He's related to the lead singer of legendary eighties soul outfit Imagination and knows everyone who's anyone in the music business. My brother – sensing an 'it's who you know, not what you know' opportunity – tells him all about his kid sister's band. My brother has the gift of the gab. By the end of the cab ride – Gants Hill to Buckhurst Hill – he's convinced Russell to bring some record company hotshot that he knows, the aforementioned Lincoln, to see us perform. I had always wondered how this part happened. How that magic connection from ordinary world to superstar world was made. And now I knew. It's easy. You get the guy who knows the guy from Imagination to take a £5 taxi ride in the back of your big brother's cab.

The surprising thing about this early brush with the music business is that Russell and his industry pals actually bother to turn up. I see them walk in, or rather I see my brother's thumbs-up from the back of the room, and feel my stomach lurch, cold with nerves. Everyone I know is in this room – this dank dingy space where Tanita Tikaram got spotted and signed – even my mum and dad. They're here to cheer us on, because this is the big one, the moment that will change all our lives. There's still a vague Latvian element to my songwriting but I'm hoping the record company will overlook this and recognise our raw potential. To help them in their task I'm wearing my new cropped leggings and I've been at work on my hair with a can of mousse and a heat diffuser for several hours.

We never meet Lincoln Elias. He leaves after two and a half songs. In the dressing room afterwards, my brother breaks the crushing news that the man from Sony isn't going to give us a record deal after all. Female folk rock is on the way out. There's something new called baggy coming in. I am broken. How are we meant to go forward? It might only take six months to master this newfangled thing called baggy, but it could easily be 30 years before another record company executive gets into a car driven by one of my immediate family.

Rocked by this defeat, Jon and I return to our shared house. They're an odd collection of souls, our London housemates: the peer's daughter who lusts after Barry Grant from *Brookside*, the landlord's daughter with recurrent pubic lice, the Australian rent-boy who goes out cruising for punters every evening and returns in the early hours to sleep off his heroin daze in our dishevelled front room. On the top floor there's a big-boned American virgin who cries herself to sleep every night listening to Suzanne Vega's 'Luka', and down in the basement is the normal one, the straight one, who works in telecoms: a sweet boy called Jim who keeps himself mostly to himself.

One afternoon, a few days after the Mean Fiddler gig, Jon and I come back to the house to find Jim is the only person home. He's sitting in the front room next to a beautiful black girl with a very high forehead and the two of them are cracking up over a video of *Beverly Hills Cop*. I think I recognise the girl from somewhere and as soon as we sit down, Jon starts nudging me. He looks like he's desperate to ask her something but she's engrossed in the film and immediately it finishes she picks up her bag, kisses Jim goodbye and she's out the door.

'Was that who I think it was?' Jon says.

'Who?' I say.

'Sade.'

'No way!'

All eyes on little Jim.

Jim is nonplussed.

'She lives up the road in Highbury. We're mates. We've known each other for years. We went to school together in Colchester.'

I could cry. I can't *believe* little Jim is friends with a superstar like Sade and I can't believe I didn't realise it was her. I love Sade. I loved *Diamond Life*. Just think of the questions I could have asked her! The advice. Think of the contacts we could have made. She didn't just hire my mini-cab; Sade came round to my house!

'Will she, you know. Be coming round again. Any time soon?'

'Nope, unlikely. Off to America, on tour.'

'Oh.'

Jim slips off his loafers and smiles. 'And anyway,' he says, 'you might as well give up. There's no chance you two will be successful now.'

I ask him why not.

'Statistically impossible,' he says, yawning and flipping over to an episode of *Moonlighting*. 'Think about it. What are the chances of someone like me being friends with more than one famous pop star?'

I have to admit, Jim has a point.

THE GROUNDHOG
DAYS

How long is this supposed to take? How long are you meant to give it? Two years? Three years? Four?

It's 1992 and Jon and I have moved into our own flat. It has no central heating. The winters are bitterly cold and in the mornings I don't want to get up. There is frost inside the windows and the dash from the bed to the living room – to turn on the electric fire – is so bone chilling and raw, it makes me feel like Scott of the Antarctic.

We have bought our own cutlery. And crockery. We have had friends round for dinner and cooked them a vegetable chilli which they ate on the sofa that feels like a rock, and turns into a spare bed if you kick it hard enough. This was meant to be a good thing. Finally out of shared bathroom land, and into a bathroom of our own. I miss the shared house, if I'm honest. It's a bit quiet up here, just the two of us. Yesterday there was a power cut while Jon was out at work and I sat here all evening in the dark, waiting for someone to come round and fix the meter. Sometimes we run out of 50-pence pieces. Must remember to go to the bank for 50-pence pieces.

When I look back on this period now, I can't work out exactly what I was doing. I know I worked. Intermittently.

I had office jobs. I was a tea lady and briefly a cleaner but mostly I signed on and waitressed. And lived in that ugly, cold flat.

I am wasting my life. I can feel it. I didn't use to be able to feel it but I can now. Every day is the same. Get up. Drink tea. No time for tea. Breakfast shift. Rush into town. Put on uniform. Serve a hundred portions of egg. Or is this a signing-on period? In which case I can really feel the wastage. Sleep in. Sign on. Go to the Workers Cafe on Upper Street for a bacon sandwich. Watch daytime TV. Get stoned.

Jon is dealing weed to supplement our income. He sometimes goes out for whole afternoons and I have no idea where he goes. Perhaps he's having an affair. We argue a lot these days. Raised voices. Things smashed. We still kid ourselves we have a grand plan, some big ambition, but the truth is, we hardly ever gig now. Once every few months at most. When we lived in the shared house we rehearsed in the basement all the time. Now we have to pay, we only rehearse when we can afford to. We take the overground train out to Stratford, to a place called Broken Lives, and try to sneak through the ticket barriers without paying. The rehearsal room is on an industrial estate which seems funny because it's full of the least industrious people you will ever meet. Us. And some unsigned heavy metal bands. I suppose they think they're all grunge now. They're not grunge. They are just heavy metal.

I am drifting. Increasingly I hate myself for it. Part of growing up is knowing when to put childish ambitions to rest and this ought to be the year to do just that. I am 25 years old in 1992; it's already beginning to feel too late. It might help if I got better at playing the guitar but I never do. All this spare time and I never sit down and really work at it. I know lots of people coasting like this and I'm beginning to hate them for it too. Ex-students in bands swearing that they will never bow down to 'the man' (chance would be a fine thing) and endlessly drawing up and reinventing their 'manifestos'. Seriously. Like *anybody* cares. And for the record, six hours in a Holloway pub arguing about whether The Wedding Present have sold out by signing to RCA does not a mission statement make. Forgive me. I'm not interested. Buy me another can of fizzy pop and I'll tell you a funny story about how I thought I'd be Kate Bush by now.

We can't work out what we want to be. We're never going to fit in among the north London shoegazers – and wouldn't want to – but where do women fit into this whole Seattle grunge thing that seems to have taken over the world? I have a crush on the new riot grrrls, Hole and Bikini Kill, and I loved it when the singer from American band L7 pulled her pants down when they played on *The Word*. I thought it was nothing short of heroic. Confounding and seditious, exactly what rock music should be. Paula Yates would have done it if she'd been in a band. Even so, I don't want to be in the kind of group that is all about agenda. I get enough hectoring in the Holloway pubs.

We ought to shut up shop but we don't. Music has become our refuge. A place for two people who don't have the will or the imagination to do anything else. We live out our version of groundhog day. The days turn to months, the months turn to years, each of them blurring into one another: waitress for six months, office temp for six months, gig a few times, record new demo tape, write new songs, form new band, dump old songs, sign on, sign off, waitress, temp, gig again, save up to record the definitive demo tape.

Band members come and go, we change names, styles, format, arrangements and try to give it up but somehow I never quite can. We forget about performing for a long time, nine months, a year, but nothing comes close to replacing it: that visceral desire to play music on stage, the egotistical emergency to be famous. And before you know it, it's winter all over again and we *have* to get out of this flat and find another one, but Jon thinks we should stay where we are, because we're back in a signing-on period, and moving out now will fuck our housing benefit up forever.

It's utterly pointless and futile. Hawaii, it turns out, is not a life plan.

There was a cafe on Upper Street called The Dome that was a constant through the groundhog days. We'd stop in there, off the train after rehearsals, with whichever band mates we had at the time, order a cappuccino – very exotic – and make it last the whole afternoon. The Dome was posh: you could tell it was posh because it sold frites instead of chips, and you got a free brandy-snap biscuit with your coffee. Who knows, one day we might be in there with our very own rock 'n' roll manager, having high-powered music-business pow-wows: just like Blur.

Four pretty indie boys, with requisite floppy fringes, stir sugar into their tea across the room from us. We recognise them but don't pay much attention. We've met lots of bands on the circuit, bigger and smaller, with record deals and without, and they can never do anything useful for you. They might pass your demo tape to their manager; more likely they'll throw it straight in the bin. Blur are on the skids anyway. They've had one top ten single but only disappointments after that, and rumour has it they're weeks away from being dropped by their record label. The four of them seem animated nevertheless. If I had to dissect the mood of that band meeting, by body language alone, I'd say they'd decided to give this pop lark one last chance.

Good on them, I think. Good luck with all that. My coffee mug is empty. I look at my watch. Time to go home. It's going dark.

MOVING ON

The winter is full of unfamiliar sounds. The clink of oxygen cylinders being delivered, the rasp of laboured respiration. Dad loses his hair after the second round of radiation therapy. It grows through again, soft and fuzzy, like a duck's. I sit by the bed. I trim his hair with nail scissors. He watches in the mirror trying to make sense of his changing face. Fading away. Skin and bones.

It's the small things I remember. How he lived on lemon sherbets towards the end. The shape of his hand as he tried to eat a piece of toast; how he'd wake in the night every hour or so and ask to know exactly what time it was. That winter was cold, thick snow all the way through to March.

The first thing he did after they gave him the retirement watch was sign up to study for a law degree. I don't think I'd ever seen him so happy. He was a natural student; he earned top grades in every course. Sitting there in the lecture halls with kids young enough to be his grandchildren, upright at the kitchen table with his piles of open textbooks, writing essays.

He'd been studying nine months when his hand shook at dinner as he tried to lift a scoop of mashed potato. They removed the tumour from his brain but the cancer had come from his lungs and there was nothing they could do about those. We almost laughed about it in the beginning, in the early days when we still could. A hypochondriac getting a brain tumour – what were the odds? I'd never even seen him smoke a cigarette. He gave up long before I was born. But they all smoked in the air force. They thought it was good for you. Gave out those cigarettes for free.

It took a year all in all. Commuting from north London to the suburbs while he was mobile, moving home to be close when he took to his bed. Some days crawled by so slowly I was desperate for them to end, and other days raced by so fast I'd have done anything at all to hold them back. Often we'd talk in the afternoons. He'd tell those same old stories, the ones I'd heard a million times before: but every time he told them he'd reveal some bright new detail and I'd collapse inside with sadness, realising I would never know him enough.

His funeral is a tiny dab of anarchy. Jewish funerals are plain, they don't have flowers, but we bring bunches and bunches of white lilies, laid out on the coffin, held in the grandchildren's arms. There is poetry and laughter and speeches and tears, and even a little music.

We play Duke Ellington's 'Take The A Train'. He would have got a kick out of that.

THE BUZZ

It could have gone one of two ways. The sensible thing is to grow up and give up after Dad's gone; to pack away the guitar, ditch the music fantasy and get a proper job. Of course, his passing has the opposite effect. I realise ambition and curiosity are not the preserve of youth, that they continue always, that they are what keep us growing and moving forward. Dad's lost opportunities are lost forever, and I grieve for them as well as for him. I am fiercely aware of time passing, grateful of growing up with so many choices, and all those wasted months suddenly seem like an affront. I'll make it just to prove that I can, for all the ways that Dad couldn't. Twenty-five is still blissfully, innocently young. Too young yet to turn your back on a thing you love.

Even so, our pop clock is ticking. We have to refine and raise our game and I think it makes sense to put a time limit on how much longer we do this. Six months. Another year at the most. If we haven't been signed by next summer then the chances are that we never will be.

I've seen what else is out there. I know the competition inside out. The glut of unsigned bands with their songs about moody girlfriends, forever repeating their vows about keeping it real and not selling out. But I am dying to sell out. Here I am. Sell me. I'm yours. You lot play to six people and a dog, in a pub, for the rest of your lives if you want to, but I want to meet David Bowie. I want to be on *Top of the Pops*. I don't want to shoplift ham from the Co-op and live in an unheated flat where I can see my own breath from October to March for the rest of my life.

Somewhere in the recent weeks and months the self-doubt has vanished; there is nothing at all to be lost. I am fearless in this period, a living, breathing streak of brunette ambition. We're done with second best, through with playing to drunks and their dogs. If there's not someone from a record company in the audience that can sign us when we play, I'm not going to bother going on.

The difference between sink or swim in this business is word of mouth. It's all about creating a buzz and I am certain we are ready for ours. The new songs are written; the chord changes are mastered; we have our full and final band line-up. Jon and I have been joined by two others, Diid Osman on bass (four strings), Andy Maclure on the drums. We have recruited them from an advert in the back of the *Melody Maker* newspaper and this time we showed we meant business by commissioning a box-ad in bold. We cited our influences as The Pixies and The Partridge Family and auditioned everyone who sounded promising and not obviously mentally ill. This isn't a foolproof selection process. It's surprising how many rock musicians can sound entirely normal over the phone then turn out to be utter crackpots in person.

But this time I think we have it right. Andy has been playing in bands since he was thirteen years old; he is cool and ambitious and fantastically charismatic on stage. Diid is experienced, sanguine, rock solid; half Somali and unfeasibly handsome. He's also a little bit eighties. I like him because he comes to the audition wearing a pair of knee-high leather boots festooned with straps and buckles that wouldn't have looked out of place in Duran Duran's 'Wild Boys' video. Most importantly, Diid Osman has previous. He's been in a signed band before. Not only did his old band tour America, they actually appeared on the *Wogan* show. An American tour *and* an appearance on national TV. We have to have him.

It wasn't easy getting Diid and Andy to join the band. I think they were a bit suspicious when I told them how long we'd been at it and things very nearly fell apart when I accidentally played them a demo from our doomed funk/baggy period featuring a masterpiece of confused styles and lyrical gibberish called 'Where Is Jones?' Answer: who cares, this is terrible, is it Latvian? In the end it hardly mattered. I had the ultimate hook in my pocket, ready to reel them both in.

Just as Diid and Andy are beginning to look doubtful, I bring out the review in the *New Musical Express*. The review is accompanied by a picture and features 200 words of text that proclaim us as pretty bloody fine. Note that it doesn't say we're brilliant. Note that it points to a couple of weak spots, while subtly implying we're the next big thing and on the cusp of certain greatness, if only we can find the perfect bass player and drummer. This is because I wanted it to sound realistic when I wrote it. When I was faking that review – writing it and searching out someone with a computer who could copy the *NME* font, overlay our photo onto a copy of the newspaper and photocopy the finished page so it all looked genuine – I thought it might be going a bit too far if it said we were brilliant.

A positive *NME* review is worth a thousand words. Diid and Andy are in. Encouraged by this skullduggery, I send out our latest demo tape, along with the fake *NME* review, to half a dozen record companies. It works. On the basis of pure cheek and some cut-and-paste fakery, a couple of A&R scouts have agreed to come to our next gig.

A&R scouts have the easiest job in the world. Anyone could do it. A five-year-old could do it. The job is essentially this. Turn up at a club with seconds to spare to catch the first few songs of an unsigned band's set. You always turn up late because it makes the band nervous that you're not going to come, and it makes you feel powerful to make the band feel nervous. You will also be late because you are seeing half a dozen other bands on the same night, most likely on different sides of London. You are also late because you're stoned. And a bit confused.

If you make it to the gig on time, you light yourself a top-up joint and watch the band from the safety of the shadows, unannounced and anonymous. This is where the job gets easy. Even easier than getting stoned and watching music for a living. Most unsigned bands are awful. You know within moments whether they are any good or not. You are looking for a couple of things: a lead singer with a decent voice who is preferably good-looking and a band that can play well and have stage presence. Above all things you are hoping to hear a tune, preferably several tunes: some indication of long-term song-writing ability within the band. A tune is the A&R scout's holy grail. Voices and image can be worked on, but a tune is either there or it's not. If you hear a 'hit' you will phone your boss immediately and he will jump up and down

and run to get his boss's chequebook while mentally super-
imposing *Chart Show* boxes over the band's – as yet to be shot
– debut video.

The thing is, I can *see* our *Chart Show* boxes, I really can. I
think we've got it now, the image and the tunes and the requisite cocky attitude, but there's something else that isn't quite
right. I've heard that A&R scouts like to see some indication
of a local following, some small but tangible proof of popularity. We don't have any following or popularity. We sell
tickets to our friends; we beg, borrow and plead to get an
audience.

This time, we're going to need a little extra sparkle. We
need to create an atmosphere to impress the A&R scouts and
represent a semblance of a following. I decide to conjure one
out of thin air. A week before our first gig with our new band
line-up, I place an ad in the actors' newspaper, *The Stage*. I list
the date and location of our gig and claim to be auditioning
dancers to be in a video. Respondents should turn up at 8pm
sharp and mosh about at the front. Wear cool clothes. Be
animated and enthusiastic about the band.

The scam sort of works. Record companies are drawn by
our fake review and impressed by our man-for-hire audience.
The crowd is respectable and there is more dancing than usual,
by which I mean there is *actually* some dancing. We don't get
signed at that gig but we do get approached by several A&R
scouts who ask for our manager's number. Whatever it is
that happens – some magic tilt of the universe – has finally
happened. We are on people's radar, at last. Surrender
Dorothy – because that's what we're called now – are officially
creating a buzz. All we need now is a kick-ass manager. There's

only one choice. I remember that moment in the back of the mini-cab with the guy from Sony. I tell the record companies to call my big brother.

A few months later, we play a gig back at the Mean Fiddler in Harlesden. I forget the words to the new song we've just written. We stop and start it over again. The A&R man doesn't mind this. He likes that we're not thrown by the mistake, that we pick up, shrug it off and carry on. I'm wearing a swirly prom dress and Dr Marten boots. When I dance about on stage, I employ a jaunty sideways hopping motion, more curious than cool, but unique and patented by me. The man from BMG seems to like us. He doesn't mention the curious hopping. He likes the tunes.

Later, we showcase for his bosses. We hire a swanky rehearsal studio in west London, one that doesn't stink of mould or make you cough in the cold, with real lights and a stage and a coffee machine that also makes hot chocolate and chicken soup. We play our six best songs to three men: two in jeans, one in a suit. The man in the suit is key.

We hear nothing after the showcase. A week passes, maybe more. My big brother, firmly ensconced as our manager, finally calls. BMG records have offered us a deal. We will be the first signing to their new Indolent label. The offer they make us is small and riven with conditions, but there's never any question that we'll turn it down. For the princely down payment of £12,000 we'll offer up worldwide recording rights for two EPs and six future albums. With the dash of a ballpoint we'll commit to them for life, make and sign away our career.

None of this matters. Not for now. The legal papers come

in the post. They drop through the letterbox one lunchtime on a Saturday, at the studio bedsit in Kentish Town that Jon and I now share. I pick them up and read them, then fold them away into my pocket. I walk to Camden Market on my own. It's the end of the summer: sunny, still warm, the market stalls filled with weekend shoppers. I wander about in a glow.

I buy a celebration jacket – second-hand black leather – and show my record deal to the man who sells it to me, taking out the precious envelope as he packs the musty cloth into a musty plastic bag.

'My band got a record deal today,' I tell him.

'Congratulations,' he says.

'It's not a very good one,' I say. 'We're signing for the world. And the universe. And all territories unknown and yet to be discovered.'

I show him this bit in the small print. The bit that says BMG own our profits, even if extraterrestrials discover us years into the future and our music becomes popular on Mars. Where money is concerned, record companies like to have all bases covered.

'Well, even so,' he says, rubbing his chin at the ET segment, 'your band got a record deal! That's brilliant.'

And it is. It really is. It's a relief. Whatever happens now it means those groundhog years weren't wasted. We were good enough. We weren't delusional. We have bulldozed our way in. Opened a door to a realm that seemed impossible. In this envelope is our chance. We will take this little deal and run riot with it. I am determined not to fuck it up.

In the evening we get drunk and celebrate. The band, my big brother, our friends. I go to sleep giggly and pissed, singing the words to 'Wuthering Heights' over and over. The following week we sign the papers and go to a record company party. We are taken to the toilets where another, smaller envelope is ceremonially unwrapped. We are offered our first line of cocaine. Nine months from now we'll be on tour with Blur. A year from now we'll be touring the world and appearing on *Top of the Pops*. The gates to the dream factory are skidding open. Pack your overnight bag.

Pop life beckons…

PART II

The ultimate revenge is being on Top of the Pops.

Siobhan Fahey, Bananarama

OUR NAME IN CHALK

It's not time to move to Hawaii just yet, but we have our deal and we have some cash and given that funds had reached an all-time low, we are feeling remarkably flush. We have money to pay the rent and buy some curries, and to restock our higgledy-piggledy stash of band equipment. Jon wants to buy a guitar amp that isn't held together with gaffer tape and I'm going to buy my first electric guitar. I'll master the art of playing it on stage, balancing with one foot poised defiantly on a monitor, the classic rock-star pose.

'Why do men call them axes, anyway?'

'You know, *because*.'

'Well, what sort of axe shall I buy? I quite fancy that nice green one that Karl played at the Falcon the other night?'

'*A Gibson SG!* No way are you getting a Gibson SG. I am *not* being in a band with someone who plays a Gibson SG. You'll have to get a Telecaster. Telecasters are the classic rhythm guitar. Bob Dylan plays one. Joe Strummer, Keith Richards…' And so on.

Jon is a boy. He is very particular about amps and guitars. He's surprisingly reluctant to base his selection criteria on a) which guitar looks the prettiest, b) which guitars come in green, c) what guitar Courtney Love is currently using.

*

The four of us arrive at our new rehearsal studio in Camden Town. Our record company have put us in here for a six-week stint and the idea is that we'll write and play for hours every day, and improve and develop to the point where we'll be ready to record our first single. It feels like the first day at school: new equipment, clean T-shirts, a pocket full of shiny plectrums, a world of expectation on the brand new term. The rehearsal-room manager shows us round. He's more accommodating than they usually are because our bill has been paid in advance. Overnight, we've stopped looking like the kind of band that pack up all their instruments and make a run for it halfway through the day.

'Coffee machine's there,' he says. 'Toilet's down the corridor. There's never any bog roll, so bring your own.'

'What's the video machine in the corner?'

'Splatterhouse. It's wicked. When you slaughter the ghouls they spray green blood and moan like it's *really* hurting.'

'Who's rehearsing in that room?' Jon asks.

'Suede,' says the no-bog-roll man.

'And that one?'

'The Wonderstuff.'

'And room five?'

'That one is yours.'

I walk in first. It's dark and perfumed with damp and the microphones smell of other people's spittle, as they always do. So far so familiar. I set up my new amp and plug in my new guitar and Jon tries to coax a decent sound out of the battered PA speakers. We can hear other bands playing in the rooms next door, and the music that filters through the walls as we untangle our leads is a song that I've heard on the radio. I'm not used to rehearsing with bands who have been on the radio.

The bands I'm used to rehearsing with have names like Clawhammer and song titles like 'Revenge Of The Beasties'.

The bands who rehearse here are cool. Their jeans are the right shade of denim, their trainers the right kind of vintage Adidas. They smoke cigarettes with the kind of studied nonchalance I never quite mastered, and wear their guitars strung extra low across their hips. I feel slightly awkward about playing, knowing bands with nonchalant cigarettes who've been on the radio can hear us experimenting through the walls.

'So,' Jon says, 'shall we run through the set?'

'Maybe... you know... we should all have a coffee first. And a game or two of Splatterhouse.'

The four of us drink cups of watery Nescafé and play many, many rounds of Splatterhouse. We play until the ghouls spill their blood and moan like it's really hurting. When we run out of every spare coin in our jeans pockets we head back to our room, shut the door firmly and get going. It's fine once we start. We stop listening to Suede and The Wonderstuff, and stop worrying about them listening to us. What I realise over the course of the next six weeks is that Clawhammer were inadvertently keeping us down: there is nothing like rehearsing next to bands that have been in the charts for making you knuckle down and up your game.

Now we're together, in each other's pockets every day, there are more things for everyone to get used to. Jon and I are arguing again and our relationship is visibly creaking. When we rehearsed once a week it was easy to keep a lid on our tensions and play them out in private at home, but there's no way to hide our bickering now. We needle each other. Like an old married couple.

'You can't put that verse with that chorus.'

'Why can't I?'

'They're in *different* keys.'

'We need to ditch the intro. If we ditched the stupid intro it would work.'

'My intro is brilliant!'

'It's six minutes *long*!'

'It's *experimental*.'

'I thought we agreed.'

'About what?'

'Not smoking spliff every day, before rehearsals.'

We give each other the look: eyes narrow, brow furrowed, mouth turned down at the edges. There's nothing more to say once we've issued the look. I know exactly where I was when I first saw it.

When Jon and I signed the record deal – right there at the table with the fountain pens – there was a moment when we caught each other's eyes and hastily glanced away. It was the kind of look a couple might give one another at the altar when the vicar asks if anyone objects to the marriage, and the bride and groom both want to shout, 'Yes, me!' For all the satisfaction and elation of that day, the punch-the-air feeling of finally nailing it, there was a sense that we were shackling ourselves together in the drying of the ink.

Our relationship was the kind you start at the edge of your teens, a tester relationship that bridges you on into adulthood. You fall madly in love and stomp about in the puddles of life. You travel and study and get high, and experiment with commitment by playing house. It might, at a push, be the one that takes you on into marriage and kids but both of us know there's no chance of that. We are worn out, used up, long past the flush, and the reason we're still together is because of this. What we said with our eyes in those posh Putney offices was, *How the hell are we ever meant to break up now?*

I think Andy and Diid are being pretty relaxed about our rows. They put down their instruments and step outside for cigarettes when the bickering starts. Every so often one of them will pop their head around the door to see if things have settled down, then they waltz back in and tune up. Over the course of a couple of weeks things settle into a pattern. The skeleton of a song that Jon or I write – a melody and some chords – is quickly fleshed out with sonic skin and bones.

We are a disparate bunch like most bands are, brought together under false pretences, but somehow it seems to be working and this period is happy and fruitful. Days spent writing and experimenting with our music no longer feel wasted, because they're validated by the fact that we have a record deal. We are starting to walk differently. Talk differently. We are nodding at signed bands and they are nodding back at us.

'The bloke from The Shamen just offered me an E.'

'Did he?'

'Yeah… he seems alright.'

The rehearsal studio is our place of work now, we belong here, and I'm enjoying being part of this gang. After so long on and off the dole and all those crappy part-time jobs, the need to be somewhere every day, to collaborate and achieve something, is a revelation. It might not be the kind of job most 26-year-olds have, but for the first time in years I'm doing something productive. The room where we play is as mouldy and dark as our old one, but I couldn't love it more if I tried. There's even a tiny corner of this place that belongs to us. Outside, in the corridor, sits a rusty metal cage where we store our amps and drum kit instead of having to lug them home at the end of every day. It bears the name of our band in big bold letters, sketched out above it in chalk.

The record company come to see us from time to time, to see how we're getting along. By the end of six weeks we've ditched every song we had when they signed us. We sound harder, grungier, and have given ourselves a brand new name, Sleeper, after the Woody Allen film. We have passed the first test, fulfilled our commitment to develop and, for now at least, Jon and I are putting our disagreements behind us.

It's time to leave the security of dank walls and Splatterhouse machines and go out and play some proper gigs. We'll record our first single at the end of the autumn and this winter we will go on our very first tour.

NEW BOOTS AND PANTIES

How is it possible to be this cold? Glasgow in January, weather sleeting and raw, loading our amps from the van to the street, down the deep, icy stairwell to the tiny venue. Our jackets are thin, our trainers are wet, my fingers are starting to turn blue.

'Come on, hurry up. We're on in less than ten minutes.'

'The place is still *empty*.'

Same as last night.

I have an idea. I sprint to the loos and lock the door and get the band to say no one can find me. I only emerge when I hear the room begin to fill up. There's no point being the warm-up act when there's no one around to warm up.

I'm discovering it takes a certain amount of improvisation and ingenuity to make a success out of being a support band. We are ballast and filler. We have no perks. Most nights we play to a half-empty room, and the headline band – who regularly steal our sound check – are the only ones who get a dressing room or a rider. Given that we're driving up and down the country in an ancient rust bucket, subsisting on a diet of Ribena and service-station pasties, we could use the odd Chipstick and a can of lager by the time we rumble up to the venue. The trick, we soon realise, is in shamelessly flattering our hosts so they share their paltry booty with us.

'Your lyrics are *genius*, Gerald.'

'Really? Do you honestly think so?'

'Absolutely. I can tell you're deeply influenced by Dylan.'

'*Exactly!* Why does no one else seem to get that?'

I cram my cheeks with crisps as we talk and Jon stuffs a bottle of the headline act's whisky into his jeans jacket pocket. Fleecing our hosts of their spirits is the ultimate goal every night. It gives us something to aim for and makes the whole British boarding-house experience, with its stained sheets and freezing rooms, seem marginally more amenable than it really is.

When we run out of pilfered whisky at the end of each night, we bed down in a local B&B. In lieu of any entertainment or a mini-bar, we wrap ourselves in blankets and share out the little pots of UHT milk next to the kettle. We encounter a few surprises along the way. One night, in a new take on *Goldilocks*, we return to our rooms to find a fat man snoring loudly in Diid's bed.

'Those pyjamas don't really fit him, do they?'

'No they don't. You'd better kip down on our floor tonight.'

I'm betting Madonna doesn't have this kind of problem when she goes on tour.

At the end of these gigs I get some small indication that our tours won't be this skanky forever. My big brother calls to say our record, the three-track EP we recorded a few weeks ago, is to be broadcast on the radio. Geoff and the band gather up at our flat, and we listen to the DJ, Steve Lamacq, introduce our first single, 'Alice In Vain'. I think it was a Tuesday. I think he described it as a grower. And there they are, those first ragged chords that I play, before the band kicks in hard over the top. Three minutes later it's out in the ether, cast into the world to sink or swim. It might be the best moment of everything that happens ever after. Hearing a song of mine on the radio for the very first time. It's the most incredible thing.

'How d'you think it sounded?'

'Different. Slower. I might need to hear it again.'

We hear it again the next week and the next. I'm in a band that gets played on the radio.

On the back of a few weeks of radio play we begin to attract the attentions of the music press. Our debut interview is with the *NME* or the *Melody Maker*, I'm not sure which – both are interchangeable to me. Jon, Diid and Andy have grown up on these papers but they've never been part of my musical landscape. Fake reviewing aside, all I know about them is this: they operate as self-styled arbiters of cool and apparently it's important that they like you. I can't see this being a problem. I'm certain we'll get along famously.

The journalist who comes to meet us doesn't strike me as a natural arbiter of cool. He's balding, pudgy and pale faced, and addresses all his questions to the boys. His interview technique is a test of their musical hobbyism, to see if they pass muster or fail.

'Who are your influences?'

'Most obviously The Pixies. But in my teenage years, bands like Devo and Kraftwerk.'

'Oh, really? I preferred Cluster and Can. And what about you?'

He moves on to Andy.

'The Smiths, The Clash, Tom Waits –'

'Yeah, all the obvious... and you?'

Go on, Diid. Say Duran Duran and ABBA. Tell him you grew up in Somalia with a single mix tape of 'Rio' on one side and 'Dancing Queen' on the other. Diid bottles it under the glare of Mr Know-it-all and offers up Blondie and The Beatles.

It goes on like this for another half hour. Endlessly on about favourite rock guitarists and obscure German electronica and not a single question directed to the girly singer. No enquiry into songwriting or lyrics. No discussion of the hidden merits of the theme tune to *Rocky III*. I'm bored now. It's time to pipe up. I think I'll start with the pudgy man's badge.

'Is that a Lenin badge on your lapel?'

'Yes it is.'

'Are you a communist?'

'I'm a revolutionary Trotskyite revisionist Leninist.'

'I see.'

He's been bugging me in other ways, this journalist. He hasn't stopped banging on about political correctness since he got here.

'You use the phrase "right on" quite a lot, don't you?'

'Any reason that I shouldn't?'

'Well, I don't know… it's a bit prescriptive. A bit Orwellian?'

He rubs his chin.

'I like to think of myself as being thoroughly reconstructed,' he says, folding his arms.

'Do you?' I say. 'That's interesting. How about we have another round of drinks.'

Very important notes to self:

a) Don't order extra rounds of drinks in interviews. Drinking makes you swear. Saying *fuck* and *bollocks* repeatedly makes you sound a teeny bit loopy in print.

b) Don't be sarcastic to your interviewer: it doesn't translate. Ditto irony and any attempts at humour.

c) Remember why you're here. Even when you're being excluded from the conversation, keep the interview to the subject of music. If you express a cogent argument about *anything* else, you will henceforth be described as opinionated, feisty and controversial.

d) Do not, under any circumstances *whatsoever*, get it into your head that these very important notes to self should be roundly ignored and that the route to securing much-needed column inches in the music papers is in speaking your mind and pressing people's buttons.

Our first interview comes out a week later. I dash to the newsagents to pick it up and wince as I read through the text. It runs along the lines of, 'Look out... mad, ranty pop bird on the loose.' It can happen as easily as that. One minute you're sitting in a Camden hostelry minding your own business, the next you're sowing the seeds of a cartoon pop persona that will come to define your band for the next four years. On the plus side – should I choose to live up to it – I will never have to do earnest interviews about my influences and am duty bound to bait the pale-faced commies who populate the music press to my heart's content forever after, just for fun. On the down side, it's a tricky game to get right. Girls are still a novelty in the indie-guitar world, as rare as a drum solo in an ABBA song. Attention-grabbing soundbites might be the lifeblood of a band at the beginning, but you challenge the orthodoxy at your peril.

THE DEVIL'S HAIRCUT

It's been a steep learning curve already and I'm ever so slightly disillusioned. More than this, I'm disappointed that I'm disillusioned. It seems ungrateful – and I don't want to seem ungrateful – but I'm not prepared for the romance to be over quite so soon. I am all about the romance; the romance is why I am here. It's hard to be romantic with the feeling that, six months in, you've already got everything wrong. First wrong thing: I play in a band whose very core is founded on a relationship that's disintegrating. Things are approaching crisis point. When we come home from gigs or rehearsals these days, Jon and I disappear to opposite ends of our flat. Our flat only has two rooms, which means its opposite ends are quite close together. Jon avoids the tension by smoking dope and playing guitar and I deal with it by sitting in the bedroom writing songs. We need to address what's going on, but neither of us can pluck up the courage. How does this work after we break up? Does the band carry on if we don't? Maybe it's better the way it is. At least the two of us are used to it.

Second wrong thing: I have the faintest suspicion that we've signed to a duff record label. Indolent is a mock independent, one that affects to be an 'indie' but is financed and backed by a major label. This makes no difference to me, I'll take anyone's money, but it turns out to be significant to other people. Indie labels are credible in the music press but our label isn't credible since it's clearly and clumsily a fake.

Never mind that. Swings and roundabouts. We might lose out in the credibility stakes but surely we'll make up for it by reaping the benefits of BMG's well-oiled, corporate machine? It seems not. Indolent is a boxroom at the end of a corridor and receives funding and backing commensurate to a small village bun shop. No one in the parent company gives two hoots about it.

Third, and most important, wrong thing: I have fatally failed to comprehend the geography of the indie-rock landscape that we've wandered into. It's my error entirely; mine and Sade's and Bananarama's. I've naively assumed that the indie world – which peddles itself on its rebellious, anti-establishment nature – will be the free-thinking, equal-opportunity, emancipated centre of the musical universe. Big mistake. Huge. This gang are deeply conformist: Smithers-Jones would have felt right at home.

Here is what I've learned about things so far:

1) To flourish in indie world, it helps to be deemed 'credible' by the music press.

2) To be deemed credible by the music press it is recommended, nay essential, that you sign to an independent record label (see things we got wrong, number two).

3) To further prove your commitment to the indie cause, you must adhere to its code of practice at all times. Your first single should be a limited-edition run of 1000 vinyl copies, with a cover made from brown paper, preferably a ream you've fashioned by hand, all by yourself.

4) You should publicly eschew all trappings of fame and fortune and dress like you are still signing on, despite secretly employing a stylist to help you get this look just right.

5) Regardless of your upbringing, you should have a cockney accent or similar.

6) You should avoid writing songs about non-specific periods of heartache and concentrate, instead, on singing songs about chip shops and council estates.

7) You should look miserable in all photographs and scowl a lot. When you go to other people's gigs you should stand at the back and look bored, impassive and moody. Never *ever*, on pain of death, have a dance at the front and throw your arms in the air like you don't care. Because you do care. You care a lot. You just have no idea about what.

Even though your record company is shelling out many thousands of pounds on your behalf – videos, photo shoots, record recordings, producers, PR gurus, tour budgets, marketing and drugs – you can, and must, remain unsullied by the stench of filthy corporate lucre that surrounds you by virtue of having once fashioned your own record cover out of brown paper.

The indie sensibility smells bad to me from the start since it's patently all so much artifice. All labels employ corporate tactics these days. All bulldoze their artists' records into the charts by releasing them on three different formats and selling one and giving two more away for free. When you make music a commodity, however you make it a commodity, the end result is the same. Money and profit, and loss.

All bands peddling the indie ethos know this (the savvy ones do anyway; there are some poor suckers that actually believe in it). But never mind them, they've got no chance. Spend ten seconds in a room with any of the bands poised on the starting line in the early days of Britpop when they called it the 'new wave of new wave'. Share a line with Elastica, sup a spritzer with Gene, split a pasty with These Animal Men. They are all of them, every man jack of them, committed to being famous, desperate to get to number one. They would all sell their grannies to get a higher chart position than the other and while they're all skulking around in their leathers and Adidas, archly pretending 'the music's all there is, man', a thousand backroom deals and deceptions are taking place.

Bands are bribing their press officers to screw up rival bands' record releases. Journalists are writing good things about the bands that offer them the most cocaine. Bands that claim to be the coolest of the cool are busy at headquarters fretting over focus-group responses to their latest single. Celebrated 'indie' bands are performing material written for them by other people, and blithely passing it off as their own.

Of course, this all happens behind closed doors, off the record. The final head-spinning sting in the tail of the indie ethos is that bands and artists must, at all times, feign total ignorance of the inner workings of the music business on which their careers depend. In public they are as innocent as babies. In private they're peddling faster than a Tour de France cyclist. It's a sickening, delusional mess.

But if that's the way it has to be, you can count me in.

GOOD VIBRATIONS

Andy dives fully clothed into the outdoor swimming pool. We are recording at a studio that has a swimming pool! I take back everything I said; this is great. You want romance, here it is: this grand old house in the middle of the English countryside with tennis courts, croquet lawns, stables and barns, and a cleaner and a cook and a ghost. It is much, *much* nicer than my bedsit and is the nicest place I've ever been on holiday. Except we're not on holiday, we are working: we have three weeks living here, in which to record our first album. Actually, I was right the first time. We're on holiday.

We have the twelve songs written – all albums should be twelve songs, it's the law – and I'm fairly sure I know how I want them to sound. But wouldn't you know it, when you get in that plush room with the 48-track recording desk that looks like the flight simulator of a space shuttle, and the engineer is plugging in leads, and the record producer is pushing faders, and each of you is locked in a soundproof booth flanked by microphones, it all begins to sound completely different. I'm used to the way our music sounds on stage – loud, raucous, unrefined – but in here it's like our instruments are wrapped in cotton wool. This isn't a sticky club with sweat on the walls; this isn't a grubby rehearsal room in Camden Town. I am crushed by the very idea, but perhaps this joint is a bit too posh for us. Of course, the thing to do, once we're over the novelty of being here, is to make the place our own: bring it down to our level and experiment.

'I think we should all record stoned today.'

'Or drunk?'

'Stoned *and* drunk.'

'No... wait, I've got it. Let's sleep all day and just record at night!'

We steadily work through our list. We record high, pissed, early in the morning, by candlelight, in darkness, at dawn and in the middle of the night. We record for 36 hours in a row. Sometimes I fall asleep in a corner after the 36 hours and wake up to find the rest of the band have re-recorded the song we've just spent 36 hours recording, and now it's twice as fast, or twice as slow.

'I can't fit the vocal in now.'

'Sing it quicker then.'

'I can't. The lyrics won't fit. We'll have to start all over again.'

'Wait! I need to fetch my lucky trousers. I'll never find my studio vibe if I'm not wearing my lucky underpants and trousers.'

A good studio vibe is the foundation of every great album and must be sought out at all costs. To summon the vibe gods, some bands will only ever record after dark surrounded by crystals and burning incense. Some vocalists will only sing between the hours of four and six because those are the times when their voices hit their sweet spot. Some guitarists will only play on a Tuesday, or outside under the stars, attached to their amplifiers by a very long lead. If the vibe gods aren't with you, the recording will reflect this, and your album will sound flat and lifeless. It's a conjuring trick. You record on your own, in isolation, but you don't want the record to sound like you did. Somehow you want to fuse the tape with the kind of passion, energy and intimacy experienced at your best ever gig. Right now, our vibe gods are missing in action: getting them back is our only hope.

'My voice sounds weird and breathy today.'

'Your voice *always* sounds weird and breathy.'

'Why have you recorded all those extra guitar tracks? It makes everything else sound muddy.'

'Exactly. I'm aiming for muddy.'

Perhaps it's the ghost in the attic that's putting us off. Perhaps it's the massive bag of weed that never seems to get any smaller. We have a magic rejuvenating bag of weed. Am I alone in thinking this is amazing? Here's a good idea: perhaps we should record out in the stables. Let's spend the day getting pissed and playing croquet while all our equipment is moved out to the stables. It all sounds shit in the stables. Let's put everything back the way it was.

The recording has stopped feeling like a holiday. Jon and I are marking time, sleeping in separate rooms, and everything feels out of sorts. Even our young producer looks done for. One morning, after working without a break for the best part of two days, he actually faints. We have done this to him. We have pushed him to the edge of a nervous breakdown with our constant mind-changing and vibe-seeking and experimenting, and now he's got to spend fifteen hours of every day tied to a mixing desk sifting through the 72 layers of guitar takes that Jon has secretly recorded over every track, in the hours when I couldn't stay awake any longer to stop him. It might be time to head back to the city. It might be time to seek out a more experienced producer. When you make your debut album it's vitally important that at least one person knows exactly what they're doing.

We meet the producer Stephen Street in a recording studio in west London. He's looks immaculate and zen in his Fred Perry shirt, like a person who knows exactly what he's doing. Stephen Street is a very experienced producer and has just remixed our three-note riff song, 'Inbetweener', the song everyone thinks should be a single.

'What do you think, guys?' he says after it's finished playing.

We shuffle about a bit, trying to look unimpressed and nonchalant but I've never been very good at this. After a few seconds I blurt out: 'Bloody hell, you've made it sound amazing! Can you do that to the rest of the album?'

We listen to the final mixes of *Smart* on a pair of giant speakers in the mixing studio. It sounds brilliant, but everything sounds brilliant played very loud on giant speakers so we take a cassette out to Diid's car and listen to it on his crappy stereo while we drive around. We're grinning from ear to ear because whatever happens now we have made an album, an *actual* album, and it's ours and it belongs to us and we love it. This is what I came for. This little reel of tape. It looks like nothing by itself, flat and grey on its spool, but it really is the beginnings of everything. I think things have turned out OK after all. We've discovered our vibe after the fact.

When we record our next album, *The It Girl*, we will ask Stephen Street to produce it. There will be no swimming pools, no all-night benders, no 72 guitar takes, no croquet. We will start at 10am sharp and finish no more than twelve hours later because this will stop us all from losing the plot. I'll remember that I've given up marijuana for good and stop smoking it, even when I'm nervous.

When we take a break for lunch, at a reasonable hour, we'll ask Stephen how it was with The Smiths when he worked on *The Queen is Dead*. What prima-donna techniques did Morrissey employ to get himself into the recording mood? Stephen will tell us that there weren't any. Morrissey would turn up on time in the morning, have a cup of tea, put on his headphones and just get on with it. These are some of the best, most expressive, most charismatic vocals ever laid onto tape. Great artists have it right there in front of them.

I always knew that whole vibe thing was bollocks.

THAT THING WITH
THE GENDARMES

There are tourists milling around outside the pavement cafe where I'm drinking cheap wine with my band. I feel slightly superior to the tourists with their baggy shorts and their disposable cameras. We're not here to sightsee like they are, we are here to play a gig on national radio. If my French was any better I'd tell the waiter who is pouring out the wine. I don't want him thinking we've driven all the way to Paris in our brand new band van just to eat snails and climb the Eiffel Tower.

Tonight we are playing a Black Session, which is something like a French version of a Peel Session. We've never done a live radio broadcast before and we want it to go well so we'll be asked back to do some proper gigs in France.

The atmosphere at the radio station is subdued and polite, and the 100 or so people in the seated audience look more like theatre goers than music fans. It's not the kind of gig I'm used to but there's something about the excitement of playing abroad that breaks down our inhibitions and we duly steam into our set.

I think Diid might be steaming into it a little too much. He's jumping up and down with his bass and Jon is issuing the kind of look he gives when he thinks that one of us is playing too fast. In the middle of a song, Diid ups the ante and attempts a wild, and not altogether successful, New Romantic flourish. His feet tangle in his lead and he tumbles over his monitor, crashing to the floor, taking several microphone stands with him and halting the gig. It feels like forever until we reconnect the mikes and start the next song. The DJ has to fill the dead air. He says something like: '*Mon Dieu! Zut alors! Diid, la bass!*'

'Hey... don't worry about it.'

'Really, no one even noticed.'

'Who cares if you fell over? We're in France. We've got a night out in Paris to look forward to!'

Diid seems annoyed with himself. He's very quiet. A little too reflective.

We're still tourists at heart and so after the gig we drive to the Eiffel Tower in our van. My brother and his Italian girl-friend are with us too, as are our British label bosses, Ben and Steve. It's good to have everyone together and the feeling tonight is one of celebration because we're growing, this little band of ours, we are widening our domain and we want to raise a toast to the future. We drink lying down at the base of the Eiffel Tower looking up at the steel and the stars. We go to a bar and then another and someone is ordering absinthe, that evil green liquor, and then it's off to another bar in Pigalle to watch some fantastic French crooner in a purple velvet suit, who must be 80 if he's a day, sing gloriously emotional torch songs while the audience cheer and weep into their Pernod.

We sing. We order Pernod. I fantasise about moving to Paris and living in a garret like Edith Piaf. I think we might have forgotten to eat.

It's not until we get back to our quiet hotel, sort of a French boarding house with knobs on, that it becomes apparent how much Diid regretted falling over at the radio gig and how much absinthe he may or may not have ordered. The thing I don't know about Diid yet is that he's really not much of a drinker. His lack of experience means he's yet to master the classic drinker's trajectory: merry, dancing, hugging, morose, unstable, vomiting, comatose, Alka-Seltzer. He's going for a more truncated style: straight from mild-mannered to lunatic.

I can hear shouts in Diid and Andy's room. It's 3am. First there was music and singing, now there is swearing and thrashing. Someone is thumping the wall with a shoe. Someone is moving furniture around. Someone else is yelling, *'For fuck's sake... don't be so stupid, put that fucking TV set down!'*

Andy bursts into our room. He's drunk, like we all are, but his face is red and he seems out of breath.

'Come quick... Diid's *completely* lost it.'

'What's he doing?'

'Hurry *up*... he's trying to throw the telly out of the window.'

This is preposterous! What can he be thinking? It's much too soon for throwing TVs out of windows. We haven't been in the top 40 yet. We haven't even been on *Top of the Pops*. We can't play the telly card now; it's too soon, it leaves us with no room to develop. At this rate we'll be in rehab by the end of the week. We'll have choked on our own vomit and died before the first album comes out. Slow down, Diid. Refer to your classic rock timeline!

Diid doesn't care about the timeline. He is grunting and moaning, face down on the floor, and giving off primeval roars. Now he's up again, cursing and crying and taking off all of his clothes.

'Diid... *no*, don't undo your trousers... Oh, OK then. You have.'

Diid is big. Diid is tall. He is out of control. It's going to have to be a group effort.

'Go and get the others. We'll have to wrestle him.'

'What do you mean?'

'Tackle him. Take him to the floor.'

'But he's got... no *pants* on.'

'Never mind that, there's no *time*!'

You can't blame the landlady for calling the police. How else is a small hotelier meant to protect the wear and tear on her television sets? I hear the *gendarmes* marching up the stairs, heavy boots, guns in pockets, making a beeline for our room. Jon, Andy, Geoff and the guys from our record company are sitting on Diid. He is naked. The TV is teetering on the ledge of an open window, the floral curtains are fluttering gently in the breeze. Everything OK here? the *gendarmes* ask, seemingly unfazed by the sight of five men sitting on a naked one, in a tiny hotel room decorated in pale pink chintz, in a seedy Parisian backstreet. Yes officers. All OK here. No need to take away our passports. The room is suddenly still and quiet. Somewhere around dawn, Diid, *la bass*, had finally passed out.

He didn't feel well in the morning. He lay in the back of the van, silent and still like a corpse. He wouldn't speak. He couldn't open his eyes. He stayed there all day while we trooped off to have lunch in Montmartre and see the sights, and loaded up on booze and cake for the journey home. Paris duly experienced and explored, we climbed into the van, found a space among the debris and headed for home. We opened a bottle of wine and passed it between us, and I remember thinking, This is exactly what band life should be like. This is probably the way it's going to be every day now: jetting off to exotic locations, plugging in my guitar, flouting the law and having adventures. And that's when we saw him, jogging through the streets near the Louvre in a string vest and highly indecent shorts... Look! *Yeuch!* Is it? It *is*. It's Mick Hucknall!

A tiny squeak. We can't really hear it. Then suddenly a roar from the back.

'Run the ginger *FUCKER* down!'

It was Diid. He hadn't uttered a word for eleven hours. For his sake, and the sake of the wider world, we tried as hard as we could.

THE FAB FOUR

We meet Blur on our second sortie into France, this time at a festival in Rennes. There are dozens of music festivals dotted around in Europe: next summer we will drive to ones in Italy and Denmark and Norway and one in Spain, where we'll sit and watch Iggy Pop crowd surf from a giant stage in the foothills of the Pyrenees. But today it's northern France and there they are, the fab four: Damon, Alex, Graham and Dave.

I think, as a courtesy, to start things off on a friendly footing, it might be nice to go over and say hello. Blur have asked us to support them on a UK tour and the dates are just a few weeks away. I spot them lined up against a wall wearing matching bovver boots and Fred Perry shirts, bottles of beer clutched in their hands.

'Hi,' I say, 'I'm Louise, good to meet you. We're going on tour with you lot.'

They don't say anything. They are silent, this little gang, surly and still and suspicious: Mr Blond, Mr Brown, Mr Spectacles, Mr Ginger. Finally, after a long time, time enough to scuff my heels and wish I'd stayed put on the other side of the venue, Damon sighs and says something like: 'Yeah, right.'

I say, 'Well, good then. Just wanted to, you know... say hello or something.'

That was weird. Like walking over to the cool table in the school canteen and nobody offering you a seat. Maybe they'll soften up when we go out on tour. Or maybe the Blur boys will turn out to be the goal-attack girls of indie.

I'm a little bit nervous about this tour, to be honest. The fab four don't seem like the friendliest bunch, and I doubt very much we'll be able to con them out of their whisky by hanging around their dressing room and complimenting them on their mumbly poetry. This lot are a little more sophisticated than that. I know they're sophisticated because I've just seen their laminated 25-page detailed tour itinerary, and it has become clear to me that not all bands travel the country staying in spunky B&Bs, surviving on Ginsters pasties and wine gums.

Blur are staying in posh hotels every night. They have a team of caterers travelling with them to make them teatime treats and cook their dinners. They have a giant truck to carry all of their equipment – the lighting rig, the sound desks, the monitors, the instruments – and a tour bus to transport their sound people and their lighting people and their roadie people, not to mention the pushy man with the briefcase and the brick-shaped mobile phone, whose sole job in life is to ensure his charges' day-to-day tour happiness and comfort.

This is something else; it's very impressive. Blur must be big if they can commandeer a set-up like this. A number-one album is one thing but by these standards you'd almost imagine they were about to become the biggest, most successful, all-conquering band in the nation.

Blur's catering smells very good indeed. I wouldn't mind some of that shepherd's pie. I wouldn't mind some of that jelly and custard. Have you seen what they get in their dressing room after they come off stage? You ought to see it. Platters of exotic fruit and buckets of champagne, posh crisps and dips and new underpants and sweets and the biggest, sweatiest cheese plate you've ever seen, laden down with foreign cheeses, accompanied by a crate of fine red wines. We get some beers and some towels. Yesterday we had a small bowl of Twiglets.

I realise that Blur are chart toppers with two monster singles behind them – 'Girls And Boys' and 'This Is A Low' – and now this new one about the pigeons with Phil Daniels. I know we're only indie squibs, yet to trouble the top 40 singles chart, but even so, this headline band versus support band caste system they've got going on is beginning to get to me. I mean, it wouldn't kill them, would it? They're full up with jelly and custard as it is; they wouldn't miss the odd tub of tzatziki. Maybe I should say something to them. Maybe I'll mention it when they're playing all those Elastica songs at sound check.

Cheese envy aside, we make the very best of this tour – a half-hour set, seven songs, all a rush – and the chance to play to Blur's captive audience. They're a tough crowd at first – they chant '*Blur, Blur, Blur*' as we strike up our first chords – but we're learning how to win them over and we're turning the corner a little earlier each night. It's a good feeling. I'm oblivious to every weakness at this stage, utterly up for it and unselfconscious. If my guitar playing is ragged I don't seem to notice. If my vocals are off, I can't care less. For now, it's all about the challenge, about proving ourselves, about willing them onto our side.

On the fourth night we have the crowd moshing from the start, hot and sticky for rows into the distance, singing along to our recent indie chart hit 'Delicious', and afterwards Damon stops by our dressing room. He stands in the doorway as we cool down, rubs his chin like some portly uncle and bestows a grudging compliment.

'You lot did alright tonight,' he says. 'They seemed to quite like you.' I think, Sod you, Damon Albarn, I'll be bigger than you one day, you patronising, cheese-eating mockney. I really believe this is true, the bigger-than-Damon thing, I mean. I don't say it out loud, though. Word is that Blur don't take kindly to insubordination from their support acts.

The fab four take to the stage a while later, in this big boxy barn of a civic hall. The atmosphere is brittle and charged and when the band come on there's that telltale, almighty, eruptive roar. They love them. They *love* them. 'Girls And Boys' is their song, 'Parklife' is a riot, the girls have tears in their eyes for 'End Of The Century'. I can barely hear Damon singing any more, the adoration is so fervent, so intense. The lead singer crowd surfs and he's pulled across the moshing audience, floating overhead on their hundreds of outstretched hands. Both his shoes are gone by the time he's back on stage and I wonder how he got there, safe and sound and intact, with a thread of cloth left on his body. They are chanting at him, now: '*Jesus, Jesus, Jesus*', they sing, and Damon just stands there staring out at them, like a kid at Christmas, half elated, half overwhelmed and lost.

I watch them every night; it's like a fix. I'm studying what they do, working out if I can learn how to do it too. It's just like that night watching The Jam at Wembley Arena only this time we're in the vortex, peripheral and slight, but close enough to feel the turbulence. I watch from the wings, or at the sound desk, or buried deep in the centre of the crowd. Even now, I only have to hear those five little glockenspiel notes at the start of 'To The End', and I'm immediately back in the glow: with that sense of it all taking off, with that feeling of everything just about to begin.

Sometimes I stand and watch the band with Andy. The two of us are getting on well this tour. He's been the engine of our confidence on stage, playing his drums standing up. And back here, sharing a beer, watching the band, he has the kind of infectious ambition and positivity that I can't help being a little captivated by.

BOHEMIAN LIKE YOU

If I'm going to be bigger than Damon Albarn, and I definitely am, it might be a good idea to start taking notes on this tour.

Note one: Things have become distinctly more cordial. Graham Coxon has asked me to marry him. He is drunk. He asks everyone to marry him. Graham Coxon is great company at the start of the evening, funny and gentle and sharp. But you have to tread carefully when Mr Spectacles is on the sauce; there's a moment when he tips over to splenetic. He has a tendency to insult people to their face. Strangers. Passers-by. Couples quietly drinking in the hotel bar. He is a harsh critic. It is sometimes uncomfortable.

Note two: The way to get groupies, should you require the attention of such, is to ask your tour manager to go out into the crowd, select the best-looking girls and give them passes to your after-show party. In this case they're called Blur-job passes. Mostly the tour manager is spot on with his choices but every so often a lesser specimen gets through. No matter. Alex James is magnanimous in these cases. He walks up to one girl with glasses and cheerfully informs her: you're ugly but I'm going to fuck you anyway. She looks grateful.

Note three: All manner of rock-star excess is to be encouraged on this tour but you must never, under any circumstance, mess with Blur's sweaty plate of foreign cheeses.

'Come on, they'll never notice. I'm sick of Twiglets and besides, they've got loads.'

'I dunno, they're much more observant than... *ooh*, look at that, they've got Jarlsberg!'

We only meant to eat a Dairylea triangle-sized amount. We didn't mean to decimate the entire plate. I'm hoping that by rearranging the grapes and organising the crackers into an elaborate fan-shape we might have gone some way to covering our tracks, but I don't think we have. Dave the drummer has been sent to find us. He looks like a dog chewing a wasp at the best of times but he really looks like one now that he's chewing us out. The band are properly angry, he barks. They may have to drop us from the tour. We scuff our feet like we're in front of the headmaster, but honestly, I don't know what their beef is: it's not like we touched their champagne buckets, it's not like we messed with their fruit. Even so, it's a major transgression. The fab four lock down. For 48 hours, Graham stops asking me to marry him.

We're all drunk and merry at an after-show party.

'Don't worry about it.'

'I won't, then.'

'It's forgotten about.'

'Good.'

'But *don't* ever do it again.'

With customary generosity, now the Jarlsberg episode has been safely put behind us, Damon would like to provide me with notes four and five all by himself. He hangs his arms around me, and gives it to me straight.

'Course, the way to be successful in this game,' Damon slurs, 'is to make all the boys wanna *be* you and all the girls wanna *sleep* with you. In your case... that'd work in reverse.'

'I see.'

'And anuvver thing,' he says, jabbing his finger in the air for extra emphasis, 'you shouldn't be shagging someone in your own band.'

'Shouldn't I?'

'Nah. Always fucks everything up.'

I'm about to tell him how right he is when he spots a grand piano in the hotel foyer. He spends the rest of the evening merrily tinkling away, playing show tunes from *Pirates of Penzance*.

They are, I can't help thinking, an odd and annoying and intermittently disarming bunch. Damon bossy and arrogant; Graham shy and sweet with the black dog inside of him; Alex louche and pompous. And Dave, the straight man who doesn't seem as mannered as the rest. You don't catch him with his arms wrapped around his bandmate's girlfriends; he doesn't raise his glass and clink it, salute you with his floppy fringe, and purr 'chin chin'.

On some nights it's just us and the band and various groupies and hangers-on at the after-show parties. The fab four disappear off into the shadows, with big-busted blonde girls, and skinny eager brown-haired ones. On other nights they relax with their entourage, shipped out to the provinces from the trendier climes of Notting Hill. Damon's squeeze, Justine Frischmann, Alex's squeeze Justine something else, who looks just like her, and various other confident, diffident types that gather round the bar drinking and smoking and getting high on whatever it is they're high on at this point.

It's quite a crowd. I imagine them back in their hotel rooms: the girls on their backs channelling Marianne Faithfull, the boys on their elbows doing pelvic press-ups, Mick

Jagger by way of Ray Davies. There's a cliquey, incestuous scent to it all; an easy, bohemian, moneyed odour. The mood is ruthlessly ambitious and, pose or not, they seem unquestioning in their acceptance of all that is coming their way.

We flit in and out, as observers and guests, wanting what they have, dipping our fingers in and seeing how it tastes, wondering how we will get it. There's a moment, quite soon after getting signed, when you stop being grateful for the chance and start feeling pathologically envious of everyone who is remotely more successful than you are. We're off the starting grid now, we have momentum, and I can feel my competitive streak hardening with every passing hour. Which must mean now's the perfect time to set about fucking the entire thing up.

THE FLEETWOOD
MAC MODEL

'Sorry the kitchen's such a mess.'

'No, no, really, it's fine.'

'And the hot water should be back on by tomorrow. Jamie forgot to pay the gas.'

'Right. No problem. I'll boil a kettle.'

'We're watching *Cracker* in the living room if you want to join us.'

'Great. Great. I definitely will.'

I don't want to go and watch *Cracker* in the living room. I want to unpack the last of my clothes, curl up under my new single duvet, eat a bar of cheap chocolate and cry.

My new shared flat could be worse. I could have ended up in that one in Archway with the bathroom along the hall. At least this bathroom is only shared between the four of us. At least there's some toilet roll, a bottle of Vosene and a half-empty can of forest-fresh Glade next to the sink. When you need to move home quickly, you make do with whatever you can get. I think I'd better go to the off licence. I might need some gin to go with the chocolate.

After seven years together Jon and I have finally split. It's a sad and ugly break-up – is there any other kind? – and everything is magnified a thousand-fold by the fact of us still being in the band. When we turned up to the first rehearsal after I'd moved out, neither of us knew how to behave. One minute we were tentatively discussing a song, the next I was arranging to come over to the flat to pick up the rest of my things.

'Oh… you've already packed them.'

'Yeah… I thought that was best.'

They were waiting for me when I turned up, everything I owned at the bottom of the stairs by the door. The history of us, neatly packed into a brown cardboard box.

It's difficult at the moment – the atmosphere is awful – but it ought to be OK in the long run, because we knew this was coming for months. It's going to take some adjusting to, but we've discussed it a hundred times now: in a pub, in a cafe, in the flat, over the phone, in the middle of working out who still owes what for the electrics and the council tax.

'It's probably not that much.'

'No, no, take fifty, just in case.'

'I found this under the sink.'

'Oh… right. That carved head from our trip to Jamaica.'

Don't look sad. He isn't. You mustn't. All you're both feeling is nostalgia.

'I thought you might like it for your new place.'

'No… no, really. You keep it.'

We've passed the screaming stage now and we've settled into an uneasy politeness. Neither of us is prepared to let the band fall apart while we wind up the loose ends of our relationship. I think, when we get over the initial upheaval, we'll begin to feel a sense of relief. At least we're not going on any tours for a while. At least we can pack up and go home to our separate places at the end of rehearsals. People split up and continue to work together all the time; why should it be any different for us? This is what I think on the good days. On the bad days I know I'm deluded. The hard part will come when one of us starts going out with someone else. Even when a relationship was as worn down and dysfunctional as ours was, there are bound to be jealousies and misgivings, and many levels of hurt involved in that.

'Christ-fuck-almighty, are you *nuts*?'

One of my new flatmates is Italian. Her name is Frede-ricka. In the weeks since I've been living here I've come to realise that she's quite highly strung.

'If Jamie did something like that to me, I would *kill* him.'

I'm certain that she would. On the night I moved in – after *Cracker* – she threw a plant pot at her boyfriend's head and bent his glasses in half because he came home late from the pub.

'This will *never* work out now. How can you all be together in one room?'

'Jon, well... he doesn't exactly know yet.'

'*Shit-fucks*. When are you going to tell him?'

'Tell him what?'

The others have walked into the kitchen: Jamie, the bent-glasses boyfriend, and my other new flatmate, Tony.

'Did you hear what she has done?' Fredericka says, turn-ing to them and throwing her arms up. 'She has chucked off her guitarist. And now she is *doodling* her drummer!'

'Diddling,' corrects Jamie. 'She's *diddling* her drummer not doodling him.'

Good. That's better. At least we've got that all sorted out.

*

It's true. Andy and I have got together. There's no excuse for this level of stupidity and duplicity and heaven knows what Damon Albarn would make of it. No one does a thing as stupid as this. No one risks the future of their band and the sanity of everyone around them for a sordid intra-band fling. You would only do something as ridiculous as this if, against the odds, you felt like you'd stumbled on a perfect fit: if you thought that maybe, many years from now, the two of you would still be together, parents to a couple of amazing kids, living on a multi-million-pound yacht, moored off the coast of Hawaii. Or living in a terraced house by the English seaside if things don't end up going quite as well. You'd only do a farcical thing like this if you had a crush on the other person the size of the one you had on David Essex when you were ten. But more so. And in a different way.

On Fredericka's insistence, I head off to have 'the conversation'. I'm going to talk to Jon and see where we all are after that. As I sit on the bus heading west from Finsbury Park to Kentish Town, I find myself thinking about seventies supergroup Fleetwood Mac. In its heyday the band was made up of two couples, John and Christie McVie, and Stevie Nicks and Lindsey Buckingham, both of whom split up during the recording of their most successful album, *Rumours*. Stevie Nicks later began an affair with fifth band member Mick Fleetwood, who in turn had just split up from his wife.

This can't have been much fun. The five of them crammed onto a tour bus. The five of them constrained inside a recording studio, their bruised psyches stuffed full of post-relationship bile, and brimming over with new-relationship insanity. It's no wonder Nicks took to cocaine so enthusiastically during this period. It's no wonder she ended up with a hole in the side of her nose the size of a cat flap.

Jon's angry but he takes it fairly well. I'm sure that he already knew. Somewhere in another part of London, Andy is having a similar conversation with his recent ex-girlfriend. I hope it's going OK. Maybe he should ask her to join the band on tambourine and percussion, just to make things feel more equal.

We all agree to take some time out. There's nothing essential that we have to do for the next few weeks so we put off all gigs and engagements and arrange to get back together towards the end of the summer and see how everyone feels. Andy and I hunker down, flitting between his new shared house and mine, living out the first flush of our relationship away from anyone connected with the band. It's the best and the worst of times. On the one hand I'm convinced that the band will break up, that all the effort will have been for nothing; on the other I'm ridiculously happy. I grew up thinking all relationships were ill-fitting and endlessly argumentative – this was the model I absorbed from my parents – but it turns out not to be true. Most days I think that if I get to keep this, then maybe all the other stuff hardly matters.

We edge back into things gradually. Bits and pieces of press, the odd rehearsal, a couple of small gigs out of London. It's odd and unnatural at first and God knows how it feels to be Diid, but gradually, little by little, when we've stopped ripping each other to shreds, we begin to impersonate a band again. Jon goes out with someone else which makes everything seem more equitable, and while I don't think Jon and Andy are going to be great mates again any time soon, we are back on our feet and almost functioning.

Our first real test is supporting the Manic Street Preachers on tour. The band are an odd mix: bellicose hammer and sickle on stage, eating Linda McCartney veggie meals and watching endless golf on TV behind the scenes. In contrast to the Blur tour, the mood is jaded and bleak and the band are often uncomfortable to be around. Richey slices into his arms with razorblades before he goes out on stage and I watch him play guitar with his skin dripping blood. Sometimes he watches us play, pale and silent, from the side of the stage. His skinny fingers nurse a plain paper cup filled with tea, his forearms covered in scars.

The Manics tour makes the four of us look and feel almost functional and what I realise as the dust starts to settle – in deep uneven drifts – is that band life is different to normal life: necessarily claustrophobic and warped. Bands that have been together for years all have their schisms and their cracks. When a band is made up of different sexes, the scars are almost always more problematic: there are a lot of lesser Fleetwood Macs out there.

Buried in the Fleetwood Mac model, however, is a small and encouraging note of optimism. At their darkest moment of emotional chaos they made one of the most successful albums of all time that sold over twenty million copies. Maybe the fallout from our bizarre love triangle will have some positive effect on the four of us. Maybe it isn't being grown-up and civil that will save us. Maybe it's becoming successful.

We've just released our new single, 'Inbetweener'. Everyone is excited about it, like it might be the breakthrough record for us. My flatmate, Tony – a news journalist – has been abroad for a couple of weeks. When he went away he thought he was sharing a flat with a girl in a struggling indie band, which he was. When he comes back to London he sees Sleeper's name plastered all over the tube, adverts for 'Inbetweener' fly-posted across Finsbury Park's empty shop windows and dank, scruffy walls.

He gets home shortly after I've taken the call from Geoff. It's a 'Thunder Road' moment if ever there was one. If my big brother had been anywhere nearby – instead of temporarily running the band's affairs from a boxroom in my mum's house in Essex – we'd have jumped into the car, taken to the open road and turned Bruce Springsteen up to full volume. The news is incredible. Our last three singles have reached 75, 62 and 54 respectively but the midweek chart position for 'Inbetweener' is number seven! This is big. This is everything. It's the culmination of a lifelong dream.

'Tony,' I say, as he plonks down his suitcase, 'you'll never believe what's just happened. This time next week, my band are going to be on *Top of the Pops*.'

IS THAT REALLY YOU?

There's been a bit of a screw up. Our single is selling out in the shops but, with typical aplomb, our record company haven't pressed enough copies and can't re-stock the shelves fast enough. This is the kind of thing they do. The other thing they like to do is go on holiday when they know we've got a record coming out. We won't end up at number seven in the charts after all, but at number sixteen instead. Even so, we still make the top twenty, we're still going to be on *Top of the Pops*.

The studio set is smaller than I'd imagined, the building scruffier, but just looking at the iconic *Top of the Pops* sign above our stage makes my knees start to wobble. Other bands are wandering around, drinking tea, eating sandwiches and chatting to their managers on the phone. They all seem very relaxed. I wonder why they're not all jumping up and down shouting, 'Oh my God, I'm on *Top of the Pops*!'

The atmosphere is ever so slightly 1950s: ordered, fusty, spick and span. The canteen smells like a dinner hut at school, and the breeze-block corridors are lined with neatly arranged tea trolleys loaded down with plates of stale sandwiches. I have the feeling Jimmy Savile might leap out of a cupboard at any second. I am sure I can smell his cigar smoke.

'How do you want your make-up?'

'Oh... you know. Sort of natural.'

I'm not sure the *Top of the Pops* make-up lady reads natural the same way as I do. She looks like she's been doing this for a very long time. I wonder if she helped Bowie do his zigzags. As she smothers my face in orange pan stick and slicks my eyes with an inch of greasy kohl, I sit back and fantasise about Pan's People doing an interpretive dance routine to our single. I picture them in neon leg-warmers and short, swirly skirts. They may or may not be carrying umbrellas.

After make-up, I wait outside in the corridor until our name is called and then we're ushered onto the stage. The audience seem young and overly excited; they gaze up at us as if we're alien creatures even though most of them have no idea who we are. My heart pumps as we're introduced and we're suddenly playing much too fast, because we're so nervous and amazed to be here. I wonder if somebody, somewhere is taping this at home, with the aid of a hand-held tape cassette recorder.

When my mum goes shopping in Ilford the following weekend, 'Inbetweener' is playing on the stereo in Clarks. Mum is overcome with pride and tells the shop assistant that it's her daughter singing on the radio. The assistant has seen us on the television. She's so impressed, she offers my mum a free pack of innersoles.

The innersole moment feels significant and in light of our debut appearance on *Top of the Pops*, our relationships with our families are subtly changing. My mum has stopped reminding me that I have useful retail experience from my days working at Mothercare and Jon's dad is no longer asking him if he's thought about getting a job on a cruise ship. Mum's nearly 70, she doesn't follow pop music or care for it much, but I can tell she's getting a thrill from all the cousins and aunts and uncles calling up to say they've seen me on *Top of the Pops*.

I think she's wondering where it's all come from. She knows I've been in a band for years but that roughly translated as her daughter deciding to drop out and become a hippie. Now she's on first-name terms with the music publishers and record-company executives who call the house every five minutes, while her son – the music impresario – searches for an office space in London. She is loving the excitement and the fuss. She's keeping that retail experience speech tucked securely in her pocket, though. Just in case.

My relationship with the outside world is shifting too. Last week I noticed two girls pointing and whispering as they sat opposite me on the tube, and just the other night, a group of boys chased after me and Andy in the street as we made our way to the pub. Half of them were belting out the chorus to 'Inbetweener', and one of them was shouting, 'Look, it's *her*.'

In the midst of this burgeoning attention, we go on tour to promote our first album. *Smart* has entered the charts at number five and the awkwardness that's still weighing on the four of us is beginning to lighten bit by bit. As long as no one asks us about it we can pretend nothing's changed. As long as a tactless DJ doesn't get us all together at a regional radio station, nudge me in the ribs and ask me when I'm going to start going out with Diid, things are largely OK.

There's a seismic shift in the air, a sense of things turning our way. We're coping with our personal fuck-ups – surviving them at least – and the venues we booked in to play months ago seem much too small for us now. All the gigs are sold out and most nights there are people queuing round the block, trying to fight their way in.

When we go on to play, the almighty cheer belongs to us and for the forty-five minutes that we perform, I feel like we're hosting a party. Everyone knows the lyrics to our songs and they sing them straight back at me, word perfect. Afterwards they wait around to have their album covers signed and one glamorous evening, outside a Travelodge in Hull, a girl who looks a bit like me – same haircut, similar clothes – breaks down and cries when I talk to her.

'I can't believe it's you,' she says, tears streaming down her face. 'I just can't *believe*... that it's you.'

It's beginning to feel a little odd. I'm not sure what to make of this stuff. We've been everywhere this past couple of weeks, on MTV shows, doing radio interviews and now on the front cover of a magazine.

'I'll take all of them, please.'

'Why do you want all of them?'

I would have thought that was obvious.

I buy a dozen copies of the *Melody Maker*. I don't know what I'm going to do with twelve. Keep some. Send one to my mum. Wrap one in a plastic bag so it doesn't go yellow and crumbly in a couple of months. I lay them out in my room, stare at them for a while, scan through the interview, then bundle them under my bed where they stay until I move home again.

The initial excitement wears off quickly and for the next few days I find myself avoiding the newsagents, because I'm sort of embarrassed to keep seeing myself, peeping out between the *NME* and *Men and Motors*. This isn't what I was expecting. I thought the day I saw my picture on the front of a magazine for the first time I'd practically live at the newsagents, wearing a big arrow round my neck pointing directly to the appropriate rack. This must be that coming to terms with fame thing I've heard so much about. I'm beginning to understand what big stars mean now, about it being complicated and strange.

One afternoon I break my curfew and go to buy a packet of biscuits at my local Spar. A boy is buying the paper with my face on the front. He sees me standing next to him in the queue and he just sort of stares and looks confused.

'What are you doing here?' he says finally, when he works up the courage to speak. 'What are you doing, you know... in the *Spar*?'

I think he expects me to live in a mansion now; that because I've been on *Top of the Pops* I commute from Hollywood to London in a Learjet.

'Would you like one of my Hobnobs?'

'Yeah... OK.'

I offer him the pack and sign his copy of the music paper with my eyeliner pencil. He seems unfathomably delighted.

I take it all back. I don't know what these big stars are on about. What's strange and complicated about this? How can fame possibly be problematic when simply by offering someone your signature and a mid-range oaty biscuit you have the power to make them inexplicably happy?

If you're properly famous it must feel like this every single day: like you're constantly doing good deeds, forever helping an old lady across the road. It's always annoyed me when famous people complain about being famous. If you don't like it, don't do it. No one asked you to. No one invited you in. This is good. This is healthy. I'm officially coming to terms with the burgeoning fame thing. But if it goes on like this, I might have to think about buying myself a pair of dark glasses.

ANOTHER FEMALE-FRONTED BAND

How does it feel to be a sex symbol? How does it feel to know boys are masturbating over your photograph? Hmmm. These aren't questions I ask myself all that much. They are questions male music journalists ask me. *All* the time. You'd almost think they were in league with my big sister. I don't think they're asking Liam and Damon this kind of question. And I'm pretty sure people are masturbating over their pictures, too.

I'm fair game, I suppose, because I do go on about sex quite a bit. All you ever hear me talk about is sex. Sex sex sex sex sex sex sex sex SEX. It's certainly all I ever write about in my sordid, smut-filled songs. Out of around 50, I can think of, ooh, nearly three.

Fame is rubbish. My emerging pop persona has taken a detour into sex-crazed and whorish, and wearing dark glasses isn't helping. It all started because of a song I wrote called 'Delicious'. From the coverage it received when it came out you'd think I'd purposely written it to be attention-seeking and 'controversial'. Why else would a woman write a frank, gorgeous, throwaway, punky pop-gem about the pure lustful joy of having it off with someone they really, really like? I know. It's nuts, isn't it? It can't be because I thought it sounded good. It must be because I enjoy doing the same earth-shatteringly insightful and revelatory interview over and over again:

'So... Louise, Sleeper. How does it feel having men masturbate over your photograph?'

'Uh... hold on a minute... didn't you ask me about this *last* time, you sad, muso loser?'

You wouldn't catch a male rock musician making this sort of elementary mistake. But then male rock stars have never written songs about having sex.

Something happens after you've been on the front cover of a magazine. Overnight, without warning, so long as you don't have buck teeth, braces and two heads – and even then – you are magically transformed into a sex symbol.

'Hey, look at this. You've been voted seventh most sexy indie singer in Camden Town.'

Fair enough.

'Hey, check this out. You've been voted 37th most sexy woman in the *entire* world by *FHM*. Ahead of Claudia Schiffer and Sharon Stone.'

'Blimey. That's surprising... but then again, Claudia does have those piggy little eyes...'

How to manage the sex-symbol label: that's what I'm wrestling with this month. On the one hand it's nice to have the quandary. I wasn't sexy in my teens, I was geeky. I wasn't sexy at college because my idea of an attractive outfit was a borrowed dinner jacket, plimsolls and washed-out black leggings that bagged at the crotch and the knee. I looked like Max Wall.

On the other hand, if you're a female sex symbol you can't ever hope to be taken seriously. Perhaps that's why the handful of women who front guitar bands have all decided it will help if we dress like men. We talk just like them, look just like them, behave exactly like them, this year. We are boy-boot, androgyny central. Denim and leather and loud: rough and tough enough to kick the indie boys' heads in. We barely own a skirt between us. No dresses. No weakness. No prisoners. We take drugs just like the boys do, we party hard, just like they do. We crave mainstream success, just like they do.

The band have a big photo shoot coming up for a glossy music magazine. I wear my usual jeans and steel toe-capped boots and top them off with a green skinny T-shirt that has *Another female-fronted band* emblazoned across it, in bold black lettering. It's a nod to female-fronted bands being seen as tokenistic; an attempt to highlight the way they are marking us out, lumping us in, obsessively comparing us with one another.

'Tell me how it feels,' the journalist says, eyeing up my T-shirt. 'Being a woman in a band?'

I shift in my seat. Over the course of the next three years, I'll be asked this question more than any other.

'I don't want to be a *woman* in a band,' I say, gruffly. 'That's the point. I just want to be in a band.'

'Right. I see. And how does it feel having men mast–'

'Seriously… these boots have steel toe-caps.'

I leave the interview having come to a decision. The unwritten rule is that women shouldn't, at any point, be seen to revel in their genetic good fortune but I'd quite like to revel in mine. It's been a long time coming, and besides, this is the best I'm *ever* going to look. I'm having my Olivia Newton-John moment, mentally dressing in the inky black, skin-tight satin pants that delighted me and worried my mother. I am strutting my stuff on that wobbly fairground ride and John Travolta is scraping his tongue off the floor.

I know my looks aren't classic – the big wonky nose, that bright red birthmark I'm saving up to get lasered off – but, blimey, in the right light, with the right make-up, all sweaty after a gig, giving off steam, hair stuck to my face, limbs shiny and slick, I look pretty fucking fantastic. There's a rumour going round that I put ice on my nipples to make them stand out in my T-shirts before I go on stage. I don't need to do that. I have great breasts as it is. I have wonderfully erect nipples already.

How does it feel to be a sex symbol? How do you think it feels? Bloody great. At least it would if you'd stop asking me how it felt. It would if I could be one like every male rock star ever from the year dot has been, without the analysis and the sniping and the whispering. If it was taken as a given; as being something powerful instead of something diminishing. I'd like to be one and not have it be the single thing that defines me. I'd like to embrace it without being constantly needled into defending my position.

I am officially at war. With this mediocre, backwoodsman thinking. I will need bigger dark glasses. Much bigger.

BIG IN AMERICA:
PART ONE

New York is beautiful. It is very early morning, just out of the airport and we're riding into town in a limousine, feeling sleepy and smiley and calm. I'm listening to *The Bends* on my Walkman. Whenever I listen to 'Fake Plastic Trees', I remember this still morning in New York. The dawn is coming up, we're on the lip of a hill, or some sort of bridge, and that skyline is shimmering in the distance: the towers and the skyscrapers, the river and the steam, baked bronze in the late summer sunlight.

The first time I came to New York I was twenty, and Jon and I were on our way to Boston to sing songs on a tourist boat for geriatrics. We stayed overnight in the YMCA on Times Square and tramped the streets for hours, bug-eyed at all the sights, fuelling up on hot dogs and slices of delicious, oily pizza. I saw a man performing tricks on the sidewalk. He hid a ball under one of three cups and you had to follow the ball while he shuffled the cups, and bet money on where it would end up. I was certain I knew where that ball was going. I bet half my holiday money on that hustler with the cups. In the end Jon had to forcibly drag me away or I would have given him everything I had.

This time there will be no sidewalk hustlers. We are here to meet our American record company. We're staying in a beautiful hotel on Central Park and there are bottles of champagne waiting in our room. First stop Camden Town and *Top of the Pops,* next stop, the rest of the world.

I think this is all going rather well. Everyone seems to know exactly who we are. The doorman, the receptionist, the kid who made us coffee, the mailman, the cleaner and every single person in every single office that we've met on our tour of the swanky Arista building. They all want to shake our hands and congratulate us. They say things like:

'Hi, I'm Tod, vice president of East Coast Radio. Great record, man, todally awesome. Love that rockin' chorus on "Twisted".'

'I'm Tad, vice president of markets. Sick beats, man. Love those cool astronauts on the cover. You guys are gonna be huge!'

Everyone has something good to add. The entire building has been primed to greet us like old friends and slap us all soundly on the back. Arista Records love our debut album. If Arista love it, then so will America.

At the end of the guided tour we take our seats in a penthouse conference room, its windows smiling over Manhattan, while the president of artist development, or some such, outlines his plans for the band. This guy is big in the company. I know he's big because all the vice presidents seem a little afraid of him and hang on his every word.

'Welcome to Arista,' he says. 'I want you all to know, this is a priority record for us.'

The vice presidents nod their heads in unison.

'I speak for everyone here when I say we're one hundred and ten per cent behind it.'

More nods and a couple of 'hell yeahs'.

At this point he rises to his feet and begins to mime swinging a baseball bat.

'What we're going to do,' he says, lining up with some tentative swings, 'is knock this thing *out* of the *ballpark*!'

As he says the word ballpark, he swings the imaginary bat above his head for extra emphasis. The vice presidents begin to whoop and cheer. One of them stands and claps, then punches the air and shouts 'Awesome!'

This is all very peculiar indeed. I feel so English and uptight in the presence of such unfettered Yankee enthusiasm that the most I can manage when the time comes to respond is: 'Nice one. How bloody lovely.'

I've been warned by every band I've ever met that on arrival in America we must keep our bullshit detectors set to maximum at all times, but this relentless positivity has chipped away at our hard-bitten British cynicism. I know we're only a limey indie band but these guys have us pencilled in for world domination. They are clearing a shelf out for our Grammys! And now we have three days in Manhattan with nothing much to do but meet more vice presidents, attend a photo shoot with *Rolling Stone* and perform a late-night gig at the legendary music club CBGB. Everyone is on a bit of a high and we disband to a bar to drink our weight in White Russians and celebrate.

We are nicely imbibed by the time the vice president of 'Where the hell has that dumb-assed, English band disappeared to?' manages to find us. He is, as the Americans say, a little pissed at us. Didn't anyone tell us we weren't supposed to leave the building? Don't we realise we're running late on our itinerary? Don't we know that every second of every minute of every hour that we are over here has been filled with very important promotional tasks?

The *Rolling Stone* shoot has been mysteriously cancelled but never mind them, they're not important. A sci-fi cable channel wants to spend two hours grilling us about the space race instead, because they like the astronaut design on our album cover. After that, the record company would very much appreciate it if we spent the next three days locked in a windowless basement doing 700 phone interviews with fanzines and college radio stations, all of whom are immensely keen to learn how to spell each of our names, hear our favourite knock-knock jokes, and have us guess the colour of various rock stars' underpants.

On the day we're meant to leave, the Americans go into a panic: they've spotted a one-hour window in our schedule. In a flash of inspiration they drive us to Tower Records, find us some acoustic guitars and get us to busk our entire album outside on the street. We earn $1.67. A couple of the vice presidents have accompanied us, partly to watch, partly to make sure we don't pack up and run away and spend a lone hour staring bug-eyed at the sights and eating slices of pizza.

They nod their heads in time to the music. They mouth the words 'out of the ballpark' while we're playing. Across the road, tucked into an alleyway, I spot a man at a table bent over three cups and a ball. It's him again, that old classic con. Fast-moving hands, all slick talk and light patter, a consummate lesson in misdirection. He encourages the tourists to take a punt. He tells them it's simple, all they have to do is keep their eye on the ball to win the prize. He's right. It's easy to know where the ball is; I should have remembered from the first time. It's always directly opposite the place you think it is.

We're home for two weeks then straight back across the Atlantic. We have a US tour coming up and the record company want us to squeeze in a short promotional trip beforehand.

The route to success in America, they inform us, is radio play. There are, as you might imagine, an awful lot of radio stations in America but some are vastly more influential than others. The key, according to Steve, our affable and charismatic radio promotions man, is to schmooze the important ones first and foremost. To this end we'll be embarking, with him, on a short six-day national radio tour of the United States. Brilliant. I like the idea of this. A few flights, some meet and greets, some handshakes and a couple of acoustic sessions where we turn up and play a song and talk about British music on the radio. Steve says no, not exactly.

'Are you hungry?' he says, as we drive up to our first meeting. 'This all works a whole lot better if you're hungry.'

It emerges that the route to the heart of American radio is through its stomach. To this end, we will spend the next six days eating lunch and dinner several times a day. On Monday we'll eat lunch in New York then fly to Boston to eat it again, before driving down to Providence to eat dinner, then on to Rhode Island for late supper.

The New York lunch is a breeze. There are lots of people coming, the whole radio station in fact. The only odd thing is that none of them seem to know who we are. I think the reason is this. Pinned to a wall in the reception of the radio station we are visiting is a hastily scribbled poster that reads: *Monday 7th, Arista act visiting. Free lunch people! Everybody welcome.*

Everybody helps themselves to the burgers and steaks and cocktails and French fries and salads, while Steve encourages us to go round the table introducing ourselves and striking up random conversations.

'Can I have some more Coke?'

'Uh, no. We're not waiters, we're the band.'

'Right, right. What are you called again, The Beepers?'

'Sleeper.'

'Cool, man. Can you pass me the hot pickles?'

At the end of the table sits the radio programmer, the man we really have to impress. It's his shout whether our track gets played on the station or not. He eats a dozen or more of these free lunches every month and we need to mark ours out from all the others. When it's my turn to sit next to him, I make sure to bring the tray of hot pickles.

We leave the restaurant having bought lunch for twenty people who seemed not in the least bit interested in meeting us or asking us any questions. But Steve is happy; he thinks it went well. A few minutes later, on the way to the airport, he takes a call in his car.

'Awesome… just awesome. Thanks for letting us know.'

He punches his steering wheel and whoops: the trademark American record-company punctuation mark.

'What's happened?' I say.

'They're playing your record, check it out.'

He tunes the radio to the station we just bought lunch for. Our song booms out at full volume. Who would have thought it? It works!

In Boston the lunch is more intimate, just us and a radio programmer and his assistant. This guy is very important. His station is one of the big six – or big seven, I'm not sure which – but Steve says if you get them on your side, you're halfway to conquering the American airwaves. 'The guy's name is Oedipus,' Steve whispers as we enter the restaurant.

'Right… that's unusual.'

'That's nothing… he owns a pet wolf. Don't mention the wolf, though. Wolf is off limits. Guy gets *very* touchy about his wolf.'

Oedipus strikes me as a unique sort of fellow. He's dressed head to toe in black leather, and may or may not have a complicated relationship with his mother. His fingerless gloves squeak as he shakes my hand and I squint into his reflective Ray-Bans, trying to gauge his mood. Oh good. His mood is hungry. He orders chowder and clams and a platter of soft shell crab that he insists I share. He's clearly unaware that I've just eaten my own body weight in hot pickles.

The platter is predictably huge and I'm beginning to feel a bit bloated. Steve, who seems to have an unlimited capacity for greasy restaurant food, fills his face with gusto and keeps the conversation flowing. This is Steve's job. He eats dinner with people for a living and is unfailingly breezy and optimistic at all times.

Oedipus is a little less sociable and prone to tetchy silences in which he retreats into his leather and sunglasses and says very little. When Steve goes to the loo – perhaps this is his secret, perhaps he vomits up one in every two meals that he eats – the conversation sort of dies for a while. I'm suddenly lost for something to say yet feel compelled to say something. Anything.

'So Oedipus,' I say, 'I hear you have a pet wolf?'

On the drive to the airport, on the way to the next dinner, there's no retuning of the radio, no celebratory hand slap on the steering wheel. That's a $200 lunch down the drain.

It carries on mostly like this. On one day we take flights to four different states and eat meals in Atlanta, Austin, Phoenix and Portland in the space of twelve hours. They vary between the group outings in which no one knows the name of our band, and the small awkward ones where some power-crazed person who owns an exotic pet lectures us on how hard it is to crack America. The consensus is that English bands are lazy. They don't like putting the hours in.

I'm never sure how to behave at these things. The default setting of the British band is surly and curly lipped and distinctly anti-establishment. This is why I joined a band in the first place. I joined a band so I could stick two fingers up at freeloading executives like these. I didn't join a band so I could sit in a bland restaurant eating $30 plates of grits, making polite conversation about how stroppy the English are.

Of course, our little taster session is nothing. I'm fast discovering this is what American bands do day in and day out if they want to be successful. They spend their lives on the road, touring and eating and meeting and greeting and shaking hands and smiling and politely pressing the flesh, before and after every gig they ever do, and on every day off in between. We hear about big-league American rock bands who send radio programmers postcards from every show in every town they ever visit, just to keep them onside. Their record companies lay on meals and seats and sweeteners, and there's so much back-handing and oiling and sucking up going on that it makes the half-baked shenanigans of British indie world look positively endearing and punk rock.

If there's a chance of getting played on a radio station, no matter how slight and insignificant, an American band will take it. To this end, Steve has sent us on an unscheduled seven-hour drive from Boston to Maine to perform an acoustic session at a tiny radio station that happens to be playing a lot of English bands this week.

'He's a great guy, he loves British pop. Have him tell you about the time he met Lonnie Donegan!'

The man at the radio station has a pair of moose antlers hanging above his desk. Next to the antlers sits a perfectly mounted moose's bottom. The moose bottom has a glass eyeball stuffed into its anus. We have just driven seven hours from Boston to Maine to play an acoustic version of a song about the English suburbs to a guy who likes to shoot moose and put marbles in their bottoms. We spend less than 40 minutes in Maine. We don't even get to eat the greasy dinner.

I've decided the Americans are right. We don't have this kind of work ethic. This kind of behaviour doesn't suit the English psyche. After six scant days of eating and schmoozing and fake laughing and forced politeness, I'm tetchy and nauseated and full to the brim with antacids. If you need me, you know where to find me. Propped up at a bar, getting drunk on White Russians and muttering, 'It's just like I always said, man... the music is all there is. Everything else is just bullshit.'

YEAR ZERO

Back in Blighty, things are motoring on. We've made a video on a plane in which I've dressed up as an air stewardess (finally my career teacher's ambitions for me are met!), the boys have dressed as pilots, and we've larked around with 50 Elvis impersonators. The impersonator agency didn't have enough Elvises to meet our needs, so they sent us their Humphrey Bogarts and their Clint Eastwoods to make up the numbers. The Bogarts and Eastwoods were grumpy about dressing up as Elvis and commiserated with each other over jammy doughnuts at the catering truck. Anyone can do Elvis, they reasoned, but a Bogart, or an Eastwood, now that takes real skill.

Our second top 40 single has just come out, which means we've been on more TV shows and recorded our first ever Peel Session. The Peel Sessions are fantastically enjoyable; it's like making a record in a day. No retakes, no refining, just straight up and down and raw energy, in the hushed, hallowed halls of the BBC studios in Maida Vale. The producers are classic and old-school, and you hash it out between you, racing against the clock to fill the tape, on a diet of instant coffee and fags.

Radio tours are on the menu back in the UK too now, but we don't have to eat any grits. After Peel, we play a live set for the Evening Session, then scoot up to Manchester for Mark Radcliffe's show with 'Lard', which is full of bonhomie and always a treat. In spring we perform on *The White Room*, Mark Radcliffe's TV show for Channel 4, and there's a technical fault that stops the recording halfway through.

'What's up?'

'Power's gone. Might be a while.'

The rule is that when you're doing a TV recording, you should always bring something to read. Video shoots and TV shows are characterised by the amount of time you spend kicking your heels and waiting around. We're nowhere near a shop and no one has a newspaper, but it turns out you don't need one when you've got Stevie Wonder in the room.

Mr Wonder is on the show with us. He's sat on the opposite stage, gently warming up at his piano. The way Stevie Wonder likes to use up the waiting time, it turns out, is by performing an impromptu gig for other bands.

'You all want to hear some songs?' he says, smiling.

It is, I think, a rhetorical question.

He kicks straight into a blistering version of 'Superstition' and now he's singing 'Living For The City'. People are dancing at the front and everyone is secretly hoping that the power stays out for a good long time. There are so few of us here, a couple of dozen, that it feels like we might be round at Stevie's house. He plays 'Uptight', and 'Misstra Know-it-all' and finishes, when the power's back, with a killer round of 'Happy Birthday'.

'He's brilliant, isn't he?'

'Fantastic. I wonder if there's time for "Ebony And Ivory"?'

The show finishes late. Andy and I get chips and kebabs, and a chauffeured car takes us back to my shared flat. Life is beginning to get strange. Half an hour ago I was filming a TV show and Stevie Wonder was playing 'Superstition' a foot in front of me. Now I'm sitting on a stained carpet playing Jenga with my flatmates, my jeans shiny with dripping garlic sauce.

I have left Finsbury Park. Andy and I have decided to take the big step and move in together. After scanning many copies of *Loot* we've found a flat to rent on Hampstead High Street, a mile or so up the road from the Camden madness. And it is madness. The streets are overrun. With drugs and musicians and skinny Adidas kids: record deals and origami-neat wraps of cheap speed spilling like sweets from their pockets.

The Good Mixer, the little pub where the Britpop 'A team' used to hang out – before they had number-one albums and moved on to private members' clubs like the Groucho and Soho House – has become a tourist attraction. People stop and take photographs of the bar stools, the way they take photographs of the zebra crossing on Abbey Road.

Our Hampstead flat is four storeys up, cut off from the world like a secret. Everything is calm and quiet up here, float-ing high above the road, lit by the small attic skylights. Because of the way Andy and I got together there's a certain stiffness when we're out with the band, but up here we can exhale and relax. We haven't spent much time alone lately so it's good to doze away these few free mornings before we set off for a summer of foreign touring: wake up, fall back to sleep, ignore the phone. A mini John and Yoko. Happy.

The mornings are ours alone, but we're staying out late every night. We are looking at London differently now: from secret after-hours basement bars in Soho, from the point of view of being part of a scene.

'Where shall we go tonight?'

'What day is it?'

'Friday.'

'Let's go to Smashing at Eve's.'

Eve's is a retro sixties nightclub on Regent Street. It has fairy lights, fake palms and foliage, gold wallpaper and velvet banquettes, and all is vintage and daftness and kitsch. Best of all it has a real disco dance floor: dense Perspex squares, red, yellow and white, brightly strobe-lit from underneath. For a year or so now, Smashing on a Friday has been the winking eye of fashion and Britpop.

'Oh look, there's the girl from Powder.'

'Who's that snogging the bloke from My Life Story?'

'What's Jarvis Cocker drinking?'

'Dunno… looks like a lager and lime.'

'I'm bored now. Let's go to the Met Bar.'

We traipse off to the Met Bar in our scruffy tops and boots, to see what all the fuss is about. It's sort of just a bar. Expensive drinks being supped by coke fiends with swivelling heads, their eyes searching like radar to find the most famous person in the room. Tonight it's Mick Hucknall drinking Cosmopolitans with Cherie Blair's sister, Lauren Booth. Not quite the Cool Britannia synergy of pop and politics that's coming, but you can see which way the windsock is blowing. He is tiny in person. I could swear that ginger fucker is following me.

At the edges, in the margins, in the gaps in between, the days are becoming more hazy. Jon, in particular, is getting on famously with drugs. There's cocaine around pretty much everywhere now. It used to be speed, when everyone was piss-poor and on the dole, and now it's coke. There's not too much in our band yet, which is probably because we're still piss-poor. Lines here and there, grams stuffed into wallets, powder that needs to be finished in the toilets at airports because no one – except our roadies – is going to be fool enough to take it through customs. As time goes on, plane journeys will become increasingly manic: more grams to take, more neatly folded packets to cut and finish in the airport.

The other important thing we have to do is write. We'll record a new album at the end of the summer and there's a US tour, a Japanese tour and a European one to fit in between times. I write songs at odd hours. Andy and I write the chorus to 'Sale Of The Century' on the top of a night bus. I find the riff for 'What Do I Do Now?' on our radio tour of America and finish the song back home in the middle of the night. I wake Andy up and play it to him.

'What do you think?'

'I like it. Let's go to the heath.'

We do this when one of us writes something good. We take the last of our beers from the fridge and walk arm in arm up to Hampstead Heath to look out over London and watch the sun rise.

This morning it all feels beautiful. For the last few months it's felt like we're in between two worlds: our fingertips in the cake tin, wondering if we're about to be flung out. Maybe that was it, maybe this was all that there was. There have been days when it seemed like the band would collapse into a shapeless heap with nothing to hold it up but an old idea. But the schisms are healing over, the battle is taking shape, and I'm slowly making sense of our place in this dirty, glittery landscape. Who is on our side. Who is a liability. The doubters I'm gearing up to fight.

BIG IN JAPAN

The Japanese fans are so welcoming and kind, they are waiting for us at the airport with presents.

Oh.

They are not our presents.

They are Suede's.

We have just upset a crowd of Japanese Britpop fans, because while they would quite like to get our autographs, they don't want to hand over Suede's presents. Being Japanese they are too polite to say so and now we're inches away from inciting an international incident. If we were in London, the girls with the gifts would just say, 'Sod off, these presents are for Brett,' but this lot are mortified that they might have offended us. We try to bow out gracefully, but our exit strategy is lost in translation. We are saved by Suede's arrival, just off the plane, minutes behind us. All is forgotten; they are mobbed. I am dying to know what was in their presents.

I can tell this is going to be tricky. I have already committed my second faux pas and I've only been in the country three minutes. I just kissed the representative from our Japanese record company hello: a big, wet, double-cheeked smacker. This is largely down to the twenty Baileys miniatures I have drunk on the flight in an ill-advised attempt to stave off jet lag because in real (non-Baileys) life I'm not a kissy-kissy sort of person when it comes to greeting strangers.

My dad's side of the family were immensely tactile; overly keen on the two-handed double-cheek squeeze and the kind of bear hugs that could easily asphyxiate a small child. My mum's side openly wondered at the rationale of kissing anyone at all, at any time, ever, when a decent brusque handshake would suffice. It's clear to me that the Japanese code of physical contact sits squarely with my mother's side of the family. Our record company man looks perturbed by my unwarranted display of affection. He is, of course, too polite to say so.

Japan is unusual. On the surface it's shiny and consumerist and quintessentially modern, yet moments below the surface it's constrained by its corsets of tradition. In the lift at the airport, Andy holds the door open for two old women with heavy luggage. They don't like this. They insist the men go first. I'm used to people giving way to one another as you walk towards them on the street, but men don't seem to do that here. The pavement is theirs and they bulldoze towards you; women are meant to defer. I know that everyone bows at one another in Japan – I've known this since I watched *Whicker's World* with my dad in the seventies and longed to travel to somewhere so exotic – but it's still odd to witness it up close. The Japanese are obsessively concerned with establishing the exact status of whoever they are interacting with, so as not to offend someone who has a higher social standing. To this end, they swap business cards constantly, so everyone knows who's most important.

This is, without doubt, the most foreign place I've ever been and the thing that makes it strange is that you can't immediately pinpoint its strangeness. It comes at you in flashes, bits and pieces … The food. The orderliness. The banks of shining neon. The higgledy-piggledy back streets with their tiny irregular houses. The cigarette machines on every corner. The beer machines on every street. The cans of self-heating hot chocolate. The crowds on the tube all facing the same way. The trains that run precisely on time. The taxi drivers with their pristine white gloves. The shop assistants who greet you every time you walk in and walk out, in their lilting, girlish, sing-song voices. The films on the hotel porn channel are hardcore and disturbingly paedophilic; but never mind that, because all pubic hair has been pixilated out, which makes all those rape scenes seem so much more palatable.

The suburbs are as grey and expansive and unyielding as in any other large city, but the kids on the streets of Tokyo and Osaka are the most stylish teens I've ever come across: kitted out like exquisite punk-rock peacocks. Their uniform is one of rebellion, but their actions are obedient and conformist and exceptionally well behaved. No graffiti. No vandalism. No throwing their homework on the fire and taking the car downtown. These kids are in training for the soul-sapping work ethic of adulthood. We ask our record-company man how many days off he gets in a year. He pauses for a long time and then he says: 'Ah, yes, the occasional Sunday.'

Japan is a culture of sweetness and smiles, and service in restaurants is disconcertingly attentive, without the incentive of tips. Step out of the neon hubbub of the city centre into one of the beautiful parks, and all is calm and lovely at the ancient Shinto temples, as zen as the view of Japan's geographical masterpiece, Mount Fuji, as spied from the window of a speeding bullet train. Then metres away, in the middle of a shopping mall, we spot dirty old men taking pictures of schoolgirls, who openly pose for them, giggling shyly in their navy uniforms and long white socks. It's hard to make sense of this place. Perhaps Japan is like one giant David Lynch film. Polite and ordered and picket-fenced on the surface; secretive and weirdly seething underneath.

We arrive at our hotel and after careful discussion and tactical analysis, it's established that this time the group of fans in the lobby really are bearing gifts meant for us. They bring us bottles of sake and cool printed T-shirts, futuristic digital watches and Tamagotchis, and bits of jewellery that they've made for us themselves. They bow politely when they hand the booty over and we're sort of touched by their generosity until someone lets slip that Suede were given handmade designer suits.

'And this one is for you... guitarist.'

A girl hands Jon a crisp white letter.

'What does it say?'

'I think it says... she wants me to marry her.'

We pass the letter round. In broken but detailed English she outlines her relationship history and cordially requests that Jon marries or, failing that, sleeps with her. He pockets the proposal and – because the girl is very beautiful – promises to give it due consideration.

This is ever so slightly weird. Forget it. I didn't say that. I didn't even *think* it. If Jon's going to put up with seeing me and Andy together every day, the least I can do is celebrate his induction into the world of rock 'n' roll groupies. As it turns out, the groupie culture is aggressively well established here. A girl from this lobby will turn up months later, living on the back of our tour bus.

It goes on like this, our initiation. The Japanese are even more detailed in their itineraries than the Americans, and every hour of every day is spoken for. Even the interviews are strange here. The translator asks a question to which we give a three-minute answer, only for it to be translated back in a single sentence. We do ludicrous photo shoots, dressed in gold lamé suits and leather trousers, because the Japanese love western flamboyance and all things pop!

One evening we take part in a prime-time Japanese TV show.

'So, it's really quite simple,' our promotions man says. 'The programme is something like a quiz.'

'What do we have to do?'

'You'll be given some phrases to learn in Japanese. Afterwards you'll be asked to repeat them, to see how much you have learned.'

It turns out there's been some glossing over with his description: mostly with the judicious use of *afterwards* and *something like a quiz*.

'Who the hell is that, now?'

'Looks like… a dwarf dressed as a clown.'

'What's he carrying under his arm?'

'Looks like… a giant… padded pole.'

We stand in front of the audience while a manic Japanese dwarf roars with laughter and jabs at us with his pole, in an attempt to make us forget what we've just learned. The audience cheer wildly at our clumsy linguistic skills, while someone from our record company marches around in the background repeatedly holding up our album cover for the camera. We are on the Japanese equivalent of *Tiswas*. It's all magnificently bonkers.

I'm feeling the culture gap everywhere we go, even at our gigs in the hip Shibuya district of Tokyo. When we play, the entire audience commence clapping at precisely the same instant, and end their applause the same way. Start. Finish. Noise. Silence. It's unnerving the way they do this, like those flocks of birds that magically change direction in mid-air. Gigs start and finish early too, all done and dusted by nine or ten.

'Look at *that*... they've got the Hoover out already.'

The crowd leave immediately we finish playing, neatly and in an orderly fashion. Outside the fans wait in line, queuing up to shake our hands and offer us more Tamagotchis.

Later on we go out to dinner. Raw liver. Giant fish heads. Live prawns dipped in boiling broth by white-faced geishas. Sake spiced with terrapin blood. Then onto a karaoke booth hidden in the basement of an office block to sing mistranslated Beatles songs. Afterwards we lose ourselves in the neon brilliance of the Akihabara shopping district, loading up on newfangled technology that will never date, like mini disc recorders and DAT-mans.

And finally to bed, with a view out over a city that winks at us all night long, as if to acknowledge our confusion. There are red lights on the top of all the buildings. Blinking on and off. Regular and rhythmic. Keeping us company. We will tour in Japan three more times and like some beguiling magic trick, it will appear more foreign each time we visit.

I WANT TO BE ALONE

It's Monday, so it must be Milan. Wrong. We are ten kilometres from Milan staying in a motel on a very ugly ring road. All of our motels are on ring roads. Was it too much to ask that whoever planned this shitty tour put us up within spitting distance of more than a desolate Italian ring road? No matter. Even though the nearest restaurant is a service station, it's bound to have something restoratively delicious to eat, like a prosciutto panini or a plate of shiny, grilled vegetables. It's not like Julie's Pantry over here. It's not like eating at a Little Chef. In Italy the truck drivers drink Chianti with their lunch and splatter olive oil on their salad. They don't base their entire diet around lard and mechanically recovered meat.

It turns out we're not going to the service station. We are, instead, heading for the nearest Irish pub. The same thing happened yesterday. We were twenty miles from Florence. Did anyone want to go and look at it? Did they hell. Where's the nearest Irish bar? Brilliant. Aces! I love an Irish bar, me, let's go there! I wouldn't mind, but it's not like any one of you are even remotely bloody *Irish*.

We are new to the European tour circuit but this is what I've learned so far from our erstwhile educators, The Boo Radleys, with whom we're touring. After gigs, before gigs, on days off between gigs, an Irish pub must be sought out as the place to sit and chill and spend the band's per diem of 'shit-ters'. A shitter is the generic name for whatever currency the tour manager gives you to spend in the country you wake up and find yourself living in that day. It stops everyone having to worry about whether it's lire or francs or guilder in their pocket, but I'm happy to worry about lire; they're confound-ing and childish, like the nation they represent and one day, very soon, you will miss them with a sadness you can hardly stand to express when you turn up in Rome and have to buy your pizza with generic sodding Euros.

But back to the Irish pub question. Why do we want to go there? We want to go there because it feels a bit like home and we like this and our crew also likes this. There are British programmes playing on TV and pints of chilled Guinness to drink. We can sit and get hammered and talk endless bullshit all day.

'The Beatles, man?'

'Yep, yep, the Beatles. B.E.A.T.L.E.S.'

'"Glass Onion"?'

'"Glass Onion."'

'"Blackbird"?'

'Yeah, "Blackbird".'

'"Piggies" though?'

'"Piggies" is the best thing George Harrison's ever done!'

'Bullshit it is.'

'Bullshit... it *is*!'

'More Guinness?'

'More Guinness.'

'Shit, yeah.'

It's enough to make you weep. It's enough to make you nostalgic for Alex James's exotic cheese plates, but fuck me if we're not in some of the most beautiful, historic cities in all the world with no time or opportunity to inhale the merest scent of them, surrounded by a gang of complete and utter rock bores and pissheads.

There's something about a tour itinerary that lists Barcelona, Milan and Berlin in its dates that's making me hysterically resistant to the lowest common denominator, herd mentality of rock-band touring: the endless communal meals where we have to find a cafe that serves egg and chips because half the crew are vegetarian and egg and chips is all they will eat. The living in each other's pockets on the tour bus, smelling the tattooed roadie's farts, listening to each other's shitty music and filthy night-time snores.

This is my first time touring on a sleeper bus. A glorified caravan with coffin-like compartments to sleep in and everyone huddled up on a banquette at the back, smoking and drinking and watching *Spinal Tap* for the 53rd time. There are rules on the tour bus. Don't poo in the toilet; it can't take it. Sleep with your feet facing forward, in case you crash like they did in Bucks Fizz. Respect each other's privacy and space. Difficult one, this: save for the sliver of curtain by your bunk there's no real privacy be had.

There is nowhere to wash on the bus. Nowhere to hide. No escape. I miss the boarding-house days already. At least there was a bedroom to escape to. At least after gigs you could go out and have a look at the town you'd been dumped in for 24 hours, even if it was Wolverhampton. There are no nights out now. Only nights in. Get off stage in France, get on the bus and drive to Belgium. Get off stage in Belgium, get on the bus and drive back to France. We are a travelling circus. There is no abroad, there is only in here: the confines of the bus and the confines of the gig venue's walls.

I'm missing female company, but not in the way that the men are. To stack the dice a little, we've employed a female sound person but Bob's been doing this so long now – this touring, shitters, larky, musical bloke-fest – she is ostensibly a man. She calls herself Bob, for God's sake.

'Cheer up, it's Dusseldorf tonight. We can all do bongs on the *autobahn*.'

'What time is it, Bob?'

'Nearly noon.'

'I need coffee.'

'Watch out for the milk, it's turned to yoghurt.'

'I need a piss, then.'

'Wouldn't if I were you.'

Great. That's just great. Someone has broken *the* fundamental, unbreakable rule of the tour bus and taken a giant unflushable dump in the stinking loo.

I think touring is getting to me. Band life is getting to me. All of it. The entire fucked-up, charmless, shallow, egotistical shit-show thing of it. Grown men acting like babies. Moaning to their tour managers that they feel sick, or feel grumpy, or need a wee, or can't go on stage without another line of 'gack'. This is no life for a grown-up. Who wants to be a pop star past the age of 25 anyway? By the age of 25 you can wee on your own. You can poo on your own. You've long since got over having to prove something to your parents because they didn't pay you enough attention when you were three.

The days are frustrating and repetitive. Playing the same songs night after night. Same chords, same notes, again and again for an hour each night, then 23 more hours in between that you have to get through with nothing else to do but drive

600 miles along an *Autobahn*, look for egg and chips and sit and get pissed in a fucking Irish pub.

This is why people are drunk all the time. This is why they want to get high. Because touring in Europe, which should be a blast, you'd imagine it would be, is the most miserable, execrable, soul-sapping activity I have ever undertaken. On tour with my boyfriend and my ex. All the simmering tensions of that madness that we foolishly thought we'd been dealing with are magnified a million times by the claustrophobia of the bus. Jon and I know the exact way to wind each other up. We've had more than seven years to practise.

'Where's my new Hole CD gone?'

'I roofed it.'

'What d'you mean you roofed it?'

Jon points at the open skylight on the ceiling of the bus.

'*Right*... that's it, where's your jacket? I'm roofing your last gram of coke.'

It isn't healthy: the four of us crammed on board with our crew, stopping every fourth day to spend a few hours in a real bed and grab a shower, and admire the view of another ring road. And for what? So German rock journalists in leather trousers can ask me why all my songs are zo damn zexy! I want to get off. I'm on the wrong trip. I don't remember signing up for this. This isn't rock and roll, it's a cross between an 18–30 holiday and an escorted old age pensioners' coach trip.

Apologies. Forget it. Rant over. You just sort of caught me at a bad time. No doubt I'll feel better after an afternoon getting pissed in another Irish pub.

BIG IN AMERICA:
PART TWO

Another town another tour bus. A new place to sleep and rest and snore, and contemplate the fact it seems to be taking an entire week to drive the length and breadth of Texas. We have inherited our latest tour bus from The Fall, who took it out on tour in the weeks immediately before we did. They have left us some gifts; I'm not sure if this is intentional or not. There are a couple of ripe socks on the floor and a carton of cream in the fridge and buried down the side of the seat cushions at the back there is a little metal tin filled with hash. We never said thank you. I'd like to say thank you to them now.

We've played gigs in America already this year, at the Whisky A Go Go in LA and CBGB in New York. CBGB was once a legendary music venue, the birthplace of American punk, home to all the greats: Blondie, The Ramones, Iggy, The Stooges, Television, Talking Heads. It doesn't seem that legendary now. It's filthy and smells strongly of piss.

'Oh great… the toilet's overflowing. I have other people's wee on my trainers.'

'Watch out for that tampon by the door. Looks like a skidder.'

I'm keen enough to imbibe the seventies spirit of old punk rock but not, you know, quite this literally. Everyone goes on and on about how amazing CBGB is but God knows why. The Ramones might have played here once but it's not like they're here now, is it? It's not like Debbie Harry is propping up the bar while Patti Smith hands round the cheesy puffs and canapés.

Today the bar is being propped up by a fantastically sulky sound man who seems hell bent on making our band sound like shit.

'Don't worry about it,' he grumbles. 'Everything will sound cool when the place fills up.'

This is the club sound man's mantra. They have this lie tattooed across their gnarly eardrums at birth, in place of any appreciation for the concept of decent sound. I suppose if you spend the bulk of your professional life with other people's wee on your shoes, your main pleasure might well be in making bands you don't like very much sound like a bag of spanners. Especially when their lead singer is tramping around the place, merry on The Fall's hash, yelling, 'This place is pants, I don't see what all the fuss is about.'

Grumpy sound men aside, the gigs in New York are always good: stuffed full and sweaty and steamy, and there's enough of an anglophile contingent to make it feel like a gig at home, only with better cocktails and later opening hours. The head of artist development has come down to watch us. He has a few words of advice.

'Great gig, guys. Great gig. One hundred and ten per cent. Now, Lou… are you a fan of Whitney Houston?'

'Uh… yeah, "Dance With Somebody". I used to love that.'

'My boss signed Whitney Houston. I've just signed a girl called Brandy. She's gonna be the new Whitney.'

And your point is?

'Communicate, communicate, communicate,' he says, smacking his fist into his palm for extra emphasis. 'Sing every word like you mean it. Straight out from *your* soul into *their* soul.'

'Like Whitney?'

'Awesome, you got it!'

You're going to whoop now, aren't you? Please don't whoop.

New York and LA are easy pickings for English bands like us but away from the cosmopolitan cities on the coasts, the concept of Britpop seems a little less widely appreciated.

Our all-conquering debut tour of the United States of America begins in a shopping mall in Virginia. Sleeper are playing in a shopping mall. Finally the pop dream is realised! This is like being Tiffany or something. We play. People shop. We go back to the tour bus. We sleep.

Our second stop is a weenie roast in Georgia. What in God's name is a weenie roast? It turns out it's some sort of outdoor festival where bands play music while rednecks barbecue sausages and drink many cans of cold beer. They do this by shaking their cans very hard, piercing a hole in the bottom, then putting their redneck lips to the hole so the entire contents shoot down their throat in seconds flat.

The drunk frat boys we are playing to are naked from the waist up, bodies toasting in the fierce Atlanta sunshine. Their skin is lobster pink, their torsos are muscle bound, and many of them have mistakenly thought it wise and interesting to shave their chest hair into complicated shapes. I plan to win them over by playing my jaunty three-minute pop-punk songs about suburbia and sex. Amazingly, the plan isn't working. They shout, 'Get the chick off stage, man!' Over and over.

Next stop is a music festival in Texas, supporting rock heroes of the moment, a band called Bush. We are first on the bill, as is fitting. Ten minutes before we're due to go on, someone from the Bush camp comes to our dressing room. Bush have been double booked and have to fly to LA tonight. Their tour manager pops in to see us.

'Great news for you, guys. You're gonna go on *after* Bush!'

This isn't great news. Bush are huge in America. They are awesome and they *rawk*! And I've just looked at the audience, more frat boys with funny chest topiary who've been baking in the sun for so long now their puffy heads look like they might spontaneously explode.

We go on after Bush. There is anarchy. We play as loud and as hard and as *rawk* as we can, but it's a bit like that scene in *The Blues Brothers* where John Belushi and Dan Aykroyd are so scared of their audience they have to play behind a metal cage. I wish we were playing behind a metal cage. The crowd are throwing bottles and beer cans, and a couple of them even throw shoes. Andy is hit on the shoulder by someone's Converse trainer all the way at the back, on the drums. This crowd have good aim. This crowd really hate us. They hate us so much they are prepared to walk home without shoes. In a vain attempt to turn things around, I try to channel the spirit of Whitney Houston. It isn't working. I think I must be doing it wrong.

It gets better and worse than this. Good gigs in Seattle and Austin and San Francisco, difficult ones almost everywhere else. And it sort of makes sense. I mean it *really* makes sense. This music doesn't translate. You can see that on the long drives, on the grand horizons, in the sheer romantic vastness of this place. It's no surprise they don't know what to make of us. America loves its categories and we're not really a pop band and we're not really alternative rock. We are small. We are niche. Our niche is England.

I have a looming sense of this now, a clear view of our unimportance that is nicely liberating. I can see how bands that are big in Britain have their egos crushed by coming to America and playing to unresponsive rednecks in shopping malls, but I sort of decide it's a fight we can't win this time and soak up all the good stuff instead. The long drives across the desert, the gigs in beautiful places; a beach in San Diego, a mountain in New Mexico, a gig under the stars in Mississippi. In Dallas we spend a happy afternoon making our own version of the legendary Zapruder film on the grassy knoll, alternating the roles of JFK and Jackie Onassis.

'Lou's being Lee Harvey Oswald.'

'I thought *I* was?'

'Who's playing the magic bullet this time?'

'Diid.'

When we arrive in LA we make straight for the water, jump out of the tour bus and dive head first into the Pacific Ocean. Freed up from another band's touring agenda, we are learning how to make and mend our own. No ring roads, just one long road movie.

Our final stop on this tour is a sold-out gig at the Whisky. Afterwards, we waste some hours at the Viper Rooms on Sunset Strip, then head to a party at a mansion in the Hollywood hills to play poker with Courteney Cox and members of Blondie.

'Check out that cupboard.'

'I know. It's full of drugs.'

'Some bloke in a thong said we should help ourselves.'

I get high and gaze out at the sparkling sweep of Los Angeles, a vast plain of fairy dust that looks fantastically pretty under the influence of some sweet Californian grass.

We make it back to our hotel after dawn. We spend the next few days lounging among the palms, doing photo shoots for tragically hip, west-coast style magazines which mostly seem to involve jumping into swimming pools in designer threads, cocktails perched in our hands. We are not going to be big in America this year, of that there is no doubt. There is also no doubting that if you are, it is endless layers of fun.

We fly back from LA and the very next day we perform on stage at Glastonbury. There are thousands of people in the crowd. It is blindingly hot, with no trace of festival rain or mud, no sign of any oddly shaped chest hair. No one throws shoes. They all sing along. It feels good to be home.

HELLO MILTON
KEYNES: PART TWO

Something extraordinary is about to happen. Sleeper are going to play a rock stadium. Today – 30 July 1995 – our band will take to the stage in support of rock gods REM at an open-air concert venue that holds upwards of 70,000 people. No matter that at the time we're scheduled to go on – four in the afternoon – half of those people will still be queuing up to get in. No matter that we are the first of three support acts, seemingly culled at random to make REM look like they're bang up to date with this funky new movement called Britpop. No matter that Thom Yorke from Radiohead is skulking around backstage throwing suspicious sideways glances at everyone he passes, quite possibly because he believes Delores from The Cranberries is a CIA operative in disguise. Tonight I am playing a rock stadium and nothing, not anything, can spoil the moment. Except that it can. I am bothered by something. What's bothering me, what's nagging quietly at the back of my mind, is that the stadium in question is in Milton Keynes.

My problem is this. I can't be certain, but I have the feeling this might be the one and only stadium gig Sleeper will ever get to play. Despite our growing UK success, internationally famous rock acts aren't in the habit of asking us to support them on sell-out tours in which the preferred mode of transport, in and out of the venue, is helicopter. If I'm only going to play one rock stadium in my life I want it to be one of the good ones: Wembley, say, or Shea, or Budokan. I'll take any of those ones, I'm not picky; it's just that when I'm old and grey and my grandkids ask me, 'Where was that rock stadium you played back in the day, Nan?', it would be cool to say New York, Caracas or Tokyo, not 'just off the A5 near Furzton, two miles up the road from Newport Pagnell'.

Of course, I'm being ridiculous. This is the same venue where I came to see David Bowie play all those years ago. The fact that we are playing here is possibly the very best thing about the gig. But, still. Milton Keynes... It just doesn't have the right ring to it.

It's like a small village backstage. Dozens of trailers used as dressing rooms, vast marquees and catering tents. Hundreds of roadies and technical crew, lines of articulated trucks. People are marching purposefully from one side of the giant stage to the other; wearing headsets, gesticulating and yelling. In the hours before we go on, I wander from bar tent, to catering tent, to dressing room, trying to stay cool and calm. It's so big out there. There are so many people back here. I've been up and down to the side of the stage and back again several times, and the place looks almost full to me already. I head to the dressing room one more time. I chew off all of my nails. I'm just dealing with an obstinate bit on my thumb when REM pop by to say hello.

'Hey,' says Michael Stipe, 'I'm Michael Stipe. Thanks for joining us today.'

He's thanking *us* for playing. He's compact and beautiful. He's genial and friendly but even so, he still wears his fame like a suit. I'm fascinated by it. I want to touch it. I want to know what this level of fame does to a person. If there's a bubble in my head I feel compelled to pop it these days, so I find myself asking him what's it like. What's it like to *be* Michael Stipe? He's touchingly unfazed by my sudden attack of social gaucheness. He smiles and says, in a low-key southern drawl, 'You know... today, it's pretty fucking cool.'

Before he leaves us to our fretting, Mr Stipe cadges a light for his cigarette. Diid snaps open his lighter and the gentle superstar takes our bass player's hand as he puffs his tobacco into life. We decide, after they've gone, that Diid and Michael Stipe have shared a moment.

'Come on.'

'Come on, what?'

'I think he fancies you.'

'Don't be ridiculous.'

'He held your hand!'

'To light his *cigarette*.'

'It wasn't just that. He was definitely checking you out.'

Diid is getting cross with Jon. He gets cross with Jon quite a lot. Jon likes to get drunk and goad him.

'If you sleep with him, he might take us on tour.'

'Leave it, Jon.'

'I'm only saying... for the good of the band... I think you should overlook your preferred sexual orientation and offer yourself up to Michael Stipe.'

We drink more. We fret more. I think I'm coming round to Jon's argument. If Diid gets off with the rock god that is Michael Stipe, it might mean we get to play another, cooler stadium. It's good for us sometimes, this goading. It helps the nerves.

We are finally ready to go on: our guitars held protectively like weapons across our chests, our hearts palpitating wildly beneath them. At the side of the stage we hear our name announced and we are doing this, we are actually walking out there.

For the first ten seconds it's exactly like that dream when you're standing at the front in school assembly and you've just discovered you're naked. We don't deserve to be here. We are indie intruders. Sleeper aren't stadiums and sunshine, we're sweaty clubs, fag ends and lager. We are gleeful pop-punk thrashers, and have no songs that would prompt you to hold your lighter aloft and sway, unless you were hell bent on setting fire to the person in front of you's hair.

But the nerves are short lived, soundly beaten down by the crowd. It's a party out here and there is only good feeling, and for hundreds of rows, far into the distance, the crowd jump up and down and cheers us on. We turn to each other and shake our heads. Jon picked up his first guitar when he was twelve. Andy started playing drums when he was ten. Diid spent his childhood with his cherished ABBA and Beatles compilation tapes for company. Now here we all are in the sunshine, doing this, everyone singing along. It's unimaginably thrilling and because I have a habit of forgetting to enjoy things until they are already over, for once in my life I remember to be happy right now. We leave the stage hardly more than 40 minutes later, sodden with sweat and still vibrating with pleasure.

*

Much later, as the sun dips and the day cools, we return to the side of the stage. On top of everything it's my birthday today. I am 29 years old and there can be no better way to mark entry to the final year of what can usefully be described as my youth than by watching one of the world's greatest rock acts, REM, perform their greatest hits at close range. The band are wonderful, muscular and lithe but in the middle of the gig, after 'Losing My Religion', there is an unexpected break in proceedings. Michael Stipe has abandoned his post and is striding off stage, blue eyes twinkling in their rings of black eyeliner.

'Look… he's heading straight for you.'

'Don't be stupid. He's heading for Helena Christensen.'

He's suddenly in front of me, holding out his small slim hand and, for no good reason I can think of, escorting me onto the stage.

It's heady out here now: the ante raised to dizzying proportions, the vista turned impossibly grand. The crowd is three times the size, its vastness magnified by the dark starry skies, the thousands upon thousands of faces illuminated by floodlights that trace their golden beams back and forth across the bowl of the stadium. The atmosphere is wilder, so much more intense, and in the midst of all this, as I stand there frozen to the spot wondering what's about to happen, it becomes clear Michael Stipe plans to serenade me by singing 'Happy Birthday' and getting the crowd to sing along. The whole experience is surreal, at once a delight and mildly mortifying. I am grinning at the implausibility of something like this happening when I sense myself drift for a moment, suddenly transported somewhere else.

What I'm thinking as I stare out at the sea of people singing is that this is exactly how it would have looked on that hot summer night in 1983 if Bernice and I had been pulled onto the stage by David Bowie. In my head I am sixteen again, hair stiff with lemon juice, high heels splattered in mud, belting out the chorus to 'Heroes'. It's the moment I discover how it feels, what it looks like, to be a rock star. It happens to me here, in Milton Keynes, just off the A5 near Furzton, two miles up the road from Newport Pagnell.

SUMMER'S HERE, KIDS

The summer of 1995 was hot and sunny every single day. Actually, it probably wasn't but – much as I'm a fan of weather websites and meteorological forecasting in general – I'm not going to look back and check. It's indelibly hot and sunny in my memory.

Prior to Michael Stipe there was that seminal Glastonbury, transformed by the heat into one of those blissful festival experiences that only seem to happen in other countries. Everyone in flip-flops and bikinis and shorts, brimming with the kind of good feeling that is almost – but not quite – enough to make you tolerate the jugglers and the palm readers, and the bungee-jumping, soothsaying hippies.

The class of '95 were all there. Supergrass, Menswear, Elastica, Pulp, and the newly all-conquering Oasis.

'Look at Liam. He actually walks like that. A gorilla crossed with a Weeble.'

'Who's the blond one trailing after Noel?'

'That's Robbie. Hey Robbie! Are you glad you left Take That?'

'Yeah, deffo… mad-fer-it, cheers. Mad-fer-it, mad-fer-it. Mad-*fer*-it!'

There's Ash and Shed Seven, and the drummer from Gene chatting to the bloke out of Dodgy. Backstage, in the VIP bar, with access to the good loos, we recognise everyone playing here this year. And everyone recognises us.

The most popular question I'm asked this summer is, do Sleeper mind being called a Britpop band? I'm not in the habit of objecting – I bet Tony Hadley didn't mind being called a New Romantic – but I can't protest now even if I wanted to, because we've just been on a programme called *Britpop Now*. The epithet is made official after its airing and next month, when Blur and Oasis go head to head for the number-one slot, Trevor McDonald will be discussing Britpop on the ten o'clock news. It's not our battle, these aren't our teams, but in a weird sort of way it feels like they're talking about us.

As we walk off stage at the filming for the Britpop programme, my big brother comes in smiling, carrying a package of silver discs, one for each of us. This means we have sold 60,000 copies of our debut album. It means we have something tangible to keep, a record of our success so far. Something with a smooth glass fascia that is perfect for cutting lines of coke on. Something to hang in our toilets when we're long forgotten, to prove that we really were pop stars, once. I like the look of the silver disc; it's sparkly, it's very pretty. I am hugely proud of it. For about six and a half minutes. And then I instantly start feeling aggrieved that we don't have a gold one.

1995 is the year Britpop explodes and ejaculates; it's the summer things begin to take off for us. I can feel our egos expanding, especially mine, because I'm starting to take all this for granted. This swanning round the world playing music. The chauffeur-driven cars, the fashion shoots, the TV shows, the bumping into superstars at the backstage bars.

It's a game of two halves. On the one hand we're nipping off to Paris and New York for the weekend to do photo shoots, on the other we're all still living in rented flats and earning £1200 a month. We pay ourselves a wage from our album advances and every so often a cheque arrives from the radio play we've had, and I rush out and spend it all on a thing. A new jacket. A bag. A settee.

On the other side of the Atlantic our American label indulge in acts of insane profligacy on our behalf. My Ikea sofa cost 300 quid but Arista have just spent £100,000 on a new American promo for 'Inbetweener' that will get shown on MTV only once. That's a high price to pay for three minutes 42 seconds of airtime. Especially when we later discover that the cost of our American videos is to be recouped directly from our British royalties.

We shoot it in California in the grounds of a derelict hotel, The Ambassador, the place where Bobby Kennedy was assassinated. There's a big crew of stylists and directors and minions who all seem to think they're Martin Scorsese. The director downs tools because the caterers don't have the right type of tea. The stylists get upset because we don't want to wear any of their shiny LA togs. The hairdresser cries because we won't let him loose on our scruffy hairdos with his heated crimpers and curlers. Video people are like fashion people: very highly strung, like Chihuahuas.

There are other odd changes in our life. Some old friends are beginning – just a little bit – to look at us differently. Mostly they'd just like backstage passes to Glastonbury and an intro to Liam Gallagher, but a couple are beginning to resent what's happening to us. Begrudging words in a pub over drinks. Annoyance that we can't arrange to take them with us.

We have friends who have been in bands for years who haven't and probably never will make it now. Rozz is a stalwart from the groundhog days who briefly played bass guitar for us. He has an encyclopaedic knowledge of XTC and Pink Floyd. He knows and cares about records – their detail, their construction, their history, their trivia – in a way I never will. This equation translates as some deep injustice. How can a girl who has never knowingly listened to more than a ten-second snippet of 'Dark Side Of The Moon' have ended up making it instead of him? How can someone who is more likely to be moved to tears by Elton John than Nick Drake have ended up supporting REM?

'It's pure luck with you lot, though, isn't it? We'd be as big as you if we'd got our timings right. How about you give us the support slot on your next UK tour?'

'Well, I'm not...'

'Because we'd blow you away?'

'No... it's not that. I'm just not sure the world's ready for psychedelic skifflecore.'

I don't blame Rozz. I would resent us too, if I were him. If this had happened to a friend of mine, I'd have been so consumed with jealousy, I'd quite likely have spent the rest of my life getting over it, and only found some small modicum of solace when their career crashed and burned, and they were forced to spend a year on a sofa in their underpants weeping into their Prozac.

Even so, my sympathy is tempered. Our friends in the duff bands should have spent less time on their manifestos and more time writing some decent tunes. All I'm thinking now is that I want things to get bigger and better and wilder, and that the album we'll record this autumn will be the one to take us up to the next level and buy us some more expensive sofas.

On the first day of recording for our second album, my brother comes in with a package of gold discs, one for each of us. This means we have sold 100,000 copies of our debut album. I like the look of the gold disc: it's sparkly, it's even more sparkly than the silver one. I am hugely proud of it. For about six and a half minutes. And then I instantly start feeling aggrieved that we don't have a platinum one.

RED LIGHT. GO

We record our next album following another lightning-fast tour of the British Isles. This one is buoyed up by our fifth single, 'What Do I Do Now?', entering the charts at number fourteen. We're on *Top of the Pops* again. We're on *This Morning* with Richard and Judy. We're on kids' Saturday morning television and in *Smash Hits,* and then we're on *The Big Breakfast* being interviewed by two sarcastic glove puppets called Zig and Zag. We go straight from the Zig and Zag interview to the recording studio and Jon lights a restorative spliff. You can see why he'd want to. Sarcastic glove puppets can have that kind of effect on a person. They can give you cause to question everything you thought you knew about yourself.

For instance, is it a good thing or a bad thing that we're talking to glove puppets on breakfast TV now? Are Richard and Judy so naff they're cool or just plain naff? Is it OK to be almost 30 and telling *Smash Hits* my favourite colour is yellow and my favourite smell is other people's chips? Will our press office ever take no for an answer on the burning question of whether I'm ready to pose in my pants for *FHM* yet? Not. Double not.

The gloomy days of grunge are a dim and distant memory and everything this year is optimistic and vividly technicoloured.

Blur are making videos featuring farm animals and page-three models, and even the most credible bands are vying for space within the pages of the nudge-nudge, wink-wink uber lads' mag *Loaded*. Zig and Zag are on first-name terms with platinum-selling artists, and having Richard Madeley playfully thump you on the shoulder and tell you how much he loves your band – 'Tip-top single, guys. Tip-top' – is becoming a Britpop rite of passage.

This is fine. This is normal. British pop bands have always behaved like this. Even The Boomtown Rats did the phone-in on *Multi-coloured Swap Shop*. I remember it well. I was tempted to call up Bob Geldof and tell him that I didn't much care for Mondays either. Doing kids' TV, hanging out with Ant and Dec: these days we can write it off as being postmodern and ironic. Maybe it is. It's certainly no worse than discussing masturbation with cross little bald men from the *NME*.

The media circus seems increasingly confounding the more I engage with it but, after the mishaps of our first attempt, the recording studio is beginning to feel like home. The places most familiar and comfortable to me this autumn are here, in the studio, and up on stage. The gigs – since we've done so many this year – are instinctive and automatic but no less enjoyable for it. Even on the larger stages that we're playing now, the gigs still feel strangely intimate: just us and the crowd, playing music, singing songs.

The first time I went on stage, I remember thinking it was a peculiarly contradictory experience because, against all expectations, it felt like a uniquely unselfconscious place to be. You have permission to be up there. There's no fight for attention, because you're clearly the centre of attention already. So you forget about it. You lose yourself. It's egotistical, obviously, but the applause isn't the best reason to be there, it simply becomes the punctuation. The rush is in communicating with so many people all at once. The highs come mid-song when everyone is with you: the rest of the band, the hundreds of strangers who have come to see you perform, who don't feel like strangers for the hour that you sing to them. The world feels like a less scary, more generous place: on stage, plugged in, in the middle of a fast and furious gig.

Making this second album is even better than being on stage. The lights have come back on in the band and there's a period of great camaraderie between the four of us during this recording. Our problems have levelled out over the last few months, bulldozed by having no time to dwell on them, by having to knuckle down and get on with things. It helps that the music feels so good. I love these songs. I love how they sound in here. I like what we're doing to them as a band: everyone growing in confidence, each of us settling into our roles.

'That guitar part is *genius*.'

'I know.'

'Don't go over it with sixty more takes.'

'Pfft. Why would I want to do that?'

In here, in the confines of this womb-like red room, with its scruffy sofa and giant mixing desk, we while away hour after hour. Drinking. Drinking tea. Smoking. Deconstructing. Playing. Laughing a lot. There's a wonderful alchemy in starting the day with an empty reel of two-inch tape and playing it back in the evening when it's filled with voices and instruments. A whole morning lost to the muscular rhythm of a drum take. An evening given over to recording drunken backing vocals and giddy handclaps. Six hours working out the exact guitar line that fits with the newly crafted chorus. I'm getting geeky about sonics. I'm getting particular about amps and snare-drum sounds. I'm not so bothered if my guitar is green or not.

This is where the glamour really sits. The TV shows, the autographs, the parties, the videos, all the stuff you grow up thinking will be glossy and exhilarating, really aren't. The after-gig parties meld into one another after a while, differentiated only by how wasted everyone is. But making a recording is utterly different every time you attempt it. It changes from moment to moment, even in the seconds it takes to rewind the tape and try another take. You can spend hours, days, trying to recreate a simple four-track demo that you've made in your bedroom and sometimes you can never quite find it.

Music is slippery and elusive, and chasing it, taming it, making it fit together is where the good stuff is. What I love most about all this, I'm beginning to realise, is the process. The melodies that spring out of mid-air, almost fully formed. The lyrics that wake you up in the middle of the night and have to be scribbled down on a piece of scrap paper. Cutting into my Telecaster with a plectrum and having a producer mean it when he tells me I'm a good rhythm guitarist.

For a long time I've felt like a fake – my status as a musician underpinned only by a stubborn inclination to call myself one – but during the recording of this album I finally feel like I'm a match for what's being asked of me. I know what I want to hear when the red recording light comes on. I know exactly how I want this to be. We're not making *Hunky Dory* or *Transformer* or *Hounds of Love* (if *only* we were making *Hounds of Love*) but I know this is an album that I'll want to listen to. That I'll like. That I'll always feel proud of writing and collaborating on, and not just for six and a half minutes. If I could go back to one part of my time in the band, a single snapshot of pop life, one flickering beam, it would most likely be back to here. The rest of it I'm beginning to think I can take or leave.

When it's finished I call our album *The It Girl*. It's a phrase my dad used to use when we were watching black and white films together on Sunday afternoons. Dad's 'It Girls' were Ava Gardner, Jean Harlow, Ingrid Bergman, Veronica Lake and Lauren Bacall. He's been in my thoughts a lot, this last year. I still have the overwhelming urge to phone him up and share bits of good news, forgetting that he's not there to call. After the record comes out, It Girl – a long-forgotten phrase – is instantly taken up everywhere. I feel like my dad has unwittingly reinstated it, which makes me smile, though he'd definitely have taken issue with its modern, mid-nineties interpretation. Marilyn Monroe, now there was an It Girl. Tara Palmer-Tomkinson: certainly not.

TRAINSPOTTERS EVERYWHERE

'Someone wants you to record a song for a film soundtrack.'

'What's the film about?'

'Heroin.'

'Do we get to go to the premiere?'

'Yes, you do.'

'Red carpet and paparazzi?'

'I think so.'

'Black stretch limo?'

'No doubt.'

'Excellent. Tell them we'll do it.'

OK, so I'm not entirely immune to the emergent-pop-star trappings. If the parties are getting boring it must mean I need to go to some better parties. As satisfying as it is, there's only so long you can huddle away in womb world, fixating about effects pedals and drum sounds. Now that it's finished, now that our album is out and in the charts (top five again!), it's time to get back on the merry-go-round.

This week Andy and I are flying up to Glasgow for the premiere of seminal nineties drug-film *Trainspotting* and the week after that I'm presenting an episode of *Top of the Pops*.

This will swiftly be followed by a quick round of award ceremonies and another sell-out tour of the British Isles. Andy and I have moved, to a bigger, nicer flat, and given that we've recently changed our phone number it's a bit of a surprise to find out Colin Gladstone still has it.

'Hi, it's Colin. You didn't come and meet me like we arranged.'

'Hi, it's Colin. Please get back to me, urgently. About our holiday.'

'Hi. It's me. Colin. Again. I'm buying our flights to Spain this afternoon.'

'Colin here. Why haven't you called? We're still meeting tomorrow, aren't we? Call me. I am getting quite cross.'

'Hi, Lou... it's Mum. Some strange boy called Colin has been phoning me in the middle of the night.'

It's one thing having Colin Gladstone leave repeated messages on my answer-phone and track down our ex-directory number; it's quite another having him bothering my mum. This is a step too far; he has officially stepped over the line. BT are very helpful and they change our number one more time. My mum doesn't want to change hers so she buys a whistle and blows Colin Gladstone's ear off each time he calls. That will teach him to phone a 70-year-old lady at four in the morning.

I have a stalker of sorts. He's not sending me dead ferrets in the post yet, but he does seem to be under the misguided impression we're going out together and that the way to a girl's heart is a weekend break for two in Alicante. He stops calling my mum after the whistle interludes but his calls to me get more regular, even with another new change of number. There's a tape full of messages waiting after a weekend away and I'm just about to get BT to try and track him down when I get a late call from someone else:

'Hi. It's Peter Gladstone. Colin's dad. I wanted to apologise about Colin. We've found out what he's been doing and we just want to reassure you that he won't be bothering you any more.'

'I see. Good. Uh... can I ask why not?'

'He's been arrested.'

'Oh?'

'For attempting to hack into the Ministry of Defence's computer. He's very good with computers, is our Colin. He does stuff like this all the time.'

From his tone of voice, it's hard to discern if Colin's dad is cross or proud of his son. Maybe these distinctions blur when you become a parent. Still, it's reassuring to hear from Gladstone Senior, good to know Colin wasn't barmy or dangerous or anything.

Our plane tickets to Glasgow have mysteriously not arrived despite being sent by courier, and I decide not to dwell on thoughts that barmy Colin Gladstone has had something to do with it. We pick up new tickets at the airport and fly up to Scotland to attend the premiere. There's much debate in the press this month about whether *Trainspotting* glamorises drug taking or not. I vote not. Too much poverty. Too much degradation and hopelessness and throwing up. Too much Ewan McGregor's head down a shit-filled toilet. If someone were to film famous Britpack actors and musicians cutting out lines of coke in the back of a limousine wearing designer clothes on the way to walk the red carpet, now that might be deemed to glamorise drug taking. Typical, isn't it? Where's Danny Boyle when you really need him?

Andy and I walk the red carpet behind Damon and Justine. It's a novelty for us to be flashed and papped, to have photographers calling out our names. Once inside the cinema, we buy ourselves a jumbo bag of popcorn and listen out for our tracks in the film. There's a big party afterwards and Justine wants to cruise the floor looking for famous people to talk to. This is diverting enough for a while but soon gets irritating because she wants to remind me *again* what a huge mistake it was that my band signed a worldwide record deal.

'Yeah, like I was saying,' she repeats, a bit too smugly for my liking, 'we signed a UK deal. Then we signed lots more in other countries. That way you make *loads* more money.'

I decide to leave her to it. Any second now Damon's going to stroll up and start reminding me how I'm meant to make everyone want to be me, or get off with me or some such. I go back to see where Andy's got to; he's signing an autograph for a pretty girl. Her boyfriend asks me for mine. Maybe we don't have to go trawling for famous people any more. Maybe we are famous people.

I'm sitting in a greasy spoon cafe in Camden Town, going over my links for *Top of the Pops*. The show's producer, an amiable flame-haired megalomaniac called Rick (flame-haired mega-lomaniacs are big in TV this year) is vigorously stirring sugar into his coffee.

'So, Louise, first up you'll be introducing Supergrass and Bon Jovi.'

'Really, Bon Jovi?'

'But they won't be in the studio, they'll be doing a live feed from Korea.'

'Is it OK to take the piss out of their poodle haircuts?'

'Whatever you like. They're your links.'

This is Rick's big innovation, having pop stars and celebrities front the show instead of professional DJs. Jarvis and Damon have done it recently. So have Justine and Björk. And Whigfield.

I'm looking forward to taking part in this new and unlikely gig but I'm having a crisis of confidence about what to wear. Somehow I've got it into my head that big boots and jeans won't cut it and that I need to up my game and look marginally more put together, like Whigfield. I make an impulse purchase, a glittery silver mini-dress that I don't feel comfortable in, but seems like an appropriate outfit in which to introduce Bon Jovi. At the last minute, I tone it down with an old denim jacket. I don't want *FHM* calling me up to ask about the pants thing again, quite so soon.

It turns out that TV presenting is pretty jammy. There's some stuff about timings and memorising lines but compared to every other job I've ever had – admittedly mostly just waitressing – it's a piece of piss. On top of that everybody treats you nicely, pays you handsomely and makes you feel exceedingly important. I can't believe I'm actually doing it. I can't believe it's my name on the dressing-room door and that I'm walking in the hallowed footsteps of Peter Powell and Dave Lee Travis. Perhaps I should be more nervous than I am. Now I'm here, in front of the cameras, reading out the rundown, introducing the number-one single, perhaps this ought to feel like more of a *thing*. I'm not saying it isn't massively enjoyable. I'm not saying, all things considered, that I haven't had a *Jim'll Fix It* sort of day. It's just that it can rock your boat ever so slightly to discover the quixotic equation in which fantasy situations become strangely ordinary – quicker than you'd think – once you are actually doing them.

Maybe that's why the whole of the London music factory is face down in a nosebag of cocaine. To make the equation last longer; to slacken the speed of diminishing returns. Maybe that's why some of the bigger, fatter bands have decided cocaine is not enough to steady the spell. Some are moving on from the nosebag, experimenting with a tougher, harsher brew. There's no glamour in smack. Ewan McGregor has shown us that there isn't with his shitty toilet. It's just that some glamorous people seem to like it quite a lot.

VODKA JELLY

No one is taking heroin on this tour. They are too busy wrapping their foreskins over the heads of other men's penises and obsessing over the rectal administration of hard liquor. We put this down to the fact they are Swedish.

'Yes, so, it was *brilliant*. Our friend Björn passed out on the floor and got taken to hospital in Stockholm.'

'And no one knew what the big hell was wrong with him.'

'And then they found the strings.'

'Coming out of his bottom.'

'And his mistake, can you see, was in putting four vodka soaked tampons up his bottom at once.'

The Swedish contingent laugh uproariously.

'This way it goes directly into your bloodstream. Sent him into an alcoholic coma.'

Our support band on this tour are a trifle unusual. They hail from the deep frozen north, a tiny town called Skellefteå in the armpit of the Arctic Circle. They keep pouches of tobacco wedged in their cheeks at all times and engage in cultish sexual practices to get them through the long, dark winter nights. No sooner have they met a new male friend than they are waving their assembled foreskins at him like a packet of wafer-thin deli ham. Docking, they call this: part initiation right, part penile 'how do you do'.

The Wannadies are almost as odd as the Welsh band that are first on our bill. They have a lead singer with chronic OCD and a drummer who is passionate about home taxidermy. Said drummer acquired his stuffing skills by 'accidentally' squashing his pet hamster with his shoe when he was ten.

'It all went horribly wrong, see. Couldn't get its bones back in. Still, it made a really *excellent* carpet for my sister's doll's house. Took me a while to master it after that. Hamsters, gerbils. A guinea pig. Banned me from Pet World, the ba-a-astards!'

You can see why they would. There's no going back after a series of pet accidents like that. Nice friendly chap, though. Plays so hard he vomits into a bucket after every gig.

Band life is kind to eccentricity. It nurtures it and encourages it, especially when a band are on the road. Everything problematic is taken care of on a big tour like this. No obligations. No responsibilities. You can be drunk as a lord at any time of the day or night with no requirement on your time, other than to turn up and play.

Our boarding-house days are long gone – how soon you forget – and these days we have a 25-page laminated tour itinerary all of our own. We have articulated trucks, roadies for every instrument, sound people, monitor people, lighting people, tour manager people, catering people, not to mention the eight giant It Girls in scarlet swimsuits, complete with flashing lights, who have come along for the ride, and to decorate the stage. There is no need for soggy Ginsters pasties any more. Tonight our caterers are knocking up Christmas dinner – in Bolton, in the middle of May – because everyone, you know, just sort of fancied it.

A typical touring day goes something like this. Get up at eleven. Clear empty mini-bar bottles off bed. Peep round door to find full English breakfast sweating outside on the carpet because you didn't hear room service knocking on your door three long hours ago when it was delivered. Did you really order the prunes? And the mushrooms? Of course you did. You ticked every single box on the order form when you were polishing off that last miniature of Drambuie.

Force cold tea past lips. Feel sick. Put on some dirty clothes. Pack bag. Leave something important behind under bed. Ignore tour manager calling for third time this morning to see if you're awake yet. Put on dark glasses. Stumble down stairs. Wait for rest of band in lobby. Witness Jon enter lobby with his bags. Witness Jon return to his room, indignant that he isn't the last person down. Sit in big squashy chair nursing hangover and think about ordering a Bloody Mary. Watch tour manager pay for rooms. Watch tour manager argue about last night's horrendous bar bill. Watch band members argue about how much porn they did or didn't buy on the hotel film channel.

Climb into band van. Make space in rubbish. Go back to sleep. Wake up feeling unaccountably lively. Ask driver to pull off motorway and find village green so band can have impromptu game of cricket. Play cricket. Wonder why you are suddenly flagging again. Get back in van. Watch film.

Arrive at the evening's venue. Sign autographs for people waiting outside. Go to small catering area set up in front of stage. Have coffee. Force down a cake. Look up at big stage and take in giant lighting rig and enormous PA, brightly lit It Girls and various muscly men with tattoos, clambering over perilous sections of newly constructed lighting rig. They all work for the band. They all work for you. And all these beams, all this scaffolding, all these cases and spotlights and speakers stacks, travel with you every day, like exceptionally heavy hand luggage.

Finish cake. Climb on stage. Roadie hands you tuned guitar. Play three songs. Check sound. Walk off stage, drive to hotel and watch tour manager check you all in. Get cross if bass player's room is ready before yours is. Watch bass player complain that his room isn't as nice as Jon's is. Open mini-bar. Watch bit of TV. Have shower and change into clean clothes. Head back to venue and go backstage to catering area. Eat posh school dinner with assorted Welsh and Swedish people who have paid to share your on-tour catering. Wonder why your record company were too tight to buy you onto Blur's catering, back in the day.

Finish dinner. Go to dressing room. Open wine and admire own cheese plate. See what exotic fruit of the day is. Unwrap new pairs of pants. Do not have line of cocaine before gig. Remember that the only time you *did* have line of cocaine before gig you walked out on stage in Southend and said 'Hello Sheffield.' Have drink instead. Settle nerves. Pop to side of stage to watch bit of support act's set and check out the feel of the crowd. Begin to get excited. Pop to support act's dressing room and stand at door like portly auntie and say, half begrudgingly, 'Yeah… well done tonight. They seemed to quite like you.'

My lovely big brother has turned up! Allies and friends and more fun. People from the record company. Live agent. Music publisher. Press officer. Press officer's annoying minion. Minion announces there's a reviewer coming tonight, even though we've told him repeatedly not to tell us if there's a reviewer coming, because it puts everyone off. Have word with tour manager and see that press officer's minion is banned from the dressing room until further notice. Have glass of wine. Put on lipstick. Panic a bit. Think about running through a couple of scales. In motherly fashion, check that band members who need to have been for pre-gig nervous poo.

Tour manager comes to tell you it's time. Feel lurch in stomach. Head for the side of stage. Listen to crowd. Fiddle with plectrum. Wish had gone for own nervous poo. Give nod to tour manager who sends torch signal to lighting crew in manner of elusive smoke signal. House lights come down. Crowd erupts. Walk on. Nerves vanish. See a thousand people in the audience all cheering. Glance over shoulder at Andy. Think, this next hour is the most enjoyable thing that will ever happen to us in our lives.

An hour passes.

Come off stage covered in sweat. Tour manager hands you clean towels. Line of coke available before encore for anyone who wants it. Do encore. Walk off. Go back to dressing room wondering what to do with insane levels of nervous energy. Have someone remind you that you told the entire crowd which hotel you were staying in tonight. Suddenly think this might not have been a good idea. Drink. Have short back-stage party with manager and visitors and friends. Duck into band van. Drive back to hotel. Sign autograph for crowd of kids waiting outside and make no attempt to apologise to the hotel staff, who have had to draft in extra security to protect the door. Go straight to bar. Order rounds of drinks. Have line of cocaine in the loos.

Midnight and bored now. There's a canal outside the hotel. Andy and our keyboard player (we've brought extra musicians on tour to beef up the touring party and the sound) decide to jump in and swim across it. The water is filthy, freezing and full of prams. They don't seem to mind. Strange Welsh drummer is playing the hotel's piano in the foyer. He is playing it so hard and is so drunk, he's smashing up his fingers and they are bleeding. Somebody drags him away. There's a trail of blood on the hotel's pristine pale carpet, a fine splatter freckling the nearest wall.

Someone else is injured. Diid has blood spilling out of his head. He has fallen over into a glass table after too much vodka. I am hoping it wasn't rectally administered. Our number-one fan, the girl who lives in her car and comes to every single gig we ever do, is sitting alone by the bar with a giant red cake on her lap. The cake is an exact replica of our album cover. It has disturbing little marzipan effigies of the four of us on top of it. We are too scared to eat it. Hidden behind a sofa, some Swedish people are wrapping their foreskins round some other people's penises. Some groupies are milling around, a couple are heading up to Jon's room. Someone is pulling all the cushions off the chairs, leaping into them and attempting to 'fly'. Someone is explaining, in detail, the best way to tackle home taxidermy.

The bar is refusing to serve any more drinks so we will all have to go to someone's room. It's two in the morning. A couple more hours until it's time to fill in the breakfast order and drain the last of the Drambuie miniatures. Andy has hiccups. He is trying to cure them by putting the hotel hairdryer in his mouth and turning it on. It isn't working.

He has passed out on the bathroom floor where he will stay until morning.

Give up the ghost. Take off boots. Crawl into bed. Go to sleep.

Get up at eleven. Clear empty mini-bar bottles off bed. Peep round hotel door... repeat, repeat, repeat, repeat to fade.

SHE'S SO HIGH

I think we need to take more and better drugs. Bands that are bigger than us are taking a lot more drugs than we are. It stands to reason that the more class As we take, the more successful we will be.

Jon may be in the first stages of an alcohol dependency that will take him years to conquer. Diid may be getting so ruined that we recently abandoned him in Barcelona – penniless, on the floor, passed out – and flew home to London without him. Andy may be thinking about writing a thesis on offsetting the effects of cocaine by the imbibing of alcohol, thus enabling you to take yet more cocaine. But where are the crack pipes and the panic attacks? Where are the ruined nasal passages and the dirty needles?

We are letting the entire Britpop side down. At this rate we're never going to end up in rehab. We'll never have implants sewn into our abdomens to cancel out the effects of all known opiates. We'll never end up digging said implants out of our bodies with our bloody fingernails because we need to have one last fix of heroin.

We need to be more like that British band we ran into in San Francisco last year: whacked off their faces on crystal meth. So aroused and pumped up they were tearing their clothes off by the pool and shagging their weasel-faced roadies. We need to be more like that vintage American girl group we met in LA. The ones who used to get high and take Polaroid pictures of their fannies, then post them through their support band's hotel rooms at night. Guess the fanny. Get to screw it. You can almost see Bruce Forsyth doing the BBC quiz show version.

By the end of this tour, I'm having serious doubts about the more drugs equals more success theory. I've discovered that I'm rubbish at taking coke night after night. It gives me huge weepy downers in the morning and makes my nose run like I have chronic hayfever. It makes me sneeze. No one wants to unwrap a gram of cocaine in front of someone who is likely to sneeze all over it. I'm trying to show willing, now the tour is winding up, but no one is fooled by me dipping a finger into the coke bag and nonchalantly spreading a dab of it onto my gums. I am ordering tea and rounds of sandwiches at the hotel bar after gigs. I am turning down lines and settling for a shot of vodka and a custard cream. I have tried – not that hard, it has to be said – to be self-destructive but I don't have the classic rock-star constitution. I haven't the will to trawl the length and breadth of Harlesden at four in the morning because a guy called Sizzles knows a man called Pete who could sort us all out.

I have fallen at the 'my drugs hell' hurdle. If only this weakness had been thrown up by all those *Jackie* magazine quizzes that I took as a teenager, I'd have given up my plans to be a rock star there and then. You can't be in a band unless you're willing to go off the rails at some point. You can't be in a band if you have a largely non-addictive personality.

In my head there's a hardcore version of me who is poppers and pills and temazepam – crawling up the dingy walls, high as a kite on amphetamines – but who am I kidding?

I'm thinking about cutting down on caffeine. I'm too neurotic to take E. The one time I took mushrooms – in 1987 – I completely failed to comprehend the effects of psychotropic drugs and pootled off to the cinema to watch Richard Attenborough's anti-apartheid film *Cry Freedom*. I had flashbacks all week in which I thought I was living in a black township being hunted down by murderous white South African policemen. I never took mushrooms again.

Taking drugs is just like having a cup of tea. So says Noel Gallagher, but he's wrong. Tea doesn't make you try to chew your own jaw off. It doesn't make you yammer on about yourself for hours on end with your face centimetres from the face you're yammering on at, which is, coincidentally, also yammering manically at you.

'I work in PR, it's amazing. *I'm* amazing. I've screwed everyone in Menswear. Almost.'

'Oh really, who's left?'

'Shit, there goes Johnny. *Johnny*, over here. Johnny, *babe*. I *love* you… There he goes, he is *lush*… What was I saying?'

'Who cares? Oh yeah, you were trying to score the whole set.'

'Of who?'

'Menswear.'

'No way… are you *mad*? I'm done with them now. I'm onto Supergrass.'

It's wearing off already. Twenty minutes and we're down the other side.

'Let's all go on to Smashing! Shit, it's not Friday. But if we head into Soho I know someone who can sort us all out.'

'I'm here with some friends.'

'Fuck your friends… *we'll* be your friends, come with us.'

*

Tea doesn't have this kind of effect. Your tour manager doesn't mysteriously mislay £6000 of your tour budget in a week, as ours has, by accidentally spending it all on PG Tips. You don't take five years to write a follow-up album because you're whacked off your head on Earl Grey.

It's easily done. Band life can cosset and flatter you. It wraps you in warm towels and you can happily regress to a sort of dirty, corrupt state of extended childhood if you want to. Other people will make your decisions for you. Other people will endlessly spin your mistakes. You see it all the time, bands laying down in the chaos and getting comfortable, forgetting to get back up again. It's not for me. We'd never survive it. Even so, I probably need to keep quiet about this deep chink in my rock-star armour. I don't want my inability to make it as a whiny, self-obsessed drug addict to stop my band advancing to the next level.

The tour motors on around the country, all glitter and swimsuit girls and flashing lights. We call in on Essex for the night, with a date at a venue called the Ilford Island. The Island is at the end of my childhood high street; it used to house the ABC cinema. My mum is there, sitting in the balcony – equipped with industrial-strength earplugs – and I get the thousand-strong audience to say hello to her. She loves this. I love that she's there. She waves at them, a bit like the queen. I am back on home turf: 100 yards from Our Price, the record shop where I chose *Dare* over moon boots, a dash away from Bodgers department store where I put on lip gloss every Saturday afternoon and dreamed of being in Bananarama. Now I'm back doing this – with my band, with my gang – and it feels wonderful.

264 • JUST FOR ONE DAY

Afterwards Mum comes backstage and looks on at the normal carnage: Jon swigging from his bottle of Jack Daniel's, Diid and Andy sweaty and stoned. Fans and groupies and record company schmoozers all fizzing around, feral and high. She looks concerned. Maybe she's worried about the terms of her younger daughter's success. Maybe she's regretting the time she had a bizarre attack of liberal-mindedness when I left university, and let me and Jon plant all our rescued dope plants in her suburban garden next to the lupins. Dad was too blasé to care. Mum always suspected it would lead to stronger things.

'Did you enjoy it, Mum?'

'Oh, yes, it was very good. *Very* loud.'

'Did you like the giant It Girls?'

'Yes, I did.'

Her eyes flick nervously round the room. Here it comes.

'You know what I was wondering?' she says, entirely innocent to the scene. 'I was wondering if Bernice Cohen might be up here. Be nice to see Bernice again.'

I wonder where she is now. I haven't seen her for years. I didn't even think to invite her.

The last night of the tour is at Brixton Academy. Four thousand people have trekked across London to watch us play. We can see them lining up from the window in our dressing rooms; we can hear the noise and the laughter from the crowded street. Brixton is a big gig. Sold out. The largest venue we've ever played as a headline act. There are lines of kids in Sleeper T-shirts, stretched out all the way to the back. At the front are gangs of girls with my haircut, those two skunk blonde stripes in the fringe. Carbon-copy leather jackets. Carbon-copy drainpipe, skinny jeans. I'm suddenly nervous to go out there, worried we can't begin to give them what they're expecting. But it's a blast. The music takes care of things, as is its way.

Afterwards Andy's dad is backstage to join the revellers, gleefully flashing his access-all-areas pass. He spent his teens going to see Hendrix and Cream; he was in the Free Trade Hall in Manchester the night Bob Dylan went electric. I'm guessing he's slightly more tuned into the backstage madness than my mum was. He seems no less delighted for his son.

I am feeling momentarily invincible. We have held this room all by ourselves. Our record is selling three times as fast as the last and we're moving up to the higher level, still largely sane and intact. We haven't traded our souls to drugs yet or joined the growing ranks of the lost boys and girls who fell apart after their first albums. It's one of those rare moments when you step back and remember where you are, take in the scene and feel intensely lucky.

SHOWBIZ

Someone is out to get me. I know they are out to get me because they've just sat down and said: 'This time, I'm out to *get* you.'

A music journalist has just arrived at a Camden pub to interview me. I take a large sip of my drink.

'You invented the Spice Girls?'

'Yes, I did. And now Geri's stolen my haircut.'

'You're not going to vote for Tony, are you?'

'Blair will be as wretched as the other lot. I won't endorse either one.'

'Why are you always being controversial?'

'Come off it. I've just wound a few people up.'

'Vegetarians?'

'Tree huggers.'

'Feminists?'

'Dungaree wearers.'

'Environmentalists?'

'We need more roads. I like tarmac. The countryside gives me the ab-dabs.'

The journalist pops to the toilet to consider his tactics. To be honest, I think he might stand a better chance of getting me if he can remember his list of important and interrogative questions. He's been to the toilet five times in the last two hours. He takes his little notebook with him every time he goes for a pretend wee and when he comes back – after a fortifying swig of beer – he starts the conversation with:

'And *another* thing...'

This is getting ridiculous. Morrissey said it's easy to be controversial in pop music because no one ever is, and he's right. The simplest, most obvious, most tongue-in-cheek statements are blown out of all proportion in the pop world. Like all rules there are notable exceptions. Our old touring mates, the Manic Street Preachers, can do and say almost anything they like without attracting lasting opprobrium. They can say 'I hope Michael Stipe dies of Aids' and no one seems to mind all that much. They can hang out with murderous Cuban dictators – the kind that execute political prisoners without trial and imprison people for saying they are hungry – and everyone smiles and says, 'Ahh, sweet.'

Conversely, I have become a wild-eyed controversialist for such searing off-beam insights as: women like sex too, and politicians of all persuasions have a tendency to be corrupt. Things have reached such a fever pitch lately that the editor of a music paper has made it his mission statement to destroy my band and is currently printing letters from spotty teenage boys calling for me to be burnt as a witch.

The whole thing is so blatantly bonkers that the only way to make interviews bearable these days is to send out my cartoon doppelgänger – well honed over the last two years – to do them for me. She's not unlike me, this loud, loopy girl on the magazine covers; just a heightened, condensed-milk version. These days I never turn up to an interview without a few solid pull quotes in my pocket that I've prepared in advance. Having something to talk about when you get there, my mum would say it was just good manners.

We're moving beyond the realms of the music press now. Our album is about to turn platinum and we've had two singles in the top ten. I don't think there will be as much game playing on the outside, especially since I've started taking instruction from Robert Smith of The Cure. After an evening spent swapping lipstick tips and drinking Campari when we met at a party, he left me with this piece of advice. Do as much TV as you can. They can't spin you on TV. On TV they get the real you.

Excellent. One more magazine shoot, then straight on to some 'real me' TV time.

'How about you undo another button on your shirt?'

'I don't think so.'

'Come on. I'm a genius. I will make you look *very* beautiful.'

'Really. No.'

'How about you keep your jacket on. But wear it without a shirt on underneath.'

'I like my shirt.'

'Undone to the waist. I will make you look *very* sexy.'

Or a bit like Zorro.

The man taking my picture for the style magazine is a world-famous fashion photographer. I have just bumped into Linda Evangelista in his stairwell as I made my way up to his studio. She was tall but tiny; as delicate and fragile-looking as a bird. Her face was so beautiful it was almost ugly. Supermodels are alien beings; it's shocking to see them up close.

The photographer is looking troubled, decorously slumped across his chair.

'I think Linda was cross with me today,' he pouts. 'Was Linda cross with me today, what do you think?'

'Uh… not sure. I didn't really meet her… except for just now, in the stairwell.'

'How do you think she looked, though? Cross?'

'Could be cross. Could be starving hungry. Hard to tell.'

An assistant arrives to smooth things over. She massages the glum photographer's shoulders and assures him that Linda wasn't cross with him, but he's still grouchy as the two of us take our places. The only thing that has cheered him up so far this last hour is trying to get me to take my shirt off.

'But the magazine would like you to look *fashion*. That's how they asked me to photograph you.'

I say, 'This is how I look. I'm a musician.'

He huffs. He photographs me from an odd angle on the floor. Enough of this bullshit. On to the 'real' world of TV.

'Louise Wener. Can you now pretend to be a volcano. Let's see you stand in the middle of the room, in front of the entire audience and prepare to be… an exploding *volcano*!'

I am on *Shooting Stars* with Vic and Bob, who are sweet and very funny. Ulrika is on my team but she's in alpha-female unfriendly mood and barely shares a word. Perhaps to keep her cool, she has a bottle of wine stashed under her desk to swig between takes. I wish I had a bottle of wine under my desk too. It may or may not have helped in my attempts to impersonate an exploding volcano.

*

'Louise Wener. Can you pretend to be a horse. Let's hear how you would impersonate a horse!'

I am on *Never Mind the Buzzcocks* presented by Mark Lamarr. The other guests include Jonathan Ross and Noddy Holder. We have just had all our lines and cues written for us by a comedian. I have forgotten all of mine and ended up saying something inappropriate about Shakin' Stevens indulging in anal sex after a kebab. In the green room afterwards, Jonathan Ross is showing off his tight black trousers and admiring how big his penis looks in them. His penis *does* look quite big. Maybe I only think this because he wasn't the one asking me to impersonate a horse.

Our press officer calls the next morning.

'The *NME* front cover is still on.'

'Good.'

'But only if it's a picture of just you. If we ask for a band picture then they'll pull it.'

'I see.'

'And we don't want them to pull it because the front cover of that style mag is not going to happen.'

'I see.'

'The photographer said you were difficult to work with. The pictures have come out all nose.'

'All nose?'

'And chins.'

'I see.'

'How was *Buzzcocks*?'

'I had to neigh like a horse.'

'Good. Good. Now... did you happen to see *TFI Friday* last night?'

'No, why?'

'Oh… nothing. Ginger Tips announced live on air that you were coming on next week to do a sketch.'

'Without asking?'

'I know… I know… but it's nothing weird. No impersonations. If you do the sketch you get to play your single live on the show the following week.'

'If I don't…'

'They'll give the slot to Shed Seven.'

I turn up at Riverside Studios the following Friday. Someone asks if I've remembered to bring my outfit for the sketch.

'What outfit?' I say.

'Sexy school teacher. Didn't they tell you?'

It's exactly the same on the outside. It's all negotiation and compromise, bartering and dealing and blackmail, and playing one set of stooges off against another. But I can hardly complain about it now. I can't say it's our record company pressurising us to do this stuff, threatening to slash our marketing budget if we turn publicity down and don't do everything in our power to earn ourselves maximum exposure and airplay.

This would be true but disingenuous. This is our chance to cross over, our route out of the indie ghetto and into the mainstream. A contestant was singing one of our songs on *Blind Date* last week. I'm not going to turn around and get all earnest – out of the blue – and suddenly reject mass appeal. I grew up on pop. I don't want us to be indie and niche forever.

But I did lie to that idiot fashion photographer. It happens in dribs and drabs, in tiny increments, so slowly you hardly even notice it. I'm not a songwriter or a musician any more: for the next twelve months or so, I'm in showbiz.

ALMOST FAMOUS

It feels like we're characters in a computer game and I am a Super Mario brother. The aim of the game is to kill your enemies by jumping on their heads while you climb platform after platform after platform. I will be content if I play the game for one more hour. I will be happy if I play the game for one more day. I must advance to the next level and then I can relax and be content. But you know how it is: you get the extra power and the extra weapons and the temporary immunity, and you ought to take a break, go and make a cup of tea, but you can't. As soon as you reach level seven – after a brief moment of reverie – you immediately want to try for level eight.

Our moment has come, our fifteen minutes is now and the language all about us is changing. All everyone wants to talk about is playlists and pop hits and radio 'A lists', and the dogs are sniffing round us, sensing blood. We are drawing people out of the woodwork at our record company. The indie squibs who have overseen our career up to now (and I use *overseen* in the loosest possible way) are being usurped by men in suits with receding hairlines and receding chins: the kind that hang out with Robson and Jerome.

When I say they smell blood, what I really mean is they smell money. Despite our parent company taking early bets on how long it would take us to collapse and topple over, we have (almost irritatingly, I can't help but feel) confounded their low expectations. A platinum album is in the offing, which represents ground zero to the men in suits. They call us up from time to time and drum their fingers on their desks while they talk. They meet one another in the lifts and smile their sharky smiles and say: 'This Sleeper lot, were you aware that we'd signed them?'

'Hmmm, let me think... Oh yes, I remember, didn't we buy them for fifty pence and a packet of crisps back in ninety-four?'

'Doing surprisingly well. Let's send them a Christmas card this year... maybe a bottle or two of bubbly.'

They have us in their sight line and they are weighing us up. They may, or may not, be thinking about dragging us into the fold.

In the meantime, it makes sense to concentrate on publicity and radio play as a route to the next safe Super Mario platform. All the media exposure means I'm being recognised a lot more this summer. People look at me and stare and call after me, and stop me in the street to ask for autographs, most days. It's an increasingly disconcerting experience. On the one hand I feel hugely flattered and important, on the other I'm beginning to get self-conscious. The me in pictures is better looking. The me in interviews is more bolshy and entertaining. The me in Boots the Chemist being asked for an autograph when I'm halfway through paying for a box of tampons and a roll of cough drops feels like I've been caught in my nightie by the postman.

'You look much smaller in the flesh.'

'Right... I get that a lot.'

'Can you sing a bit of your song?'

'What, here in Boots?'

'Aww... come on.'

'Sorry. No.'

'Never mind, eh. By the way, you look *well* sexy in your videos. My dad even fancies you and he's *well* old.'

It wasn't like this in the Spar with my packet of Hobnobs, because back then there was nothing to live up to. I think there is something now. There's this being, this alter ego, this newly famous person, and my nagging suspicion is that the real me – not the distilled essence you get in the magazines – might turn out to be a disappointment.

Famous me is the half-formed twin that I carry around like an extra head and she is far more important than I am. People want to talk to her and celebrate her and get off with her. She's doing photo shoots for *Vogue* with David Bailey and being invited to parties by the Rolling Stones. She's analysed and criticised and gossiped about, and even though I'm fairly certain she can take care of herself, I've recently begun to engage in 'how does she look to the world' bouts of worry. I didn't care much about this until quite recently. What kind of a person takes any of this stuff seriously? Press isn't something you read; it's a confection, something you weigh.

'Did you read that bit in your last interview where they compared you to Mrs Thatcher?'

'Have you phoned up especially to tell me that, Rozz?'

'No, of course not... uh, yes.'

I shouldn't read the bad stuff in the papers because it lodges in my brain and I can't seem to shake it for days. I shouldn't read the good stuff because it's pointless: it drains away like water through a sieve. Seeking validation from people you don't know, who've never met you, who've only ever absorbed a piece of the cartoon you through the ether. It's an act of madness.

I shouldn't be surprised that it's catching up with me. I'm weeks away from turning 30 and I've long since given up using Doris Schwartz as my pivotal role model for analysing the vagaries of fame. I suspected, long before I came face to face with it, that fame was weirder and more addictive, and likely much more mutinous, than it seemed for Leroy and Coco and the gang. The point is, I thought I'd be immune. I thought I could play with it and mould it and see it for the blasts of hot and cold air that it is. But fame is slippery and seductive. It tugs at your vanity and fluffs up your ego and there are times when I'm sort of annoyed that my big brother is always on hand to puncture the bubble and bring me back down to planet earth.

'I can't go on *telly*.'

'Why not?'

'Look at it... look... at this spot.'

'More like a boil. Let's be honest.'

'See... *see*. I look like shit.'

'Bit of make-up... no one will notice.'

'But they *will*.'

My big brother sighs.

'OK then. They probably will. You'll go on telly with a giant spot on your forehead the size of a third eye, and everyone will see it. Same as anyone who has to get up and do a job and face their workmates all day long, with a colossal shiny zit on their face.'

'This is *completely* different.'

'No it's not.'

I am grumpy. I am cross. I try another tack to attract some modicum of fame-related sympathy.

'Did you see what they were saying about me in the *NME* this week?'

'Was it true?'

'Uh... no.'

'Doesn't matter then, does it? Come on... let's go. You'll be late.'

It's infuriating. It really is. It's highly inappropriate behaviour. One of the band manager's key functions is to indulge and flatter the artists he represents. It is not his job to be honest and rational and exposing of the ephemeral nature of the fifteen minutes of fame and celebrity his kid sister has patiently spent a lifetime accruing. At this rate I will never ascend to a Mariah Carey level of diva-dom. I will never be surrounded by snow-white puppies and get to say things like, 'Heavens, no sweetie. I don't *do* stairs.' It is, as I'm finding out, very difficult to get away with this kind of behaviour with the person who took the stabilisers off your first bike.

This is, of course, a very good thing. Fame and success, even at our level, seems designed to swaddle and infantilise. People have begun to treat me like a child. They don't ask me things directly any more. They talk to me through the record company, or my press office, or my brother or other members of the band. Quite often, they sidle up to Andy, like he's parent to some recalcitrant toddler, and say, 'Do you think Louise would like to do such and such?', 'Do you think Louise would mind if I asked her this or that?' Andy – for the tenth time that day – replies, 'Here's an idea, why don't you go and ask her yourself.' It's pissing him off. Going out with someone that people have started to treat with kid gloves.

Even so, you can see how it happens. You can see how famous people get addicted to entourages and flattery and the veneer of innocence and immunity that comes with making every decision through an intermediary. This isn't going to happen to me. Fame is a fiefdom of wank and I won't subscribe to it. I have my brother and Andy to keep things in perspective. When I'm mentioned in the *Sun* or photographed by a paparazzo coming out of a bar, we will heave a collective shrug and say, bollocks to all of that nonsense.

I'll stop reading my press. I'll go back to weighing it. I'll sieve the good stuff from being famous – the status, the fun, the validation of the music – and discard all of the rest. I will not, under any circumstances, spend unhealthy hours flicking through old interviews in private, feeling alternately hard done by and heroic. I will not watch five-second excerpts of myself on TV whilst staring through my fingers flinching in horror, like I used to do decades ago with *Doctor Who*. Why did I *do* that? Why did I *say* that? Why did I make that stupid face? Is *that* the face I make all the *time*! I will not, never, not once, twirl around the room in a pair of teenage legwarmers that I have secretly squirreled away in long-term anticipation of getting to this point, singing: '*I'm going to live forever*... tra la la la la la *la!*'

Fame is an uneasy bedfellow. You need the skin of an armadillo to remain untouched by it.

TURNING THIRTY

The bar is minimalist, trendy and expensive. A Japanese waiter in a sharp, Armani suit is cutting ice for our drinks from a giant block. He is using a dagger-shaped pick. I wonder why he's scowling at Andy. I wonder why he's being so aggressive with his ice pick.

'What's he looking at you like that for?'

'You're crying. He thinks I've upset you. '

'You haven't upset me.'

'I know.'

'Just tell him… you know, it's my birthday.'

I'm going to turn 30 in Japan. Right after a little detour to Singapore and Thailand. Our first port of call is Bangkok to sweat it out in the summer heat and play gigs and sign records, and eat stinky durian fruit. We perform a couple of songs at a branch of Tower Records and a gentle soul from our record company's classical music department is put on crowd-control duty. He's too nice to control the crowd. We are mobbed. We are chased through the shopping mall by squealing gangs of Thai schoolgirls, waving pirated copies of our album in their outstretched hands.

Next stop Singapore, the land of chewing-gum bans and death-to-drug-smuggler signs, and odd little toilet monitor ladies who prowl the public lavatories to check that you've flushed them correctly: they make you pay a fine if you don't. We discover that one of our crew has brought a block of hash through customs under his tongue. We send him home straight away.

After a quick check under everybody's tongues, it's back onto a plane to Japan. We scoot around the country, getting recognised on the underground in Tokyo, doing interviews on Japanese radio, trying at all costs to avoid being poked with sticks by dwarves. The band fly home immediately afterwards while Andy and I stay on to finish up a few bits and pieces of promotion. Somewhere in those few days it becomes my 30th birthday. The two of us head to a penthouse bar to drink cocktails and celebrate, and I cry.

'I think you should stop now.'

'I don't think I can.'

'That ice pick he's holding looks very sharp.'

'Let's order more cocktails. I'm sure some more cocktails will help.'

I have no real cause to be crying. It's true that I'm very, *very* past it now, and old, but I am also a pop star, on tour in Japan, and I should be elated by the fact I've made it to 30 and succeeded at the one thing I've always wanted to do. I've been like this all day, inconsolable. I can't work out what it's about. I'm having fantasies about staying here and not going home. I'm having dreams about a tiny island off the coast of Malaysia that Andy and I once visited where you can live on a beach in a shack, for months on end, for 20p.

The running-away fantasy has popped up from nowhere just this week and will build to a pitch over the coming year. It goes like this: get up, find passport, head to airport, get on plane, don't tell a soul where you've gone. It feels like an odd dream to be having in the midst of all this. If my teenage self could see me, sobbing into a martini in my birthday dress, a platinum album back home on the shelf, she'd grab both my shoulders and shake me.

Back to London. More TV shows. Practically live on the stage set at *TFI Friday*. Watch Ginger Tips from the wings, ruling his crew with a bloated mix of tyranny and fear. Begin to suffer from insomnia. Insomnia before interviews. Insomnia after interviews. Start having peculiar dreams in which every answer I give is recalled with pinpoint clarity and pored over and rejected and replaced with bigger and better answers. It's like that feeling you have after an argument when you suddenly realise what you should have said, in the car on the way home. I am having imaginary conversations with myself. I am suddenly fixating on the idea that there's a finite way to do this, a way to make things flaw free and perfect. I'm more aware of my flaws than I used to be, because, almost every week now, people are writing down – in public – exactly what they think they all are.

Out of the blue, Elvis Costello has just asked us to record a cover version of a song from his latest album, to put on the B-side of his next single. After the thrill of doing this, I pluck up the courage to call Elvis and see if he'll consider returning the favour for us. Magnificently, he does more than that. Not only does he record a gorgeous, pared-down version of our song 'What Do I Do Now?' (so simple and soulful that I have to play it 100,000 times in a row to check it's real), he asks us to support him on his up-and-coming tour of America. I leap at the chance. Another opportunity to get away, change gear and enter new headspace.

Back out west, across the water, it's entirely the same as it was the last time, with the Americans not knowing what to make of us. It doesn't seem to matter. I'm glad to be out of the UK madness for a few weeks and we're playing these grand old venues – music halls and outdoor theatres – and getting to see Costello and The Attractions play every night. They are joyous to watch. I love seeing Costello do his sound check; I love hearing him fill the room with his grit and honey voice.

We've been warned that Elvis is a legendarily moody beast, but I only bear witness to it once. His band are halfway through a gig when someone makes a small mistake in the middle of a song. Elvis stops the gig and stalks off and the band gather awkwardly around him backstage. He doesn't say a word to them, just stares at the floor looking murderous. The tension is unbearable, too much to watch, and I want to go over and puncture it, tell a joke or offer someone a toffee.

The crowd are getting restless, unsure what's going on, and the band are shuffling uneasily from foot to foot. Just when you think The Attractions will melt with anxiety and ticked-off schoolboy rage, Elvis raises his head and offers a barely perceptible nod. Still wordless, no explanation to the band or to the audience, he marches them back on stage and starts the wronged song from the beginning. They play bitter and brilliant and charged for the rest of the night.

It seems that even the most seasoned artists can find relationships stretched to breaking point by the claustrophobic nature of touring and ours are more down than up on this tour: fragile and fractious, made petty and vindictive by the constant use of drink and drugs.

Even now, Andy and I are still working out how to be a couple on tour; the best answer we've come up with is to pretend not to be. Jon's bored. He's drinking much too much and searching out powder in every port. He keeps himself amused by finding perverse new ways to wind the others up. By the others I mostly mean Diid. We have extra musicians with us to spread the load but they can't sop up the growing pool of tension. I'm not eating enough on this tour. Usually I'm my own Jewish mother, imploring myself to extra helpings: I am curry and pickles and cake. Odd things are making me happy. Missing out on lunch. Making do with an apple. Not putting butter on my bread.

Even so, there are good days and great days, and foreign touring will always surprise you and offer up its perfect, nut-sweet moments. As repetitive and dysfunctional as it is, touring has begun to feel like a refuge, a realm where the outside world can't touch us. In here, in the bunk, life drifts by outside, like a grainy Super8 film. We take a stop in LA to make a video. We drive downtown in a vintage open-top Cadillac, smiling and blissed out on weed. Someone is filming us. A policeman on a motorbike is threatening to arrest us for not wearing our seatbelts. Our tour manager is trying to talk him out of it, while the rest of us wait in the car.

'Stop giggling.'

'Can't.'

'You have to.'

'Can't. You hate me, don't you?'

'Of course I don't hate you.'

'The paranoia must be kicking in, then.'

'You can't be paranoid if you're giggling... Keep it down, he's coming back. We don't want him to know we're all stoned.'

We carry on driving. I'm wearing bright red shoes with Statue of Liberty models floating in the gel-filled high heels. I am miming, out of time, to our next single. I've decided that no one hates anyone and everyone loves everyone instead. All is good. All is warm and silly and surreal.

Fly to Seattle tomorrow. Another few weeks of gigs on our own and then home. More press and performances and show-biz pencilled in. Another single release, another short UK tour to shore things up and maximise the life of the album. I'm looking forward to the home gigs. I want to go on stage and see my gang. I want to sing loud and make my ears ring. These gigs are like rocks; solid footholds. As the gloss, spin and fakery build around us, it's the one place we still feel utterly like ourselves.

After we're done, at the end of the year, Jon will head back to America. He's fallen in love and plans to hole up in LA with his new girlfriend through the winter. The new year will be busy back in London. Time marches on, there are schedules to be met. Success must beget more success. They want us to move on this quickly. The men in suits have stepped up and they want another album started by the spring.

WHO'S THAT GIRL?

This isn't any way to write an album: they don't suit being made in a rush. I have sat down, post touring, post year of merry madness, and I've looked at my guitar and conjured… nothing. The melodies are a mish-mash of styles. The lyrics are coded and empty. The songs have no centre, they have no heart.

The writing is coming out all wrong this time round and to make matters worse, nothing else is in its proper place. Jon is thousands of miles away and relations with Diid are distant and strained. At the start of '97 we're so rattled with one another that we barely have a functioning band. It's something you don't see while you're on the merry-go-round, but as soon as you stop spinning, you instantly sense how rotten it's become. The intensity of this year has left us splintered and cracked, and it's stupid to imagine we can make another record without taking time off to gather up the pieces.

Because no one is communicating, the usual rehearsal process – the playing, the arguing, the working things out – has been replaced with something more pedestrian. Andy and I have filled our spare bedroom with recording equipment and make hurried demos of one song idea after another in the hope that something good will stick.

'I've done something with that chorus riff you wrote.'

'Excellent. What are you going to call it?'

'"She's A Good Girl".'

I play it. I sing the words. Andy nods.

'Yeah… the melody works. But what's it about exactly?'

Good question. Fucked if I know the answer.

Time drags on and pressure from the record company mounts. Because our advances are so small, we are beginning to run out of money, and won't get paid again until we record the new album. When the final tally comes we'll have sold over half a million records but our deal is so paltry and ill-conceived that we'll never make a penny in royalties. At this stage there's still hope. If we make an album quickly, capitalise on our success, they are offering to renegotiate the deal and make it more fair. It's hard to resist that kind of carrot.

What this record needs, to get it off the ground, is a hook – some kind of anchor – but I can't seem to grasp what it is. Our first album was written over the course of a relationship breaking down; our second was written under the influence of the fallout. Both were coated in a cheap shell of confidence and cheek: they were the very incarnation of that girl in the big boots with the scruffy haircut, stomping to the damp rehearsal room, guitar in hand, on a quest to conquer the world. The girl in the big boots has left the room. I'm not sure when it happened but it did. Somewhere in the showbiz, Zig and Zag, tour and tour again months, she's been usurped by a weary imposter.

It feels like we're writing this record on shifting sands and in the rush to start recording I can't seem to focus on a direction. The atmosphere all around us is changing and there's a darker, more reflective mood emerging. Blur have set out their stall with 'Beetlebum', and Pulp are spirited away working on something similarly pared down and introverted. Oasis are pompous on cocaine, about to spin off into the buffers with *Be Here Now.*

In the opposite corner, Elastica have surrendered to their heroin stupor, and that coterie of frank, gutsy women fronting guitar bands has been watered down with giggly 'girl power'. What happened to that battle? That slice of rock and roll sexual equality that we came for? It started with an attempt to level the playing field, but ended in something altogether tamer and more dilute. You wake up one morning in the midst of the beer-swilling, coke-fuelled, self-important, macho parody that is Britpop's death rattle and say, haven't we been here before? Justine aping Christine Keeler on the cover of *Select*, Sonya Echobelly falling out of her shirt in *i-D*, Cerys Catatonia pouting half naked on the cover of a lads' mag, and how the hell did I end up being photographed in a wet-look PVC catsuit carrying a gun? I look ridiculous. Like sexy liquorice.

This wasn't part of the plan. This isn't the girl from L7 pulling her pants down on *The Word* to reveal her big hairy bush. This is neutered and neat. Conformist and traditional. Same as it ever was. Indie Playboy. Don't be stupid. Look what we've won. The right to go out on the town with Zoë Ball and throw up until we puke, and rave all night and take our kit off in *Loaded* and call ourselves ladettes. The right to have celebrity fashion photographers ask us to undo extra buttons on our shirts every time they take our picture. The right to be replaced by airbrushed, apolitical, muppety versions of ourselves like Natalie Imbruglia. It's not how I saw it. This feels like a corruption. I don't think I like what we've started.

The sexy liquorice picture falls out of a pile of magazines when I'm moving things around in my flat. It's from ages ago but it annoys me to see it and these days I'm frustrated with myself. In the midst of clawing our way up, battling with the record company, keeping the band together and winding up the numbnuts in the inkie press, I feel like I've forgotten what I'm doing here. Indie world was rife with contradictions and conservatism, but mainstream pop world, like a giant emery board, has ground down all my rough edges.

We pull the songs together in the end, but the process isn't a happy one and somebody has to be the fall guy. We drag Jon back from LA a couple of weeks before recording starts but replace Diid with a new bass player, a friend of ours, Chris Giammalvo, from the American band Madder Rose. The feeling is that something has to change and in lieu of taking much-needed time out, stepping back and rediscovering our mojo, we settle for reshuffling the band. This new line-up doesn't work particularly well. Jon is drinking heavily in the studio and everything is taking much longer than it should. Chris is a great player, but we have no history together, no real cement. It turns out that a broken bond is better than no bond at all.

I know for sure that the album isn't good enough when Robbie Williams plays us a song called 'Angels'. Robbie is recording his debut album in the studio next to ours. We've just spent a couple of hours playing a video game called Cool

Boarders in the TV room and now he wants to know if we'll come next door and listen to some of his stuff.

'I'd really like to know what you think,' he says, nervously. 'You're cool, aren't you, you indie bands? You know what's what.'

An indie band. Pfft. That's what he thinks.

'Yeah... all right then,' I say. 'We'll come and have a listen, if you like.'

I think I'm going to hate it. I think I'm going to be sniffy about it whatever it's like because, you know, it's by the soppy dancer from Take That. But it's hard to be sniffy to someone who's so friendly and insecure and that skilful at Cool Boarders.

Robbie takes us into his studio. He has reviews of Gary Barlow's album (all stinkers) taped up on the wall, which makes me like him even more. (I wonder why I never thought to do that with Echobelly's?)

'This is the one,' he says, looking rather more sure of himself. 'The record company think it's an eleven out of ten.'

The song starts to play but I'm not paying it much attention until that big chorus kicks in. You can't argue with a chorus like that. You know from the moment you first hear it that he'll always have to sing it, for the rest of his life, just like Tony Hadley must always sing 'True'. I don't think Robbie needed our opinion after all. I think he just wanted to show off.

It's Andy's 27th birthday, early June, and Robbie hangs around to celebrate with us one last time. His album is almost finished and tonight there's a car coming, courtesy of Elton John, to whisk him away from the temptations of coke and booze to the safety of rehab.

'Vodka and champagne mixed,' he says wistfully. 'That's my drink.'

He's bought Andy a magnum and a bottle of Stoli – a sort of 'I can't any more, so you should'.

After he's gone we head back to the studio and listen to what we've recorded so far. Nothing I hear makes me smile. 'Angels' is a torch song. It's emotive and maudlin and sentimental but, love it or hate it, it's big. What it isn't is some rushed indie fug, about no one and nothing at all.

YOU OWE IT ALL TO ME

'Sorry,' the driver says. 'Traffic's pretty heavy this afternoon.'

'Aren't we going the wrong way? Isn't Park Lane in the opposite direction?'

'It's next to Mayfair,' the driver says.

I have the feeling he's only saying that because of Monopoly.

Andy and I are late for an awards ceremony: the annual shindig held by *Q* music magazine at the Grosvenor House Hotel in London's swanky Park Lane. Of all these celebrity bashes, the *Q* awards are immeasurably the best: champagne, red carpet, paparazzi, petits fours, none of your indie cider and stale Chipsticks. This is lunch with proper cutlery and crockery and a guaranteed seat in nerve-tinglingly close proximity to rock-star royalty. In 1995 David Bowie (the *actual* David Bowie!) sat two tables away. In 1996 we were in bread-roll-throwing distance of U2.

The whole giddy affair is a bit like a gig meets a Jewish wedding meets an, admittedly glitzy, end-of-year works do. There are gilt-backed chairs and detailed seating plans, embarrassing speeches and petty rivalries and by the end of the evening some young pup always gets drunk and makes a show of themselves. Last year it was Liam Gallagher, flicking cigarette ash at

Mick Jagger's head, then getting arrested on the way home for possession of cocaine. As tabloid-worthy as this was at the time, my own personal high point was beating Patsy Kensit to the last of the mini-hamburger hors d'oeuvres and getting stuck in a lift with Rod Stewart.

This year, things have started out badly. The car booked to ferry us up to the West End has got lost. We've missed the early drinks reception, our press officer has mislaid our invites and no one knows where we're meant to be sitting. Just find an empty chair, someone with a walkie-talkie tells us. Anywhere. It's about to start. And so we do.

In retrospect I should probably have headed away from the stage and settled for a spare pew at the back. But I'm arm in arm with Andy, a waiter has just thrust glasses of champagne into our hands and I'm feeling pretty confident and cool.

'Here,' I say, spotting two spare seats at the front. 'These will do. Why not sit here?'

We should have looked at the place names in front of us. It would have been sensible to have looked at the place names.

It's only as I slip my denim jacket off my shoulders that I notice I'm sat next to Bob Geldof. Undeterred, I offer him a smile. It's the kind of smile you might offer up on a tube train or the bus: it says, 'Is this one taken, do you mind? And while you're at it, would you like to try one of my chips?' Bob's response is decidedly chilly and my approach seems inadequate all of a sudden. He raises his eyebrows and folds his arms.

'You can't sit there,' he says, curtly. 'That's Sir Paul McCartney's chair. He's just nipped out to the loo.'

It's hard to know how to take this. I'm not sure which is most awkward, the fact I've purloined Paul McCartney's chair or the fact that all I can think about now is an ex-Beatle going to the toilet. I try to come up with something pithy and appropriate to say, but all I can manage is 'Oh'.

Minutes later the lights will dim and the ceremony will begin and Andy and I will dart around like that couple who turn up late for the cinema, muttering oops and sorry, is that seat taken, until we score a couple of empty places next to Sharleen from Texas. In the meantime, while Sir Paul busies himself with one of the Grosvenor House Hotel's finest hand dryers, Bob Geldof asks me a favour. He'd like my autograph, not for himself, but for his daughter Peaches who's nine and likes my band. I'm delighted with this turn of events and ask for Bob's autograph in return. He obligingly flips his invite and signs it and, in spidery ballpoint letters, scrawls the words: *You owe it all to me.*

With seconds to spare, and McCartney heading towards us looking suitably refreshed, we elbow our way past Patti Smith to take our places at the Texas table. As the presenters walk on stage, I turn Bob's autograph over in my hand. I'm happy to have it but I'm ever so slightly irked by what he's written. In part, this is because I am deep in lead-singer egotistical territory where I don't think I owe anything to anyone, thanks very much, but it is also because I know it isn't true. I loved 'I Don't Like Mondays', who didn't, but The Boomtown Rats were always runners-up on my C90 compilation tapes: if I owe a debt of inspiration to anyone in the Geldof camp, it isn't to Bob, it's to his platinum-haired ex-wife, Paula Yates. But what irks me most of all, what leaves me feeling gloomy and despondent, is that a month or two from now, there might be nothing left for us to owe.

*

I am having a recurrent dream. The entire Britpop clan is on board a giant ship, not unlike the *Titanic*. An iceberg has hit us, and the raft my band is clinging to has no oars. It's come to my attention that Sleeper have been travelling in steerage the entire trip, and now Jarvis, Damon and Liam won't let us over the side of their first-class lifeboat where they're merrily quaffing back the last of the Moët. I'm just about to make it, I am inches from safety, when I slip. I'm dragged under the icy water to drown, by Rick Witter from Shed Seven, and an irate Bluetone.

The odd thing is that everyone loves the album in the beginning. The record company give it the hearty thumbs-up; the men in suits tap their loafer-clad feet and nod and smile, and rub their receding chins in time to the beat. The advance reviews are the best we've ever had and the first single, 'She's A Good Girl', seems to be going down a storm on the radio. Maybe it was all paranoia and insecurity; perhaps we have unwittingly turned up a gem.

On top of all that, those doubts I've been having, my wavering unease with pop life, I think they've been entirely normal. There's a breaking-in point, a period of adjustment. We just need to steady our nerve, find a new platform and knit the new band back into shape. I might have been feeling wobbly about being almost famous, but at least I haven't resorted to schmoozing up to Tony Blair and his brigade of crooks and cronies at Number Ten.

Noel's obsequious smile is everywhere this month. Rock and roll is bopping – like your dad at a disco – with the newly elected political establishment. It's dispiriting to see the elder Gallagher brother hobnobbing at Downing Street because he's instantly neutered in the process. If you're in a band the only place to be, always and to everyone, is in opposition: not tucked up like a neatly folded hanky in Tony's breast pocket. But all isn't lost. At least I'll have the benefit of standing up six months from now – when everyone's snivelling about the great betrayal – and saying I told you so.

I am sticking to my guns. I have shorn all my hair and cut out my blonde bits and I'm putting my catsuit days behind me. I have a good feeling about this. We can weather the storm and put this broken record back together. The girl in the big boots is coming back.

It's six in the morning and I'm on the way to make a video for our first single from *Pleased to Meet You*. The driver, a woman, is crying. I ask her what's wrong. Haven't you heard, she says, mopping at her eyes with a tissue. Princess Diana has been in a car crash. She's dead.

We buy the early papers, the ones that think she's injured but still alive. We turn on the radio and know she's not. We spend all day flitting between video takes and watching the news on the television. It's wall-to-wall coverage, the same scant facts over and over, the shock and hysteria slowly building. It's pitifully sad, a young woman, a mother, in a horrific accident, but the response – a nation rending its clothes over a person they don't know, have never met – feels uniquely alienating. The pavements are made of flowers, the newspapers are blackened with grief, and all but the most benign love songs are being pulled from the airwaves. Our old label mates, The Wannadies, can't get their record played because their band name is deemed inappropriate for broadcast. Everyone is jittery and defensive and labels that can are putting back album releases until the mood has subdued and settled down.

It's into the atmosphere of a country gone momentarily mad that we release our first single from what will be our last album. Things feel awkward and unsteady to me as it is, but just at this moment, with days to go, our record company make a ruinous decision.

Part of the reason Britpop took off with such a flourish is that it coincided with record companies slashing the cost of singles and selling them for as little as a pound. They no longer sold in their millions like they did in their eighties heyday, and came to be seen as a loss leader, an advert for more lucrative albums.

The new edict comes down from on high. The chairmen of our parent label BMG thinks music fans have had it too good for too long. He imagines he can buck market forces – put the genie back into the bottle all by himself – and make the fans reach deeper into their pockets overnight. It's no wonder the record companies ended up in such a state. They really had no idea what was coming.

After much to-ing and fro-ing we are sent out as pricing guinea pigs for our label and, for this week only, our single will be double the price of everybody else's. I can't help but feel that now is not the time to be greedy and all in our camp are convinced it's a suicidal move. Can it be true? Were the manifesto kids right all along? In the end and with no way to fight it, my band are being fucked over by 'the man'.

I wait for the call from my big brother.

'Hi.'

'Hi.'

There's something about the way he says hi. I don't want him to tell me. I don't want to ask. I know the result can't be good. I want to be back in my flat in Finsbury Park waiting for that magic number seven. I want to be right back at the beginning, calling Geoff up and persuading him to manage my band.

'Nah... I'm not sure.'

'Come on... you'll be *perfect*.'

'I don't know anything about the music business.'

'You don't have to. You're a natural scammer. When we lived in Gants Hill, you made me watch *The Godfather* sixty-seven times.'

'You think the music business is going to be like the Mafia?'

'Definitely. Worse. The two of us will be just like the Corleones.'

'We'll have people killed?'

'No. We'll sell loads of records and buy ourselves big houses in Lake Tahoe.'

I take a deep breath.

'Where's it gone in?'

'Number twenty-eight.'

It's a long way from being a 'Thunder Road' moment.

THANK YOU
AND GOOD NIGHT

The music business is a cruel and shallow money trench,
a long plastic hallway where thieves and pimps run free,
and good men die like dogs. There's also a negative side.

Hunter S. Thompson

It doesn't sound catastrophic, a fall of eighteen places – last single to current one – but it is. Things are different by the autumn of '97. The record industry is brittle, avaricious, less forgiving, and certain things are required of a platinum-selling band. Top ten or nothing, that's what's demanded; anything less and you're written off.

I think the experiment is over. We have failed to deliver on their terms, so the men in suits will wash their hands of us and slither back into the shadows. There's a well-trodden path to be followed by a major label in such circumstances: support is withdrawn, the label will let the album die, and the people who signed us – our supporters – will be edged out of the company. It's only a matter of time until we're dropped. Three months? Six? Certainly not as long as a year. We might pick up another deal further down the line but it's unlikely: to get this close and stumble, whatever the reason, is considered unforgivably bad form.

I shouldn't know this yet but I do. It comes from having a manager who never wrapped his charges in cotton wool or sought to insulate his kid sister from the insane asylum fisticuffs of the music business. Geoff has been our brilliant secret weapon, our Jake LaMotta and our Rocky Balboa all rolled into one. He won't countenance defeat, it's not in his nature, but he knows not to sweeten the pill. In the instant I put down that receiver I know – as surely as if Dick Dastardly had appeared in front of me and ripped my medals from my shirt – that my band are done for.

How to respond to a call like that? What do you do when the pop dream is torn out from under you, in the space of 60-odd seconds? I have things to do today: a radio show with Jo Whiley this lunchtime, more newspaper interviews this afternoon. A TV show on Friday, then a friend's gig and their after-show party where all the industry and press will be hanging out.

People are looking at us differently already; they have their heads tilted slightly to one side. The ones who like us are sympathetic, up to a point. The ones that don't are gleefully sharpening their knives. For our contemporaries – given that we all loathe each other beyond redemption – our stumble is a cause for celebration, one less competitor in the ring. I'm not sure what's worse, the sympathy or the knives, and did that person at that party really blank me and pretend to be talking to someone else? My band have a virus, the virus is failure: everyone knows that we have it and no one else wants to be the next to catch it.

I coast for much of that month. I feel nauseous and panicky, regretful and bitter; now here comes maudlin and sad. I was only just getting the hang of things. I'd only just worked out that it didn't matter if my guitar was green! All this stuff to come to terms with and learn and make sense of, and now it's roaring away at such a speed that I can't hold it back for a second. I worried too much, and fretted too much, and the further pop life recedes into the distance, the more I think I didn't grab it and snog it nearly hard enough.

All pop careers, like political ones, end in failure and I knew we would reach this point sooner or later, but the pace with which it happens is shocking. One moment you're elated and immune on a platinum tour, the next you're clinging to the rock face, trying to stop yourself falling. The record company have shut us out, the album is tanking and we can't fill the venues that we've booked for next year's tour. We will have to reschedule and downscale.

After a couple of months of this – the pulled interviews, the withdrawal of funds, the failing tour – I come to a decision. I call a band meeting at a cafe 100 yards from our old ground-hog haunt, The Dome.

'Split up the band?'

'That's what I'm saying.'

We look at each other. Jon sits back and lights a cigarette. Andy stands and heads to the bar. He doesn't ask what anyone is drinking. He says: 'I'll get us a round of White Russians.'

It doesn't take long to hash it out. Despite all the history, or because of it, there's an instinctive shorthand between the three of us: a depth of friendship that, whatever happens now, I am certain will long outlast the band. I can hardly stand to voice it out loud, but I won't let us slide away slowly. One last hurrah and then out. We'll book into smaller venues for the new year but we'll keep the date at Brixton Academy and we'll sell it out – just – and that will be the last gig we ever play. We'll limp on until the tour starts, fulfilling obligations: last time on *Top of the Pops,* a quick jaunt out to Japan, then we'll blow pop world the biggest, fattest, sweetest thank-you kiss we can muster, and bow out gracefully.

If I thought it was all about timing and record-company fuck-ups I'd stay. If I thought it was just about facing down the fallout, I'd simply start polishing my boots. But other bands are catching our virus. The Britpop kids in steerage are sinking behind us one by one, and the reason it's happening is because the cycle is ending. The Cool Britannia party is over – all that's left is an ashtray of stinking cigarette ends – and the music that we're making isn't enough to carry us through. Pop music is intensely democratic, which is much of what makes it wonderful, but when your time's up, you listen and move on.

If this is to be our last tour then we had better make sure it's a good one. There are more drugs and more drink and everyone is as ruined as they've ever been, but more so. It's grubby and filthy and oddly glamorous still, but just as often it's the land of the stupid, corroded and difficult to love.

The groupie situation steps up another level. Our support bands are all boys, pretty ones, some of whom take a lot of cocaine. One night we are holed up in a hotel bar halfway through the tour, and the pretty boys are holed up in the toilets. The groupies are here, hunting in slack-jawed, mini-skirted packs: traipsing back and forth, through the bar, to the toilets and back again. I lose count of how many girls there are and how often they traipse back and forth. Jon's mum is in the bar with us; she has just been to see us play.

'Did you enjoy the gig?'

'Oh… yes, I loved it.'

Her partner nudges her on the shoulder. He seems distracted.

'Where are those lot going, then?' he says, suspiciously.

'Um… who?'

'All those young lasses. Back and forth to the toilets all the time?'

'They've got no tights on either,' adds Jon's mum. 'It's January, it's freezing outside. Why have none of them got any tights on?'

What can I say? They are both lovely people. I've had Sunday dinner at their house. I can't tell them they've gone to snort the support band's coke off the cistern and give them repeated rounds of sex and blow jobs.

'I'm sure it's nothing,' I say, unconvincingly. 'They've probably all got cystitis.'

I'm used to this scenery now. The band members who have sex with the same girl at the same time at the back of the tour bus. The band members who hide from irate fathers, checking up on the whereabouts of their underage daughters. The hangers-on who fritter our tour budget on prostitutes, the groupies who come on to Andy when I'm sitting *right there*! The Japanese girl in the thigh-high leather boots, last spotted in the lobby of a Tokyo hotel, now evidently shagging various band members as a way to ensure free passage from Glasgow to Hull and back to London.

I'm thinking about telling her to get shorter boots. I'm thinking about outlining the benefits of a railcard. I regularly think about telling the toilet groupies that the boys take the piss out of them afterwards and they could all do much better. It's too early to say what regrets I'll have but I bet one won't be not getting enough oral sex from sixteen-year-old boys in the urinals.

It is, I think, different for girls.

The circus motors on to its inevitable end and by the time we reach Brixton I'm viewing the last gig as a liberation. I'm looking forward to going out there and ripping off the plaster. No more sweaty tour bus. No more interviews and showbiz. No more wading through the soil pipe of the music industry, gulping for air.

It's only when I get out on stage and see the huge crowd that I start to wobble. I say welcome to the last waltz and we play, and when it gets to 'Inbetweener' – the one that started it all, the one I wrote in my bedroom, the one Jon and I argued about all night, the song the crowd are yelling along to – I want to take it back and carry on.

How does it feel to be a woman in a rock band? Up here, on stage, at our last ever gig, I am sure I know. The answer, of course, is it feels fantastic. Men bore women rigid with their neatly catalogued collections of Devo and Steely Dan for the sole purpose of keeping them off their turf and diverting them from the indisputable truth. There is nothing sexier or more exciting than standing at the front of a stage, foot on monitor, guitar in hand, band roaring along full pelt beside you.

A few years from now – because that's how long it takes to come down – I'll be glad that we left it right here. It's just that at this moment, in the middle of this song, I'm that kid singing into her hairbrush, and I know a part of me will miss this forever.

NOT THE KIND OF GIRL WHO GIVES UP JUST LIKE THAT

Tomb Raider is brilliant. You can have no idea how much I love the computer game Tomb Raider and how many lost hours this year I have spent playing it. If I were to play the Venice levels again now, after all these years, I'd instantly be transported to that period in my life directly after Sleeper had just split up. The sitting on the sofa in my bra and pants days. The pretending it hasn't happened and everything is much as it was days. The remembering that it *has* happened moments, when Andy comes across a long-lost wrap of coke in an old pair of jeans, and the two of us snort a line in place of a meal, because it's bound to make us feel better than the jam sandwich we were planning to have.

Early on in the Tomb Raider months came the fulfilment of the running-away fantasy. Jon wisely decamped to LA, and Andy and I packed a rucksack – not orange – and set off for Thailand. We lived on the beaches and toured the temples for a few months, and when you're at the top of a mountain gazing out on the Mekong River it's hard to imagine that things won't feel better and much clearer when you get back to London.

They didn't feel much better or clearer. Our band was still over. Our careers were still burning. All we had to ease the blow was a suitcase full of wooden Buddhas and a tan. We still had our record deal in the summer of '98; we hadn't been officially dropped yet. Record contracts have option periods which operate as little breakers, signifying when the record company can legally let you go. It should be noted that you can never let *them* go; it's not a reciprocal arrangement.

In the meantime we're going through the motions, demoing material for our new A&R man. As expected the people who signed us have left and now we're in the care of a bored, be-suited executive who used to be the bongo player for Haircut 100. My eighties past is coming back to haunt me. When Haircut 100 stops calling, we'll move on to hanging out with George Michael.

I have come up with a spectacular new plan! I will record a solo album and come back as something altogether different and more marvellous. I will prove myself a master of reinvention in the manner of Madonna or Doctor Who. To this end I am putting together a brand new record and working on some demos with Andy in a recording studio in Highgate, north London. The studio is owned by none other than George Michael.

There are platinum discs and pictures of George on every wall and the main man pops in from time to time to see how things are going. He rolls fat cannabis joints, smokes them non-stop, and tells scurrilous stories about Princess Diana and Elton John (not together). His new best friend Geri Halliwell calls up every five minutes and most weekends the pair of them take off in a helicopter with George's boyfriend, to some palatial villa in the South of France.

He is candid, charming and easy-going, and one day he lollops in with his pet Labrador, and says he has some ideas about a song he likes that we're recording.

'You know what it really needs,' he says, stroking his goatee thoughtfully. 'Some nice backing vocals to support the chorus. I'll have a go if you like?'

I sit in the control room and listen to the takes, while George sings on my demo downstairs.

'What do you think?' he says, calling up from the vocal booth. 'Does it sound OK?'

Of *course* it sounds OK. It's George Michael, for goodness' sake! It puts a shuttlecock down the pants of the song. It drapes the chorus in a layer of sexy velvet. It's not enough to secure a solo record deal, or turn me into Doctor Who or Madonna, but what the hell: this totally makes up for that no-show night in '84, shuffling about in my dungarees at the Wag Club.

When pop life is gone for good – because it hasn't quite yet, there's a day or two left – I'll miss surreal moments like this. But our savings are running low, the speeding train of real life is fast approaching and, as diverting as it is, a girl can't hang out with George Michael and his dog chatting about 'Last Christmas' forever. The romance of pop life, what was left of it, is gone and I have my eye on a new and more grown-up way to earn a crust.

Most of all, what you realise when you hang out with proper pop stars, with their multi-million-selling albums, and their money and their houses and their jets and their hot tubs, is that our pop dream was only ever just that. As bonkers and euphoric and briefly heartbreaking as it was in the end, the love affair I'd nurtured since the age of twelve – from Kate

Bush to The Human League, to Springsteen, through Britpop and all the way back round again to George – turned out
to be a one-night stand.

But what a great one it was. Late summer. Back seat of a
Ford Capri. Pack of Fetherlite torn open on the dashboard.
'The Tide Is High' blaring from the radio.

EPILOGUE

'Damn, the babysitter's cancelled. We'll never find someone this late.'

Andy thinks for a moment.

'Let's try Jon.'

'Really? What about the last time?'

'When he let Iris stay up until midnight, watching *Mr Benn*?'

'No.'

'When he let Frankie eat an entire family pack of Maltesers?'

'No. I'm thinking about the time he let the two of them form... a *band*.'

What I need is a babysitter like Mary Poppins. The kind who can bathe two children, high on sugar and *Peppa Pig*, read them twenty-seven stories, wrestle them into bed and magic away the ensuing chaos with a few judicious clicks of her fingers. What I don't need is to come home from a rare night out to find my four-year-old singing along to Lady Gaga, and my two-year-old strumming acoustic guitar with his teeth.

'It's totally Hendrix,' Jon says, admiringly. 'He likes to lift the guitar up and slam it into the floor after he's finished. And Iris can already keep the beat to *Poker Face*, on tambourine. You really *have* to see this.'

Oh dear.

All our old musical instruments – the drum kit, the guitars – live upstairs in the attic. There's no space for them anywhere else. While Andy and I were on the way home from hospital after the birth of our daughter, an odd thing happened. Someone – possibly an employee of the Early Learning Centre, working on commission – came round to our house, opened all the doors and windows, and began shovelling primary-coloured plastic inside. I can't think how else it all got there, the lava flow of pirate ships, trains and toy garages, Lego, and broken bits of Buckeroo.

The other reason we keep the guitars in the attic is so the children aren't tempted to play them. On no account, whatsoever, do I want them thinking it might be fun, some time way in the future, to join a band. I am vigilant for any evidence of pop-star leanings. A preference for *Carrie and David's Popshop* over *Numberjacks* when watching CBeebies. A desire to stay up and watch *X Factor* on Saturday nights.

It's early days, but in years to come, any musical ambition might call for drastic action. When the time is right I plan to accompany my teenage progeny to every gig they go to, invited or not. For maximum embarrassment value I will dress as I did in my heyday – tight jeans, skinny T-shirt, skunk-striped hair – and dance about at the front with the curious sideways hopping motion I first patented on stage at the Mean Fiddler venue in 1994. It may seem cruel but it's the only way

I can be sure they will rebel against everything their mother aspired to and grow up to be something truly creative and worthwhile, like accountants.

Andy and I are home before midnight. All is quiet. Jon, our emergency babysitter, is working at the kitchen table. He's finishing off his column for *Guitarist* magazine and doing some background reading for his latest studies.

'How's the PhD coming along?'

'Good. I've just written five thousand words on John Lennon's choice of guitar strings. How's the new book going?'

'I'm almost done.'

Andy pours two glasses of wine and I put on the kettle for Jon, whose only vice these days is caffeine.

'So, how was it tonight?'

'You know... fine. Uneventful. Bit of telly. Few stories.'

'No band practice?'

'Uh... absolutely not.'

Andy and I go up to check on the kids. We stand together for a moment, watching them sleeping. Iris is still wearing her fairy dress. She has a tambourine tucked underneath her pillow. Frankie has a drum stick in his cot. And a tell-tale bottle of Fast Fret.

Downstairs, the three of us drink and gossip a while longer but none of us is a night owl any more. I'm yawning already, thinking about the 7am shift. Andy chats to Jon about the music college where they both teach and invites him to a gig he's playing in a couple of weeks. We make a note to call Geoff and ask him along.

As Jon gets up to leave, I open my laptop and click on the file for this book.

'Take a copy with you,' I say. 'Let me know what you think.'

Jon looks slightly apprehensive.

'Don't worry,' Andy says, smiling. 'It's so long ago. She probably made half of it up.'

'Did you?' asks Jon.

'Not a bit of it,' I say. 'It's all exactly the way I remember it.'